Complete Collected Intercessions

NICK
FAWCETT

kevin
mayhew

kevin
mayhew

First published in Great Britain in 2015 by Kevin Mayhew Ltd
Buxhall, Stowmarket, Suffolk IP14 3BW
Tel: +44 (0) 1449 737978 Fax: +44 (0) 1449 737834
E-mail: info@kevinmayhew.com

www.kevinmayhew.com

© Copyright 2015 Nick Fawcett.

The right of Nick Fawcett to be identified as the author of this work has been asserted by him in accordance with the Copyright, Designs and Patents Act 1988.

All rights reserved. No part of this publication may be reproduced, stored in a retrieval system, or transmitted, in any form or by any means, electronic, mechanical, photocopying, recording, or otherwise, without the prior written permission of the publisher.

9 8 7 6 5 4 3 2 1 0

ISBN 978 1 84867 763 0
Catalogue No. 1501466

Cover design by Rob Mortonson
© Images used under licence from Shutterstock Inc.
Typeset by Richard Weaver

Printed and bound in Great Britain

Contents

About the author

Brought up in Southend-in-Sea, Essex, Nick Fawcett trained for the Baptist ministry at Bristol and Oxford, before serving churches in Lancashire and Cheltenham. He subsequently spent three years as a chaplain with the Christian movement Toc H, before focusing on writing and editing, which he continues with today, despite wrestling with myeloma, a currently incurable cancer of the bone marrow. He lives with his wife, Deborah, and two children – Samuel and Kate – in Wellington, Somerset, worshipping, when able, at the local Anglican church. A keen walker, he delights in the beauty of the Somerset and Devon countryside around his home, his numerous books owing much to the inspiration he unfailingly finds there.

Introduction

'Hi Nick. Do you have something among your many prayers on the subject of schools . . . of AIDs . . . of grandparents . . . of One World Week . . . of baptism . . .?' So I could continue. I've lost count of the number of phone calls, letters or emails I've received along just such lines from friends, colleagues or readers seeking inspiration concerning a particular theme. And it's always good being able to help if I possibly can. The trouble sometimes, though, is knowing where to look. Yes, I think, I'm sure I wrote something on that somewhere, but where was it exactly? With close on a hundred and fifty books now in print, it's difficult to remember in which of them a particular prayer appears, so I end up thumbing through one book after another before I finally track it down. What I really needed, I decided, was all the prayers of a particular type organised in one place, and so was born the series of which this book is the first, with collected prayers for Advent, Christmas and Epiphany, and then for Lent, Holy Week and Easter, soon to follow.

Here you will find in a single volume all of the intercessions I've written over the years, many of them revised and adapted for public worship through the addition of congregational responses. There are prayers here for the Christian seasons, the Church year, the Lord's Supper, and for special services such as Mothering Sunday, Believer's Baptism and a Church anniversary, together with a host of prayers on themes as diverse as home and family, employment, scientists and researchers, education, health, bereavement, doubts and questions, society, retirement, and numerous other aspects of daily life. The aim is to offer a wide ranging and easy-to-use resource that will offer help and inspiration to all those charged with the demanding but vital responsibility of leading public intercession, bringing before God the needs of others near and far. Not every situation is covered here of course – new needs and concerns arise every day – but hopefully you will find what you're looking for most of the time, or discover at least material to provide a basis for your own further thoughts and reflections. If this compilation helps to articulate more fully our shared concern for the wider world, then it will more than have served its purpose.

NICK FAWCETT

Christian Seasons

Advent

1

Lord Jesus Christ,
we remember today how so many looked forward to your coming,
but we remember also how it became harder to keep faith as the years went by;
how hope started to splutter and dreams began to die
until, finally, you came –
the fulfilment of prophecy,
the culmination of God's purpose,
the definitive expression of his love.
Lord of all,
the Word made flesh,
bring hope to your world today.

We remember with gladness how you brought hope throughout your ministry,
a sense of purpose to those for whom life seemed pointless –
the poor, sick, outcasts and broken-hearted –
light shining in their darkness,
joy breaking into their sorrow,
new beginnings in what had seemed like the end.
Lord of all,
the Word made flesh,
bring hope to your world today.

Hear now our prayer for those caught today in the grip of despair –
those for whom the future seems bleak,
optimism seems foolish
and trust seems futile.
Reach out in love,
and may light shine into their darkness.
Lord of all,
the Word made flesh,
bring hope to your world today.

Hear our prayer for those whose goals in life have been thwarted,
whose dreams have been shattered,
who have grown weary, cynical and disillusioned.
Reach out in love,
and rekindle their faith in the future.
Lord of all,
the Word made flesh,
bring hope to your world today.

Hear our prayer for those who mourn,
who wrestle with illness,
or who watch loved ones suffer.
Reach out in love,
and grant them your strength and comfort.
Lord of all,
the Word made flesh,
bring hope to your world today.

Hear our prayer for those whose lives are blighted by injustice,
crushed by oppression, poverty, hunger,
and encourage all who work against the odds to build a
better world.
Reach out in love,
and grant the assurance of your coming kingdom.
Lord of all,
the Word made flesh,
bring hope to your world today.

Lord Jesus Christ,
we remember your promise to come again in glory,
the culmination of God's purpose,
the ultimate victory of love.
May that conviction bring new faith,
new vision,
and new purpose
wherever life seems hopeless.
Lord of all,
the Word made flesh,
bring hope to your world today.
Amen.

2

Loving God,
accept our glad thanksgiving for all you have given us,
and hear now our prayers for your world.

We pray for those for whom there is no celebration –
the poor and the hungry,
the homeless and the sick,
the lonely and the bereaved,
the oppressed and the persecuted.
Lord, you call us to respond to their need:
help us to reach out in love.

We pray for all those whose celebration is marred by fear –
those who are anxious for themselves or a loved one,
who see no hope in the future,
or who live under the constant threat of danger.
Lord, you call us to respond to their need:
help us to reach out in love.

We pray for all who wrestle with grief –
those whose lives have been broken by tragedy,
who live each day in perpetual shadow,
crushed by the burden of sorrow.
Lord, you call us to respond to their need:
help us to reach out in love.

We pray for all who feel isolated –
those who feel unloved, unwanted,
who find it hard to show love towards others,
or whose relationships have been broken
by cruelty, discord, division.
Lord, you call us to respond to their need:
help us to reach out in love.

Loving God,
may your light reach into the darkest places of the world,
so that there may be hope rather than despair,
joy rather than sorrow
and love rather than hatred.

Come now to our world through Jesus Christ,
to bring good news to the poor,
release to the captives,
recovery of sight to the blind,
and to let the oppressed go free.
Lord, you call us to respond to their need:
help us to reach out in love.
Amen.

3

Loving God,
we thank you for the hope you have given us in Christ,
the meaning and purpose,
joy and fulfilment,
you bring us through him.
Hear now our prayer for those who find it hard to hope,
those for whom life is testing.
Reach out in love,
and may light break into their darkness.

We think of those we label as the Third World –
the hungry and undernourished,
homeless and refugees,
sick and suffering –
human beings just as we are,
deprived of their dignity in the desperate struggle for survival.
Reach out in love,
and may light break into their darkness.

We think of those who are caught up in war –
overwhelmed by fear and hatred,
their homes and livelihoods destroyed,
each day lived under the threat of violence.
Reach out in love,
and may light break into their darkness.

We pray for those who feel overwhelmed by life –
lonely,
frightened,
sad,
weary –
many dreading what the next day might bring.
Reach out in love,
and may light break into their darkness.

Loving God,
may the message of good news that Advent brings
burst afresh into our world,
bringing help, hope and healing.
And may we, as those who profess the name of Christ,
play our part in showing his love,
displaying his care
and fulfilling his purpose,
so that he might come again into the hearts of all.
Reach out in love,
and may light break into their darkness.
Amen.

4

Lord Jesus Christ,
at this time supposedly of goodwill among all,
we pray for peace in our world –
an end to division and discord,
hatred and hostility,
death and destruction.
Prince of Peace,
hear our prayer.

We speak of peace
but in our hearts do not believe it possible.
When we look at our world
we see little hope of an end to its troubles.
We are sceptical,
uncertain,
filled with doubts,
cautious about expressing any optimism.

Even where there are signs of hope,
moves towards reconciliation,
we know it will take many years before we dare believe it is really possible.
But, we pray,
in this Advent season,
renew our ability to look forward,
rekindle our belief in the future,
and restore our capacity to hope for better things.
Prince of Peace,
hear our prayer.

Help us –
as we remember your coming,
as we serve you now,
and as we look forward to your coming again –
to anticipate your kingdom through the service we offer
and the lives we live.
Prince of Peace,
hear our prayer.

Teach us to work for that day when your throne will be established,
your justice prevail
and the earth be filled with the knowledge of you
as the waters cover the sea.
Prince of Peace,
hear our prayer.
Amen.

5

Living God,
thank you today for those who have the courage to stand up and speak out
against evil and injustice;
those who are ready, if necessary, to stand alone for their convictions,
enduring mockery and rejection,
sacrificing status and security,
willing to risk everything for what they believe to be right.

We thank you for their vision,
their determination,
their willingness to be a voice in the wilderness.
May your glory be revealed,
and all people see it together.

Thank you for those who have sufficient concern for others
to reach out and bring help –
ministering to the sick,
comforting the bereaved,
visiting the lonely,
providing for the poor,
giving hope to the oppressed,
bringing laughter to the sorrowful.
We thank you for their dedication,
their understanding,
their goodness,
their willingness to speak your word in the wilderness.
May your glory be revealed,
and all people see it together.

Living God,
you call us to reach out to your broken world –
to those walking in darkness,
wrestling with despair,
craving affection,
thirsting to find purpose in their lives.
Give us faith,
wisdom,
tenderness
and love
to meet that challenge.
Help us to venture into the wilderness ourselves,
and there, gently but confidently,
to speak your word of life.
May your glory be revealed,
and all people see it together.
Amen.

6

Lord Jesus Christ,
we look forward at this time of year to your coming again;
your return on earth to establish your kingdom,
and to bring in a new era of peace, justice and blessing for all.
Maranatha:
Come, Lord Jesus, come.

Teach us not simply to talk of such things,
but to seek to make them happen;
to do whatever we can through our life and witness
to help bring your kingdom closer,
a foretaste of heaven here on earth.
Maranatha:
Come, Lord Jesus, come.

Though what we can achieve alone may be all too small,
remind us that,
in partnership with all your people,
it may be greater than we may imagine.
Maranatha:
Come, Lord Jesus, come.

Challenge us, then,
guide, inspire and help us,
to live in such a way that does not give conflicting signals
but speaks simply and solely of your love –
a love that extends unfailingly and unconditionally to all.
Maranatha:
Come, Lord Jesus, come.
Amen.

7

Gracious God,
we pray for our world,
and for those many people who have no thought of Christ or his coming –
those who live only for themselves,
who seek fulfilment solely in material satisfaction,
or who have no spiritual dimension to their lives.
Lord Jesus Christ,
come among us, we pray!

We pray for those who profess to love
but who have drifted away from your side –
their faith shallow and empty,
their hearts full of bitterness, pride, envy,
or their minds troubled by doubts and disillusionment.
Lord Jesus Christ,
come among us, we pray!

We pray for those who work against your kingdom –
who knowingly cheat and deceive,
who serve self at the cost of others,
who spread hatred and incite violence in pursuit of their aims.
Lord Jesus Christ,
come among us, we pray!

We pray for those who long for your kingdom –
who hunger for a new beginning,
who pray for a fresh chance,
or who simply see no hope for themselves in this world.
Lord Jesus Christ,
come among us, we pray!

And finally we pray for those who work *towards* your kingdom,
who strive for peace and harmony,
who campaign for freedom and justice,
who demonstrate love and compassion in action.
Lord Jesus Christ,
come among us, we pray!

Gracious God,
we thank you for the assurance that your kingdom shall come
and your will be done –
the knowledge that we do not hope or wait in vain.
Teach all your people to live always as those ready for Christ's
coming,
so that others may hear and respond to your word of challenge.
Grant to those who despair
the knowledge that you are with them,
and to all who work to bring your kingdom nearer
the assurance that in your own time it will come.
In that faith we proclaim:
Lord Jesus Christ,
come among us, we pray!
Amen.

8

Gracious God,
we pray for those who struggle against you,
who through word and deed contend against your purpose.
We pray for those who knowingly flout your will –
those who kill, maim and destroy,
who exploit others,
who ignore the poor and needy,
who add to the total of human suffering.
Confront them with your searching presence.
Your kingdom come,
your will be done,
on earth as it is in heaven.

We pray for those who put their trust in false gods –
who know there is something missing in their lives,
but who try to deny it,
seeking refuge in money, possessions
or the trappings of success.
Reach out to them with your searching love.
Your kingdom come,
your will be done,
on earth as it is in heaven.

We pray for those who resist your call –
who have heard your voice,
recognised your challenge,
and glimpsed something of your love,
yet who hold out against you,
refusing to take the final step of commitment.
Challenge them with your searching word.
Your kingdom come,
your will be done,
on earth as it is in heaven.

We pray for those who let you down despite themselves –
ordinary believers like ourselves who each day betray your love
and deny your purpose,
the spirit willing but the flesh weak.
Restore them through your renewing grace.
Your kingdom come,
your will be done,
on earth as it is in heaven.

Gracious God,
we look forward to a time when you will be all in all –
when everything that conspires against you
will finally be overcome,
and your love will reign supreme.
Bring that day closer, we pray,
through the indwelling of your Spirit
and the living presence of Christ.
Your kingdom come,
your will be done,
on earth as it is in heaven.
Amen.

9

Loving God,
for your coming to us in Christ,
bringing love,
joy,
peace
and new beginnings,
receive our praise.
For your promise that he will come again,
establishing your kingdom and fulfilling your will,
accept our thanks.
Come afresh now to our world of pain and need,
and in the wilderness of our lives
make straight a highway for your Son to bring new beginnings –
fresh hope to all.
Amen.

10

Gracious God,
just as you came to our world in Christ,
help us now to go out for you,
to proclaim his word,
share his love
and work for his kingdom.
Help us to live in him
and for him
and through him,
until that day when he comes again
and you are all in all.
Amen.

11

Loving God,
save us in this season from indulging ourselves while a world goes hungry.
Help us to celebrate this season with our friends and loved ones,
but also to think of those who have so much less than we do,
those for whom the money we spend on little luxuries
would represent a small fortune,
able to make such a difference to their lives.
Open not just our hearts to them but also our hands,
so that they, too, will have cause to rejoice in body
as well as in soul.
Amen.

12

Loving God,
despite the apparent fickleness of fate,
and in all the complexities and uncertainties of this world,
may we continue to have faith in your loving purpose,
daring to believe that your grace will finally triumph over all.
Though so much conspires against you,
seeming to deny and even contradict your love,
may your hand continue to work,
bringing order out of chaos,
truth out of falsehood
and good out of evil,
until your will is done
and your kingdom has come.
Amen.

13

Sovereign God,
though we look forward to a new heaven and earth,
a kingdom that is yet to come,
save us from turning our back on the present,
as though the here and now isn't important
and the world around us is not our concern.

Save us from washing our hands of social
and environmental responsibility;
of loving our neighbour, both near and far;
of working out our faith in daily life;
of testifying to your love through words and deed.
Teach us that if we would truly see your kingdom
we must strive each day to bring it closer,
on earth as it is in heaven.
Amen.

14

Eternal God,
instil in us a vision of your eternal kingdom,
a sense of anticipation at the joys you hold in store.
Teach us to look forward in confidence to that day
when you will gather your people from the ends of the earth,
from every place and time,
welcoming us,
with them,
into your presence.
But save us from being so full of heaven that we are of no
earthly use,
dismissing this world
and abandoning our responsibilities towards it
through dwelling unduly on the world to come.
Remind us,
should we forget,
that though the fulfilment of your purpose lies in the future,
you are working among us here and now,
each of us,
through your Spirit,
having tasted your blessing
and glimpsed the dawn of your kingdom.
Teach us to trust in what you will do
and to celebrate what you are doing already.
Amen.

Christingle

15

In the darkness of sorrow and despair, Lord,
bring light.
In the darkness of war and hatred, Lord,
bring light.
In the darkness of pain and suffering, Lord,
bring light.
In the darkness of fear and superstition, Lord,
bring light.
In the darkness of poverty and need, Lord,
bring light.
In the darkness of famine and starvation, Lord,
bring light.
In the darkness of injustice and exploitation, Lord,
bring light.
In the darkness of death and loss, Lord,
bring light.
In every place and experience of darkness, Lord,
bring light.
Amen.

16

In a beautiful but broken world,
full of so much good yet so much evil,
so much joy yet so much sorrow,
we bring you, Lord, our prayers for others.

Where hardship has crushed the spirit,
poverty, injustice or disease having destroyed faith in the future,
Lord Jesus Christ,
may your love bring light.

Where war and suffering scar your world,
hatred, greed and intolerance erupting into violence,
Lord Jesus Christ,
may your love bring light.

Where disaster has brought devastation,
flood, famine, earthquake and hurricane shattering lives,
Lord Jesus Christ,
may your love bring light.

Where hearts are closed to you and others,
doubt, fear, dogma and prejudice creating alienation,
Lord Jesus Christ,
may your love bring light.

Come to our world, Lord, and heal its wounds,
shining in the darkness
and restoring joy, faith, hope and love.
Lord Jesus Christ,
may your love bring light.
Amen.

17

Lord Jesus Christ,
come as light into our world,
bringing food where there is hunger,
peace where there is war
and justice where there is exploitation.
Gracious Lord,
shine upon us.

Come as light into our lives,
bringing happiness in our homes,
joy in our relationships
and contentment in our work and leisure.
Gracious Lord,
shine upon us.

Come as light into our darkness,
bringing love instead of hatred,
good instead of evil
and hope instead of despair.
Gracious Lord,
shine upon us.

Come as light into our souls,
bringing faith instead of doubt,
fulfilment instead of emptiness
and life instead of death.
Gracious Lord,
shine upon us.

Come, Lord Jesus,
and shine in the hearts of all.
Amen.

18

Lord Jesus Christ,
reach out through your Spirit
and bring light to whose lives are shadowed by trouble and turmoil:
the shadow of famine and starvation,
trauma and catastrophe,
sickness and pain,
anxiety and fear,
loneliness and rejection,
hatred and violence,
death and bereavement.
Though the shadows may lengthen
and the darkness deepen,
may your light finally break through
and shine for evermore.
Amen.

19

Almighty God,
we yearn for a day when your will is done
and your kingdom come,
when your light bathes all in its radiance
and there is an end to sorrow and suffering,
darkness and death,
but we believe also that you care about us here and now,
about life today as much as life to come.
So we pray,
come among us.

Overcome with love all that undermines happiness and dignity,
and help us, wherever possible, to do the same,
doing all we can to bring you kingdom closer on earth
as it is in heaven.
So we pray,
come among us.
In the name of Christ.
Amen.

20

Living Lord,
light to the nations,
light of our lives,
shine, we pray, into our world today,
banishing all that obscures your goodness
or obstructs your will.
Amen.

Christmas

(For prayers concerning the magi, see Epiphany)

21

Loving God,
we praise you for all we have to rejoice in at Christmas,
this special reminder year by year of your coming to us in Christ.
Come to us now,
and help us to keep you at the centre of our celebrations.
Lord, in your mercy,
hear our prayer.

Come to our loved ones,
our families,
our friends,
all those we hold dear
and whom we shall share with or think of over these coming days.
Help us as we celebrate and make merry to think also of Christ,
and through drawing closer to him
to grow closer together.
Lord, in your mercy,
hear our prayer.

Come to those in special need –
the poor, the sick, the lonely and sad,
the homeless, the helpless,
the oppressed and persecuted;
all those for whom life is hard and the future seems bleak.
Reach out to them in love,
and give them something to celebrate.
Lord, in your mercy,
hear our prayer.

Loving God,
may the light of Christ break into the lives of people everywhere,
bringing your joy,
your peace,
your hope
and your love,

a song of praise on their lips
and celebration in their hearts.
Lord, in your mercy,
hear our prayer.

Come to them,
to us,
to all,
and send each of us on our way,
rejoicing in the gospel
and praising you for the wonder of your grace.
Lord, in your mercy,
hear our prayer.
Amen.

22

Gracious God,
we say that it is more blessed to give than to receive
but in practice we rarely show any indication of believing that.
We claim that Christmas is a time for giving as well as receiving,
but our gifts are usually reserved for family and friends,
the chosen few.
Gratefully, we remember today that your gift of Christ is so very different –
good news *for* all,
the Saviour *of* all,
given *to* all.
God of grace, you have given us so much:
teach us to give in return.

We thank you that you offered yourself freely,
not for any reward, save that of sharing your love,
and you gave everything,
even life itself,
so that anyone and everyone might come to know your goodness,
irrespective of creed, colour or culture.
God of grace, you have given us so much:
teach us to give in return.

We pray now for your world in all its need –
those in lands racked by poverty,
crushed by debt,
overwhelmed by famine or natural disaster.
God of grace, you have given us so much:
teach us to give in return.

We remember those who are persecuted,
denied justice,
or falsely imprisoned.
God of grace, you have given us so much:
teach us to give in return.

We remember those whose land is torn by hatred,
scarred by violence,
broken by war.
God of grace, you have given us so much:
teach us to give in return.

We remember those afflicted by sickness,
struggling with disability,
or crushed by suffering.
God of grace, you have given us so much:
teach us to give in return.

We remember those overcome by depression,
bereavement
or broken relationships,
all for whom the present brings trouble
and the future seems uncertain.
God of grace, you have given us so much:
teach us to give in return.

Gracious God,
at this time of giving and receiving
reach out in love to your aching world.
Bring comfort in distress,
courage in adversity,
confidence in uncertainty
and compassion in suffering.
Strengthen all those who work to build a fairer society
and a more just world,
and challenge each of us,
who have so much,

to share from our plenty with those who have so little.
May we not just talk in this season about goodwill to all,
but do something to show what it means.
God of grace, you have given us so much:
teach us to give in return.
Amen.

23

God of love,
we pray for all who will be celebrating Christmas this year,
enjoying presents, parties, food and fun,
yet not having heard, accepted or understood
what Christmas is all about.
Speak to them now,
and help them to respond.

We pray for those who have never heard the gospel,
or who have received a distorted picture of its message,
or who have failed to recognise it is good news for them.
Speak to them now,
and help them to respond.

We pray for those who have closed their hearts and minds
to Christ,
refusing to listen or consider further,
rejecting your Son as so many rejected him at his coming.
Speak to them now,
and help them to respond.

We pray for those who have come to faith
but barely realised what that means,
seeing perhaps just a small part of all you have done,
or seeking to know more but troubled by doubts and questions.
Speak to them now,
and help them to respond.

God of love,
come again to our world this Christmas,
breaking through our cosy traditions,
narrow horizons
and neatly packaged celebrations.
Speak to *us* now,
and help *us* to respond.

Help us and all people to glimpse the wonder of your awesome love –
a love revealed in the Christ who came and lived among us,
who suffered and died on the cross,
who rose and reigns with you,
and who shall come again to draw all things to himself.
Speak to *us* now,
and help *us* to respond.
Amen.

24

Lord of all,
we have heard again the good news of Jesus Christ,
the glad tidings of his coming,
and we have rejoiced in the wonder of this season.
But we pray now for those for whom it brings no joy,
serving only to remind them of their pain.
Come again to your world,
and turn tears into laughter,
sorrow into gladness.

We pray for the poor, the hungry, the homeless –
those for whom this Christmas will simply be another day in the struggle for survival;
for those caught up in war, violence and persecution –
those for whom this Christmas might be their last;
for the unloved, the lonely, the homeless –
those for whom Christmas merely heightens their sense of isolation.
Come again to your world,
and turn tears into laughter,
sorrow into gladness.

We pray for the anxious, the troubled and the fearful –
those for whom Christmas will be swamped by worries;
for the sick, the suffering, the broken in body and mind –
those for whom this Christmas means only another day of pain;
and we pray for the bereaved, the divorced, the estranged –
those for whom Christmas brings home the memory of happier times.
Come again to your world,
and turn tears into laughter,
sorrow into gladness.

Lord of all,
you give us a vision
through the song of Mary
of the way the world ought to be
and one day shall be:
a world in which you show the strength of your arm
and scatter the proud;
in which you bring down the powerful
and lift up the lowly;
in which you fill the hungry with good things
and send the rich away empty –
a world of justice,
in which good will triumph,
evil be ended
and the meek inherit the earth.
Give us confidence to believe that day can come
and the resolve to make it happen.
Stir the hearts of your people everywhere
to work in whatever way possible for change –
to bring the dawn of your kingdom closer
and so translate that vision into reality.
Come again to your world,
and turn tears into laughter,
sorrow into gladness.
Amen.

25

Lord Jesus Christ,
you came to our world,
but there was no place for you.
You came to your own people,
but they were not ready to receive you.
You were born in Bethlehem,
but there was no room for you in the inn.
You walked among us, sharing our humanity,
but had no place to rest your head.
You returned to your home town,
but were without honour in your own country.
You came to bring life to all,
but you were put to death on a cross.

You know what it is to be homeless,
hungry,
abandoned,
rejected,
and so we bring you our prayers for all those who endure such need today.
Friend of the friendless,
hear our prayer.

We pray for those who have no roof over their head
or no place to call their own –
waiting perhaps on council housing lists,
or evicted because they cannot pay the rent,
homes destroyed by natural disaster,
or left behind as they flee from persecution or the threat of war.
Friend of the friendless,
hear our prayer.

We pray for those who live in poor and overcrowded conditions,
in shanty towns or refugee camps,
hostels or bed-and-breakfast accommodation,
tenement blocks or run-down slums;
for those who sleep rough on the streets.
Friend of the friendless,
hear our prayer.

And we pray too for those who feel they have no place in society –
the unemployed,
the poor,
the lonely,
the oppressed,
the persecuted,
the terminally ill.
Friend of the friendless,
hear our prayer.

Lord Jesus Christ,
reach out to all who face such situations.
Grant the assurance that you care,
courage to believe in the future,
and strength to meet the present.
Friend of the friendless,
hear our prayer.

Grant your help to those who offer help,
your support to those who campaign for justice,
your blessing to all who seek to bring hope where there is only hopelessness.
Friend of the friendless,
hear our prayer.

May we, with them, make real your love
and show your compassion,
working together for your kingdom.
Friend of the friendless,
hear our prayer.
Amen.

26

Lord Jesus Christ,
born an outcast and refugee,
in weakness and frailty,
as we rejoice today,
hear our prayers for all those who have no cause for celebration.
Lord, in your mercy,
hear our prayer.

We pray for the hungry and the homeless,
the poor and the unemployed,
the oppressed and the exploited,
the lonely and the downhearted.
Lord, in your mercy,
hear our prayer.

We pray for the sick and the dying,
the sorrowful and the bereaved,
victims of violence and war,
all whose lives have been shattered by tragedy and disaster.
Lord, in your mercy,
hear our prayer.

Lord Jesus Christ,
born to set your people free,
come again to our world,
bringing reconciliation where there is division,
comfort where there is sorrow,

hope where there is despair
and confidence where there is confusion.
Lord, in your mercy,
hear our prayer.

Come and bring light where there is darkness,
love where there is hatred,
faith where there is doubt
and life where there is death.
Lord, in your mercy,
hear our prayer.

Lord Jesus Christ,
come again to our world,
and bring that day nearer when your kingdom will come,
and your will be done.
Lord, in your mercy,
hear our prayer.
Amen.

27

Living God,
we thank you for the great message of the gospel,
the glad tidings of your love,
the good news of your coming to our world through your Son
Jesus Christ.
May that message inspire us again this Christmas-time
and in the days to come.
Speak your word of love,
and move in the hearts of all who hear it.

We thank you that the good news of Christ has challenged people
across the ages,
and that though it has been proclaimed countless times,
though we have heard it ourselves so many times before,
it continues to be news for us and for all –
able still to speak to individuals across the world
and change their lives.
Speak your word of love,
and move in the hearts of all who hear it.

So now we pray for those you have specially called to proclaim the good news –
ministers,
preachers,
evangelists,
teachers –
all those with the special gift and responsibility of communicating your word.
Grant them wisdom,
dedication,
inspiration
and courage,
that they may faithfully witness to you
in the power of the Holy Spirit.
Speak your word of love,
and move in the hearts of all who hear it.

We pray also for those who hear the good news,
responding in different ways:
those who have closed their minds to what you would say to them –
may your love break through the barriers they erect;
those who have heard but failed to understand –
may their hearts be opened to the truth;
those who have yet to grasp that the gospel is good news for them –
may the experience of meeting Christ transform their lives;
those who have responded and come to faith –
may their knowledge of you continue to grow.
Speak your word of love,
and move in the hearts of all who hear it.

Finally we pray for those who long for good news,
who cry out for glad tidings:
the poor, starving, sick and lonely,
the oppressed, persecuted, unloved, bereaved –
so many people across the world who despair of ever seeing hope rekindled.
May the message of the gospel mean good news for them.
Speak your word of love,
and move in the hearts of all who hear it.

Living God,
come again to your world this Christmas-time,
through your word,
your Spirit,
your Church
and the living presence of Christ,
so that the message of the gospel may truly be good news for all people.
Speak your word of love,
and move in the hearts of all who hear it.
Amen.

28

Father God,
we pray for all who worship you today,
all across the world who rejoice in the good news of the birth of Christ.
Speak your word of life,
and be born in our hearts today.

May the reading of Scripture,
singing of carols,
offering of prayers
and sharing of fellowship
convey something of the wonder of your love.
Speak your word of life,
and be born in our hearts today.

May the faith of all your people be enriched,
and the life of the Church renewed,
by the presence of the living Christ,
so that the gospel may be proclaimed through its joyful witness,
and the glad tidings of your coming in Christ bring new hope,
joy,
meaning
and purpose
to the lives of all.
Speak your word of life,
and be born in our hearts today.

Father God,
reach out to your Church and to people everywhere at this glad time of year,
touching the lives of all with the living presence of Christ.
Speak your word of life,
and be born in our hearts today.
Amen.

29

Gracious God,
we have heard the good news of this season,
the glad tidings of the birth of your Son,
our Saviour,
Jesus Christ,
and we have rejoiced in everything which that means.
Yet we know that this message is not just for us but for everyone –
your love being for all the world,
your concern for all people,
your purpose without limits.
Help us then to go now with joy in our hearts
and wonder in our eyes,
to share the love that you have shown,
and to make known the great thing that you have done in Christ.
May Jesus be born again in our hearts
and made known through our lives.

Through the words we say and the deeds we do,
the love we share and the compassion we show,
the faith we proclaim and the people we are,
may his light shine afresh in the world,
bringing hope, healing, joy and renewal.
Grant that all may come to know you for themselves,
and so celebrate the news of great joy,
your coming among us in Christ
to bring us life in all its fullness.
May Jesus be born again in our hearts
and made known through our lives.

In his name we go,
to live and work for him,
with joyful thanks and grateful praise.
Amen.

30

Loving God,
at this time of giving,
help us to offer the worship,
thanksgiving,
service
and witness
that you alone deserve.
Lord, hear us,
graciously hear us.

At this time of receiving,
help us to open our hearts to your gift of Christ,
making his love and life our own.
Lord, hear us,
graciously hear us.

At this time of joy,
help us to celebrate the good news at its heart,
the wonder of your coming in Christ,
walking our earth and sharing our humanity.
Lord, hear us,
graciously hear us.

At this time of sharing,
help us to reach out to those whose hearts are heavy,
crushed by hunger,
poverty,
sorrow
and pain.
Lord, hear us,
graciously hear us.

At this *special* time,
open our lives to your transforming power,
your love that is able to make all things new.
Lord, hear us,
graciously hear us.
Amen.

31

Living God,
we remember today
how shepherds responded to the message of the angels –
how they hurried to Bethlehem
and found the baby lying in a manger,
and how afterwards they went on their way,
sharing what they had seen and heard.
Through our life and love, Lord,
reach out to others in turn.

Teach us, like the shepherds, to share our experience of Christ.
Help us to understand that your coming through him
is good news for everyone,
and that you want us to help make that known.
Through our life and love, Lord,
reach out to others in turn.

Enable us, then, to live each day with joy in our hearts
and wonder in our eyes
as we share the love you have shown us
and make known the great thing you have done in Christ.
Through our life and love, Lord,
reach out to others in turn.
Amen.

32

Lord Jesus Christ,
born in Bethlehem,
come afresh to our world today –
to our towns and cities,
our fractured communities,
our divided nations,
our bleeding planet.
In your mercy,
hear our prayer.

Lord Jesus,
born in a stable,
come afresh to the poor and homeless,
the disenfranchised,

the weak and vulnerable,
the outcast, oppressed and exploited.
In your mercy,
hear our prayer.

Lord Jesus,
born to suffer and die,
come afresh to those who are sick,
those in pain,
those facing death,
those who mourn loved ones.
In your mercy,
hear our prayer.

Lord Jesus Christ,
born in ages past,
be born in *us* today.
Amen.

33

For so many, Lord,
despite the glitz,
bustle,
hype
and expense,
it's not just crackers but Christmas itself
that proves to be a let-down,
promising much yet delivering little.
Awaken the hearts of all to the glorious surprise
at the heart of this season –
the wonder of your Son,
born in a stable and laid in a manger.
Instead of focusing on trivia that promises much
yet delivers little,
help us, today and always,
to celebrate your Word made flesh,
love incarnate –
a gift beyond price that will never disappoint.
Amen.

34

At this time of family get-togethers, Lord,
open our eyes to the wider family of the Church
and of all people across the world.
May Christmas truly be a time of coming together;
a time when,
remembering the One made flesh,
we grow together,
united in your love
and celebrating our common humanity,
barriers broken and divisions overcome.
Amen.

35

Living God,
save us from frittering away our money at Christmas on trivia,
while a world goes hungry;
from turning this season of goodwill to *all*
into one of good things for *us*.
Teach us to make room in our celebrations for those who,
in this life,
have so little to celebrate
and to give as generously to them
as we have so richly received.
Amen.

36

Loving God,
hear our prayer for those many people for whom Christmas stirs a sense of your presence,
reminding them of a reality beyond this world that they crave
yet all too quickly forget about.
Break through the trappings of this season,
and touch human hearts the world over,
so that instead of being briefly remembered,
you may be known and loved,
this and every day.
Amen.

37

Loving God,
though we can never begin to dispel this world's darkness,
help us to do whatever we can,
however insignificant it may seem,
to help lessen it a little.
Amen.

38

Lord Jesus Christ,
shine again into our world
and bring light to those who walk in the night-time of sorrow
and despair.
Where hearts are broken and spirits crushed,
lives overwhelmed by catastrophe, sickness, war or poverty,
be there in your mercy to bring new beginnings,
the opportunity to start afresh in the hope of a better tomorrow.
Amen.

39

Bring light, Lord, into our troubled world,
and shine in every place and experience of darkness.
Disperse the shadows of disease and disaster,
sickness and suffering,
hardship and hunger,
war and terror –
everything that destroys and divides,
alienating people from themselves,
one another
and you.
Amen.

40

Lord Jesus Christ,
Light of the world,
break into the darkness that oppresses so many.
Bring love where there is hatred,
good where there is evil,
and hope where there is despair,

your grace creating peace instead of war,
freedom instead of oppression,
joy instead of sorrow
and life instead of death.
Come now,
and shine in the hearts of all.
Amen.

41

Lord Jesus Christ,
in a world where so much holds people captive,
denying the life and light you long to give them,
bring an end to the darkness.
Comfort those who grieve,
support those who suffer,
provide for those in need,
and strengthen the weak in body, mind or spirit.
Encourage all who work to disperse the gloom,
and inspire us and others to respond in turn,
so that there may be laughter after tears,
delight after despair
and sunshine after shadow.
Amen.

42

Reach out, Lord, into our beautiful but broken world,
and cause your light to shine.
Where hatred brings war,
disaster causes devastation,
injustice leads to poverty,
intolerance breeds violence,
disease creates despair
and life entails suffering
be there in the darkness,
restoring joy, faith, hope and love.
Amen.

Epiphany

43

Saviour Christ,
shine in the darkness of our world –
into our sorrow,
hurt,
pain
and despair.
Bathe all, Lord,
in the sunshine of your love.

Scatter the clouds that hang over us –
the shadows of hatred,
violence
and war.
Bathe all, Lord,
in the sunshine of your love.

Break into the night-time of evil and injustice,
and bring among us a new dawn.
Illumine the way of all who cry out for a lamp to their feet
and light to their path.
Bathe all, Lord,
in the sunshine of your love.
Amen.

44

Lord Jesus Christ,
you promised that those who seek will find,
and in the pilgrimage of the magi we find proof of that promise.
So now we bring you our prayers for all in our world,
known and unknown to us,
who, in different ways, are searching.
May your light shine upon them:
a beacon of hope and a lamp to their path.

We pray for those who search for meaning,
their lives empty,
devoid of purpose,
hungry for something or someone to put their trust in.
In the bewildering variety of this world's voices,
each claiming to offer the answer,
may your love break through
and the message of the gospel touch their hearts,
so that they might find in you
the one who is the way, the truth and the life.
May your light shine upon them:
a beacon of hope and a lamp to their path.

We pray for those for whom the journey of life is hard,
beset by pain, sickness and sorrow,
or overwhelmed by disaster, deprivation and injustice.
In the trials they face and the burdens they struggle with
may your love break through
and the message of the gospel bring strength and comfort,
help, healing and inspiration.
May your light shine in the darkness:
a beacon of hope and a lamp to their path.

We pray for those unsure of the way ahead,
faced by difficult choices and vital decisions,
troubled by situations in which they can see no way forward
or doubting their ability to cope with the demands the future
will bring.
In the uncertainties of this ever-changing world,
may your love break through
and the message of the gospel bring a new sense of direction,
an inner peace,
and the assurance which you alone can give,
so that, whatever they may face,
they will know that nothing will ever separate them from your love.
May your light shine upon them:
a beacon of hope and a lamp to their path.

We pray for those who have gone astray –
betraying their principles,
or their loved ones,
or, above all, you.

In this world of so many subtle yet powerful temptations,
may your love break through
and the message of the gospel bring new beginnings,
so that, however low they may have fallen,
they will know themselves forgiven,
accepted
and restored.
May your light shine in the darkness:
a beacon of hope and a lamp to their path.

Lord Jesus Christ,
hear our prayer
for all who seek purpose, help, guidance and mercy.
May they find in you the answer to their prayer
and the end to their searching.
Amen.

45

Lord of Light,
we have remembered today the journey of the wise men –
how, inspired by what they took to be a sign,
they set off in search of a new-born king,
a king who would change not simply their lives,
nor merely the life of his people,
but the life of the world.
Come again now,
and may light shine in the darkness.

We remember how they persevered in their quest,
travelling in faith
even though they had no clear idea of where they were heading,
or any certainty of what they would find when they reached their destination.
Come again now,
and may light shine in the darkness.

We remember how they refused to be discouraged,
despite their reception in Jerusalem,
despite the fact that no one seemed to have any idea that a new king had been born.
Come again now,
and may light shine in the darkness.

We remember how they kept going,
single-minded in pursuit of their goal,
until at last their determination was rewarded
and they came face to face with the infant Jesus.
Come again now,
and may light shine in the darkness.

Living God,
we pray for all who seek today,
all those who are looking for a sense of purpose in their lives,
all who are searching for spiritual fulfilment,
all who long to find you for themselves.
Come again now,
and may light shine in the darkness.

Help them to keep looking,
even when the journey is demanding
and no end seems in sight;
to keep believing,
even when others seem oblivious to their quest
or scornful of it;
to keep on trusting,
even when those they look to for guidance
seem as confused and as lost as they are.
Come again now,
and may light shine in the darkness.

Living God,
you have promised through Jesus Christ that those who seek
will find.
May the experience of the wise men inspire all who seek for truth
to keep on searching,
in the assurance that they too,
come what may,
will one day complete their quest
and discover you for themselves.
Come again now,
and may light shine in the darkness.
Amen.

46

Lord Jesus Christ,
shine into the darkness of this world,
into its suffering and sorrow,
evil and injustice.
Lord, hear us,
graciously hear us.

Brighten the lives of those who wrestle with illness, pain and infirmity;
those who mourn loved ones or face the prospect of their passing;
those who are poor, homeless or hungry;
those who are oppressed and exploited;
those who are depressed, troubled or weary.
Lord, hear us,
graciously hear us.

Shine into the hearts of those who do not know you,
those who reject you,
ignoring, rejecting or even opposing your way.
Lord, hear us,
graciously hear us.

Illuminate our own path,
opening our hearts each day to the radiance of your love
and blessing.
Come through your Spirit and shed your light afresh upon all.
Lord, hear us,
graciously hear us.
Amen.

47

Lord Jesus Christ,
come among us now,
for so often we look around and see only darkness –
a shadow over our lives,
denying hope and destroying life.
Come again now,
and may your light shine on all.

Come into our hearts,
our homes,
our country,
our world,
and shine upon us,
so that we might bathe in the glow of your love
and the radiance of your grace,
your light scattering the darkness for ever.
Come again now,
and may your light shine on all.
Amen.

48

Come, Lord, into the darkness of our world,
the shadow of sorrow,
suffering,
hunger,
despair,
hatred,
evil
and death.
Bring a new dawn,
new beginnings,
the light of your love shining on all.
Amen.

49

Come, Lord, into the darkness of our world,
its hatred, suffering and evil,
and somehow, through your grace,
work within such things for good.
Amen.

50

Light of the world,
shine wherever there is darkness today.
Where there is pain and sorrow,
may the brilliance of your love bring joy.
Where there is sickness and suffering,
may your healing touch bring sunshine after the storm.

Where there is greed and corruption,
may your radiance scatter the shadows.
Where there is hatred and bitterness,
may your brightness dispel the clouds.
Amen.

51

Lord Jesus Christ,
light of the world,
shine again upon us we pray,
and illuminate the darkness of this world
through your life-giving grace.
Amen.

52

Lord Jesus Christ,
may the flame of faith burn brightly within us,
and your light shine in our hearts,
so that we, in turn, may bring light to others,
to the glory of your name.
Amen.

53

Lord Jesus Christ,
shine afresh into our world,
so that even where all seems dark we may find reason to celebrate,
cause to rejoice.
Amen.

54

Shine afresh into the darkness of this world, Lord,
and disperse the shadows of sorrow,
hurt,
hatred,
violence
and war.
Break into the night-time of evil and injustice,
and usher in a new dawn.
Illuminate all in the sunshine of your love.
Amen.

55

Sovereign God,
you turned the darkest of nights into the brightest of days
through the resurrection of your Son,
our Saviour, Jesus Christ.
Come now into the darkness of our world:
into the night-time of suffering and sickness,
doubt and despair;
into the shadows of hurt and heartbreak,
injustice and evil;
into the bleakness of violence and hatred,
fear and death.
May your new day dawn
and the light of Christ blaze to your glory
as we share his resurrection life
and rejoice in the victory he has won.
Amen.

56

Thank you, Lord, for being with us in our darkness,
your light continuing to shine through trouble and tragedy,
turmoil and tears.
Break through where shadows still linger,
into our doubt and disbelief,
our disobedience,
our flawed commitment and weakness of will.
Illuminate all through the radiance of your love.
Amen.

57

The night is turning to day,
darkness is turning to light –
it is time to wake from our sleep.
Wherever there is sorrow, fear, need or hurt,
let us reach out in the name of Christ,
and may his joy and peace,
healing and compassion,
dawn through us,
until morning has broken
and the day of his kingdom is here.
Amen.

58

Lord Jesus Christ,
there's nothing special about us,
nothing exceptional that will make people sit up and take notice.
We're not particularly good or loving,
much though we'd like to be,
nor do we possess saintly or special qualities.
We're just ordinary people seeking to love and serve you better.
Yet, with your help,
we can make a difference nonetheless.
In various ways,
no matter how small,
we can help to brighten up this world.
Shine upon us,
so that our light in turn may shine among others.
Show us what you would have us do,
and help us to do it.
Amen.

Lent

see also Themed Prayers: Social Justice – Self-denial

59

Lord Jesus Christ,
we are reminded today,
in this season of Lent,
of the time you spent in the wilderness –
facing choices,
wrestling with temptation,
experiencing a period of testing that would shape the course of your ministry;
a time that reminds us of your humanity,
that tells us you were one with us,
tempted just as we are.
In the wilderness of life today,
be present, O Lord.

We thank you that you came through that time the stronger –
more sure of the path you must take
and more confident of your ability to take it.
So now we pray for those experiencing similar times of testing.
In the wilderness of life today,
be present, O Lord.

We pray for those facing difficult and demanding choices –
choices that entail pain and self-sacrifice,
that mean letting go of cherished dreams,
that involve facing awkward facts about themselves and others.
In the wilderness of life today,
be present, O Lord.

We pray for those wrestling with temptation –
torn between conflicting desires,
unsure of where they stand,
uncertain about their ability to stand firm.
In the wilderness of life today,
be present, O Lord.

We pray for those experiencing a period of testing in their lives –
problems they fear they cannot cope with,
challenges they feel unable to rise to,
questions they would rather not face.
In the wilderness of life today,
be present, O Lord.

Lord Jesus Christ,
give strength to all facing such times –
a sureness of purpose and clearness of mind.
Give the knowledge of your will –
then courage to make right decisions
and resolve to see them through.
May each emerge the stronger for all they experience,
and better equipped to face the future.
In the wilderness of life today,
be present, O Lord.
Amen.

60

Almighty and everlasting God,
we do not always know what to ask for in our prayers
for there is so much that we do not know or understand,
yet we know that you are active in our world,
moving in human hearts
and in the events of history
to fulfil your purpose.

So we come now to you,
and, in quiet faith,
we place ourselves and our world into your hands,
asking that your will may be done,
despite everything that conspires against it.
All things are yours:
we entrust them into your keeping.

We bring ourselves,
weak,
faithless,
hesitant,
foolish.
We bring all we are and all we long to be,
seeking your help and your transforming touch.
All things are yours:
we entrust them into your keeping.

We bring those who are part of our lives –
family and friends,
neighbours,
and colleagues at work,
all those whom we meet in the daily round of life.
All things are yours:
we entrust them into your keeping.

We bring our world –
the rich and poor,
powerful and weak,
well-fed and hungry,
healthy and sick;
those who enjoy peace and those who endure war;
those who revel in freedom and those who fight for justice.
All things are yours:
we entrust them into your keeping.

Almighty and everlasting God,
we thank you that you are involved in our lives,
active in our world,
concerned about everything you have made
and holding all things ultimately in your hands.
So we leave them confidently with you,
asking only this:
'Your will be done,
your kingdom come,
on earth as it is in heaven.'
All things are yours:
we entrust them into your keeping.
Amen.

61

Lord Jesus Christ,
you gave of yourself without counting the cost,
offering even your own life for the life of the world.

So now we pray for all those who seek to love you in return,
however hesitant, partial, or imperfect their love might be.
Inspire them through your grace,
and fill them with love.

We pray for those new in their faith,
still learning more of you,
still uncertain perhaps of their commitment,
still discovering more of your love.
Inspire them through your grace,
and fill them with love.

We pray for those established in their faith,
facing the daily risk of growing complacent,
stale,
settled into a comfortable routine.
Inspire them through your grace,
and fill them with love.

We pray for those whose faith has crumbled,
no longer holding the trust they once held,
no longer feeling you close by their sides,
no longer seeking to follow Christ.
Inspire them through your grace,
and fill them with love.

We pray for those who have never had faith;
those consistently unmoved by the message of the gospel,
those who resist its challenge despite themselves,
and those who wilfully go against your will.
Inspire them through your grace,
and fill them with love.

We pray for those whose faith is costly,
those who sacrifice time,
money,
energy,
security,

health,
and even life itself,
in the service of others.
Inspire them through your grace,
and fill them with love.

And we pray for those who need something to put their faith in –
the poor, the hungry and the homeless,
the sick, the suffering, the bereaved,
all those broken by the tragedies and crises of life.
Inspire them through your grace,
and fill them with love.

Lord Jesus Christ,
your love is for all,
whoever they may be.
May it reach out then into every heart in every place,
and may we be a part of that,
learning to love you as you love us.
Amen.

62

Merciful God,
we pray for those who walk through life with a sense of guilt,
burdened by past mistakes,
overwhelmed by a sense of failure,
troubled by feelings of shame,
depressed by the knowledge of their own weakness.
Help them to understand that in you they can find true forgiveness
and a new beginning.
In your mercy,
hear us.

We pray for those who commit evil with no sense of wrongdoing,
no concept of sin,
no hint of remorse,
no sign of scruples.
Help them to glimpse what is right and good,
and to be touched by the renewing, transforming grace of Christ.
In your mercy,
hear us.

We pray for those who have been wronged by others;
hurt,
deceived,
betrayed,
let down.
Help them to be ready to forgive others
as you have forgiven them.
In your mercy,
hear us.

We pray for those whose relationships are being tested –
with family and friends,
with those at work or in their place of leisure,
with other Christians,
even in their own fellowship.
Help them to understand the cause of division between them
and to work towards the healing of all such rifts,
forgiving and seeking forgiveness.
In your mercy,
hear us.

Merciful God,
help all those who are burdened by past mistakes
to discover the forgiveness you so freely offer,
and to show that mercy themselves.
In your mercy,
hear us.
Amen.

63

Living God,
you challenge us to go the extra mile,
to do more than anyone can ask or expect of us.
Through our service and witness,
reach out and touch our world.

Forgive us that we find that so hard:
that we prefer to do as little as possible rather than as much;
that we give our help, time, service and money grudgingly rather than cheerfully.
Through our service and witness,
reach out and touch our world.

We praise you for the readiness of Christ to go not just the extra mile
but to give his all,
identifying himself with our human condition,
willingly experiencing suffering and death
so that we might discover life in its fullness.
Through our service and witness,
reach out and touch our world.

We praise you for those who have followed in his footsteps,
willing to go beyond the call of duty in the service of others.
Touch our hearts through their example
and inspire us through the love of Christ,
so that we too may be ready to offer that little bit extra,
giving as freely to you and to others as you have given to us.
Through our service and witness,
reach out and touch our world.
Amen.

64

Lord Jesus,
throughout your life you were the man for others,
always ready to listen,
always prepared to respond,
whatever the cost to yourself.
Through our life and love,
reach out to others in turn.

At your death it was the same –
still you poured yourself out,
thinking of others to the last.
Through our life and love,
reach out to others in turn.

Forgive us that we are so different,
rarely willing to listen,
even less so to respond,
fearful of what it all might cost us.
Through our life and love,
reach out to others in turn.

Always *we* are the same,
reluctant to give of ourselves,
thinking of our own interests to the last.
We do not mean to do it,
but it is the way we are,
hard though we try to change.
Through our life and love,
reach out to others in turn.

Lord Jesus,
forgive us and teach us your way,
for until we learn to serve all
we will never truly learn to serve you.
Through our life and love,
reach out to others in turn.
Amen.

65

Help us to make a difference, Lord –
if not to be salt of the earth
then at least to change something,
somewhere,
for the better.
Help us,
through serving others,
to serve you.
Amen.

66

In a self-serving world, Lord,
where greed rules,
profit is everything
and looking after number one is the all-consuming creed,
teach us your way:
the way of humility,
sacrifice
and service.
Give us the love and courage we need not just to learn of it
but to put it into practice;
to take up our cross and follow you.
Amen.

67

Lord Jesus Christ,
we proclaim you as our Lord and Saviour,
we believe you to be God's promised Messiah,
we preach the gospel of your cross and resurrection.
Yet how often do we really listen to your message –
your message that challenges and disturbs,
that calls us to a life of self-denial and sacrifice,
that speaks of justice for the poor,
liberty for the imprisoned,
hope for the oppressed.
Lord Jesus, help us to hear not simply what we want to hear,
but rather what you would say to us.
Amen.

68

Lord Jesus Christ,
we think we know what it means to deny ourselves,
but in reality we have little idea at all.
We content ourselves with token actions –
a hunger lunch, perhaps,
a temporary renunciation of some little luxury,
a few extra pounds given to charity –
and then we pat ourselves on the back,
as though we've achieved something special,
truly gone without.
Remind us of the immensity of *your* sacrifice –
your willingness to endure not only death,
but the weight of human evil,
in order to redeem us and bring us life.
Help us, conscious of that awesome love,
to understand what self-denial really means,
and more meaningfully to put it into practice.
Amen.

Holy Week

Palm Sunday

69

Lord Jesus Christ,
you entered Jerusalem in quiet humility,
taking the form of a servant,
even to the point of death on a cross,
emptying yourself so that we might be filled.
Come again now
and establish your kingdom.

Come afresh to our troubled world,
with all its needs,
its tensions,
its problems
and its evil.
Come again now
and establish your kingdom.

Bring healing where there is division,
love where there is hatred,
hope where there is despair,
joy where there is sorrow,
confidence where there is fear,
strength where there is weakness,
healing where there is sickness,
life where there is death.
Come again now
and establish your kingdom.

Lord Jesus Christ,
reach out to your Church and world,
despite the weakness of our faith
and the rejection of so many.
May your will be done on earth
even as it is in heaven.
Come again now
and establish your kingdom.
Amen.

70

Lord Jesus Christ,
you came not as a king mighty in battle,
but as the Prince of Peace,
the promised deliverer,
sent to heal and restore our broken world.
So now we pray for peace and unity between nations.
Your kingdom come,
your will be done.

We thank you for signs of hope in the world today –
for the desire to make this planet a safer place,
for initiatives that have been taken to reduce nuclear and conventional arms,
for the breaking down of seemingly insurmountable barriers,
and for a willingness to engage in genuine dialogue rather than empty rhetoric.
Prosper all such efforts,
and grant that a spirit of trust and cooperation may develop among all.
Your kingdom come,
your will be done.

We pray for those places where tension continues –
where there is still hatred,
division,
violence
and slaughter –
and we pray especially for all those caught up in the awfulness of war:
those maimed and injured,
those who have lost loved ones,
those for whom life will never be the same again.
Your kingdom come,
your will be done.

Through your Spirit of love, break down the barriers that keep people apart –
the prejudice and intolerance,
greed and envy,
injustice and exploitation
that continue to scar our world.

Overcome everything that leads people to take up arms against one another.
Your kingdom come,
your will be done.

Lord Jesus Christ,
Prince of Peace,
come again to our world
and bring the unity that you alone can bring.
May the day dawn when swords will be beaten into ploughshares,
and spears turned into pruning hooks;
when nation shall not lift sword against nation,
neither learn war any more;
a day when no one will hurt or destroy
on all your holy mountain.
Your kingdom come,
your will be done.
Amen.

71

Lord Jesus Christ,
Prince of Peace,
King of kings,
though you knew that the cheers welcoming you into Jerusalem
would soon turn into jeers of rejection,
still you continued on your way,
offering your life for those who would crucify you.
Son of David,
have mercy on us.

Come again now to your world,
though it repeatedly turns its back on you,
and bless it with peace,
justice,
freedom
and hope.
Son of David,
have mercy upon us.

Come again to your Church,
though it repeatedly fails you,
and fill it with love,
harmony,
humility
and faith.
Son of David,
have mercy upon us.

Lord Jesus Christ,
through our life and witness,
walk again among us here on earth,
and help us to serve you as the Servant of all,
Lord of all,
all in all!
Son of David,
have mercy upon us.
Amen.

Holy Monday to Wednesday

72

Lord Jesus Christ,
we remember today how your concern
throughout your ministry
was not for yourself but for others –
the vulnerable,
the distressed,
the sick,
the despised;
all those who were marginalised in society –
downtrodden,
oppressed,
rejected.
You came as the man for others:
come again to our world today.

We remember how you had a special place in your heart for the poor,
and so we pray for the millions suffering still under the yoke of poverty
with all the attendant misery that involves –
victims of failed harvests, natural disasters and civil wars,
crying to us for help,
begging for food to stave off their hunger,
homes to house their children,
resources to build a better future,
an opportunity to start again
free from the shackles of debt.
You came as the man for others:
come again to our world today.

We remember how you suffered at the hands of others,
and so we pray for all who endure violence and cruelty,
all who are wounded in body, mind and spirit by acts of inhumanity.
We pray for victims of racism and discrimination,
of verbal and physical bullying,
of assault and abuse,
intimidation and torture,
terrorism and war.
You came as the man for others:
come again to our world today.

Lord Jesus Christ,
you lived for others,
you died for others
and you rose for all.
Help us to live in turn as your people,
seeking to serve rather than be served,
to give rather than to receive.
Teach us to reach out in love
and so to make real your compassion
and represent your body here on earth.
You came as the man for others:
come again to our world today.
Amen.

73

Lord Jesus Christ,
you call us to minister in your name,
to express your care for all through word and deed,
but day after day we let you down.
Lord,
have mercy.

Through the compassion we fail to show,
the love we fail to express
and the justice we fail to fight for;
through the hungry we fail to feed,
the sick we fail to visit
and the needy we fail to clothe;
through the truths we distort,
the hurt we cause
and the selfishness we indulge in,
we inflict more pain upon you,
driving the nails once more through your hands and feet,
hanging you once again upon your cross.
Lord,
have mercy.

For all the ways we continue to break your body,
gracious Saviour, forgive us,
and help us to reach out in your name,
ministering to all who are broken in our world,
in loving service.
Lord,
have mercy.
Amen.

74

Father God,
speak again in this Holy Week of your love in Christ,
of your surrendering all for our sakes.
Lord, hear us,
graciously hear us.

Speak of his faithfulness to your call,
of his selfless service and awesome sacrifice,
and help us to remember what it cost both him and you.
Lord, hear us,
graciously hear us.

Give us similar courage to give and go on giving,
to love and go on loving,
so that we,
like him,
may be enabled to put you first,
others second,
and self last.
Lord, hear us,
graciously hear us.
Amen.

75

Lord Jesus Christ,
bruised and broken,
make us whole.
Loving Lord,
hear us.

Gracious Christ,
poured out for many,
fill our hearts.
Loving Lord,
hear us.

Vulnerable Christ,
trembling in Gethsemane,
strengthen us in time of need.
Loving Lord,
hear us.

Crucified Christ,
hanging in agony,
support those who suffer.
Loving Lord,
hear us.

Redeemer Christ,
bearing our sins on the cross,
have mercy upon us.
Loving Lord,
hear us.

Saviour Christ,
dying to bring us life,
gladly we receive and rejoice.
Loving Lord,
hear us.
Amen.

76

Lord Jesus Christ,
bruised for our iniquities,
heal our wounds.
Saviour of all,
hear us.

Lord Jesus Christ,
broken for all,
nourish our faith.
Saviour of all,
hear us.

Lord Jesus Christ,
poured out for many,
refresh our hearts.
Saviour of all,
hear us.

Lord Jesus Christ,
betrayed and denied,
assure us of your constant love though we prove false and faithless.
Saviour of all,
hear us.

Lord Jesus Christ,
abandoned in your time of need,
reach out to the lonely.
Saviour of all,
hear us.

Lord Jesus Christ,
falsely accused and convicted,
bring justice to our world.
Saviour of all,
hear us.

Lord Jesus Christ,
given over to death,
help us to walk in newness of life,
this day and always.
Saviour of all,
hear us.
Amen.

77

Lord Jesus Christ,
teach us more about the way you walked;
the path of love,
service,
mercy
and compassion.
Teach us your way,
and help us to follow.

Remind us of your openness to all;
your willingness to give and go on giving.
Teach us your way,
and help us to follow.

Remind us of your humility;
of how you invariably put others before yourself.
Teach us your way,
and help us to follow.

Help us to understand how much you surrendered,
how much you cared and continue to care,
and may that knowledge inspire us in turn
to consecrate our lives to your kingdom,
seeking always and in everything,
to know and do your will.
Teach us your way,
and help us to follow.
Amen.

78

Lord Jesus Christ,
thank you for having reached out to all in need,
entering into our darkness in order to bring us light.
Shine now.
Shine always.

Thank you for enduring hatred to show your love,
for facing death to bring life,
for bearing our sins to make possible forgiveness.
Shine now.
Shine always.

Come again into our broken world,
bringing healing to the sick,
justice to the oppressed,
guidance to the lost –
life to all.
Shine now.
Shine always.

Wherever hatred divides,
pain destroys
and evil defiles,
bring new beginnings through your transforming touch,
and make us whole.
Shine now.
Shine always.
Amen.

79

Lord Jesus Christ,
you were acquainted with grief –
help us to weep over what destroys and denies life.
Lord, hear us,
graciously hear us.

You were silent before your accusers –
help us to speak for you.
Lord, hear us,
graciously hear us.

You faced up to darkness –
help us to shed your light.
Lord, hear us,
graciously hear us.

You took on the forces of evil –
help us to work for good.
Lord, hear us,
graciously hear us.

You wiped the slate clean –
help us to start again.
Lord, hear us,
graciously hear us.

You gave your all –
help us to give something back.
Lord, hear us,
graciously hear us.

You *died* for us –
help us to *live* for you.
Lord, hear us,
graciously hear us.
Amen.

Maundy Thursday

80

Lord Jesus Christ,
who endured such anguish in Gethsemane,
hear our prayer for those who,
as was so with you,
wrestle with what the future might bring,
uncertain of their ability to meet it,
nervous,
troubled,
afraid.
Gracious Saviour,
be present in their need,
and lead them safely through.

Lord Jesus Christ,
falsely arrested, accused, imprisoned and condemned,
we pray for those who,
as was so with you,
are denied their rights,
wrongfully charged,
cruelly treated
or unfairly judged.
Gracious Saviour,
be present in their need,
and lead them safely through.

Lord Jesus Christ,
flogged, humiliated, nailed to a cross,
we pray for those who,
as was so with you,
are tortured,
abused,
victimised,
despised,
Gracious Saviour,
be present in their need,
and lead them safely through.

Lord Jesus Christ,
bearing our sins in awful isolation,
we pray for those who,
as was so with you,
feel hopeless,
abandoned,
crushed,
alone,
Gracious Saviour,
be present in their need,
and lead them safely through.

Lord Jesus Christ,
laid in the coldness of a tomb,
we pray for those who,
as was so with you,
face death
or who have passed from this life,
their earthly journey near its close
or at an end.
Gracious Saviour,
be present in their need,
and lead them safely through.

Lord Jesus Christ,
our Lord,
we pray for ourselves and all people, asking that,
as was so with you,
we may enter into the joy of your kingdom,
the beauty of your presence,
celebrating your new creation,
and rejoicing in your love for evermore.
Gracious Saviour,
be present in *our* need,
and lead *us* safely through.
Amen.

81

Lord Jesus Christ,
we are reminded today that you were broken for us,
that you gladly endured sorrow, suffering and death for our sakes.
You identified yourself with humanity,
standing alongside the broken-hearted,
accepting the limitations of life and death.
So now we pray for all who are broken in body, mind or spirit.
Reach out to hold.
Reach out to help.

We pray for those who are in pain,
racked by illness and disease,
physically disabled,
maimed or injured through war, terrorism, disaster or accident.
Reach out to hold.
Reach out to help.

We pray for those who mourn loved ones
or who face death themselves,
those tormented by fear or anxiety,
the mentally ill or handicapped,
and all who are confused or overwhelmed by the complexities of daily life.
Reach out to hold.
Reach out to help.

We pray for those whose spirit has been broken in the storms of life –
overwhelmed by sorrow,
overcome by disappointment,
crushed by tragedy.
Reach out to hold.
Reach out to help.

We pray for those whose faith has been battered by the harsh realities of this world –
their confidence shaken,
their trust destroyed,
their love grown cold.
Reach out to hold.
Reach out to help.

Lord Jesus Christ,
who endured such turmoil of mind in Gethsemane,
whose body was broken on the cross,
who surrendered your spirit to the Father,
reach out now in love and compassion to all in any such need,
bringing the assurance of your presence,
the comfort of your peace
and the joy of your love.
Reach out to hold.
Reach out to help.
Amen.

82

Lord Jesus Christ,
we remember today that you were broken not only for us,
or even for many,
but for all.
We rejoice that your love isn't for the select few but for everyone –
young and old,
rich and poor,
male and female,
black and white.
So then we pray for our world in all its need.
May your grace bring hope;
your love bring healing.

We pray for all who feel broken today –
shattered by disappointment, tragedy and bereavement;
overwhelmed by poverty and hunger, disease and deprivation,
crushed by injustice, oppression, imprisonment and violence –
all those who have been broken in body, mind and spirit,
battered by the circumstances and events of life.
May your grace bring hope;
your love bring healing.

We pray for those who long for wholeness –
bring delivery from physical pain, sickness and disease,
freedom from fear, anxiety and depression,
an answer to inner emptiness and spiritual longing,
the opportunity to be at peace with you,

their neighbour
and themselves.
May your grace bring hope;
your love bring healing.

Lord Jesus Christ,
broken for all,
reach out now to our broken world
and teach us to reach out in turn.
Show us where you would have us serve,
teach us what you would have us do,
and use us to fulfil your purposes.
May your grace bring hope;
your love bring healing.
Amen.

Good Friday

83

Lord Jesus Christ,
broken on the cross,
tortured there in body, mind and soul,
you know what it means to suffer.
So now we pray today for the broken people of our world,
all those who have experienced something of your pain.
Reach out in love, and make them whole.

We pray for the broken in body –
those injured in accidents,
those maimed in war,
those disabled by disease.
Reach out in love, and make them whole.

We pray for the broken in mind –
those tormented by fears,
those wrestling with depression,
those who have suffered a mental breakdown.
Reach out in love, and make them whole.

We pray for the broken in spirit –
those whose dreams have been destroyed,
those whose love has been betrayed,
those whose faith has been crushed.
Reach out in love, and make them whole.

Lord Jesus Christ,
you came to make us all whole,
to mend broken lives.
to restore broken people.
Reach out in love, and make them whole.
Amen.

84

Suffering Saviour,
broken for all,
we bring to you our fractured world,
scarred by so many gaping wounds.
We pray for the hungry and homeless –
victims of famine, disaster, war or oppression,
denied not just the bare essentials of life
but also the resources and opportunity to work for change.
Loving Lord,
bring hope and new beginnings.

We pray for the sick and suffering –
those wrestling with illness or disease,
those disabled in mind or body,
those coming to terms with the prospect of death.
Loving Lord,
bring hope and new beginnings.

We pray for the sorrowful –
those hurt or betrayed in relationships,
those whose dreams have been shattered,
those mourning loved ones.
Loving Lord,
bring hope and new beginnings.

We pray for all whose lives have been blighted by evil –
victims of violence, war and terrorism,
of crime and corruption,
of physical, sexual or verbal abuse.
Loving Lord,
bring hope and new beginnings.

We pray for communities and society as a whole –
racked by tensions and division,
torn by prejudice and discrimination,
disfigured by fear and mistrust.
Loving Lord,
bring hope and new beginnings.

We pray for this planet you have given us –
once seeming so solid and secure
but exposed now as all too vulnerable,
ravaged by years of plunder and abuse.
Loving Lord,
bring hope and new beginnings.

Suffering Saviour,
where we see problems to which there seem no solutions,
needs to which there seem few answers,
reach out to bring wholeness and healing,
the opportunity to learn from the past and so build for the future.
Loving Lord,
bring hope and new beginnings.
Amen.

85

Lord Jesus Christ,
you know what it is to be broken in body,
for your flesh was torn by the whip,
pierced by a crown of thorns,
skewered by nails in your hands and feet,
and by a spear through your side.
Hear, then, our prayer for all those broken today –
the sick and suffering, old and infirm,
victims of accident, war, torture and abuse.
Reach out to all in their pain,
and bring your healing, renewing touch.

You know what it is to be broken in mind,
for in the darkness of Gethsemane you faced the terror of the cross,
and you endured what followed alone,
betrayed,
denied,
abandoned by closest friends.
Hear then our prayer for all those broken today –
the anxious, fearful, hurt or disillusioned,
the lonely, bereaved, depressed or mentally ill.
Reach out to all in their pain,
and bring your healing, renewing touch.

You know what it is to be broken in spirit,
for you bore our sins,
carried our burdens,
endured the agony of separation from God
and the awful emptiness that entailed.
Hear then our prayer for all who are broken today –
those who have lost their faith,
and those who have never found it;
those wrestling with hopelessness,
failure,
doubt,
guilt.
Reach out to all in their pain,
and bring your healing, renewing touch.

Lord Jesus Christ,
you know what it is to be broken,
and you know what it is to be made new.
Grant your blessing today to all who are bruised and battered by life,
and restore them in body, mind and spirit.
Reach out to all in your love,
and bring your healing, renewing touch.
Amen.

86

Lord Jesus Christ,
broken for us,
remind us that the cross was not the end:
that from death came life,
from despair, hope
and from sorrow, joy –
your love bringing new beginnings.
And remind us,
above all,
that this same love is still at work,
here and now today,
able to take broken people,
broken lives,
and make them whole.
Amen.

87

Lord Jesus Christ,
we know that many suffer,
enduring untold agony of body, mind and spirit,
but we know also that few would do so willingly,
and fewer still would choose that course as their vocation in life.
Yet you came and walked the way of the cross with single-minded determination,
and you gave your life freely
so that one day there will be an end to suffering and sorrow;
a time when all will rejoice in the wonder of your love
and experience the joy of your kingdom.
Until then, Lord, reach out into our world of darkness,
into every place of need,
and bring the comfort, strength, peace and hope
that you alone can bring.
Amen.

Easter

88

Loving God,
this is a day that changes the way we think,
the way we act,
the way we live –
that changes everything.
And so we pray now for change in our world,
in all those places where there is human need.

We pray for the poor,
the homeless,
the sick
and the hungry.
Lord of life,
hear our prayer.

We pray for the victims of war,
for refugees,
for divided communities and countries,
Lord of life,
hear our prayer.

We pray for the sorrowful,
the fearful,
the troubled in heart and mind.
Lord of life,
hear our prayer.

We pray for the oppressed,
the persecuted,
the imprisoned
and the exploited.
Lord of life,
hear our prayer.

Living God,
may the truth of Easter break into each and every one of these situations,
bringing help and healing,
strength and support,
comfort and courage,
hope and help,
faith and freedom,
love and life –
the change that you alone can bring.
Lord of life,
hear our prayer.
Amen.

89

For all who have lost faith in love,
may your dying and rising, Lord, rekindle trust.

For all who have lost faith in truth,
may your dying and rising, Lord, rekindle trust.

For all who have lost faith in justice,
may your dying and rising, Lord, rekindle trust.

For all who have lost faith in good,
may your dying and rising, Lord, rekindle trust.

For all who have lost faith in life,
may your dying and rising, Lord, rekindle trust.

For all who have lost faith in themselves,
may your dying and rising, Lord, rekindle trust.

For all who have lost faith in others,
may your dying and rising, Lord, rekindle trust.

For all who have lost faith in God,
may your dying and rising, Lord, rekindle trust.

However much faith may be a struggle,
and however much hope may seem in vain,
may your dying and rising, Lord, rekindle trust.
Amen.

90

Lord Jesus Christ,
we remember the trauma which your suffering and death brought to your followers,
a grief that went beyond words
and that seemed beyond healing.
We recall how Peter wept bitterly when he realised he had denied you as you predicted;
how women sobbed on the way to the cross
and as they watched you die;
how Mary broke down in the garden,
overwhelmed with grief –
each one a symbol of the desolation and despair so many felt at your death.
But we recall also how Peter rejoiced as,
three times,
you repeated your call,
how your followers celebrated as you stood among them,
risen and victorious,
how Mary's heart soared with wonder as you spoke her name.
Gracious Lord,
wherever there is sorrow,
grant your joy.

We pray for those who suffer today –
all who endure constant pain,
who wrestle with illness,
who are victims of violence
or whose bodies are broken by accident or injury.
Gracious Lord, wherever there is sorrow,
grant your joy.

We pray for those who feel betrayed today,
cheated by loved ones,
deceived by those they trusted,
hurt by those they counted as friends,
or let down by society.
Gracious Lord, wherever there is sorrow,
grant your joy.

We pray for those who grieve today,
their hearts broken by tragedy and bereavement,
their lives torn apart –
many for whom tears are a constant companion,
laughter and happiness like some distant memory.
Gracious Lord, wherever there is sorrow,
grant your joy.

Lord Jesus Christ,
reach out into our world of so much pain, heartache and sadness.
May your light scatter the shadows,
your love lift the burdens,
and your grace bring life in all its fullness.
Gracious Lord, wherever there is sorrow,
grant your joy.
Amen.

91

Lord Jesus Christ,
in this world where hopes are so often dashed
and dreams so often broken,
we remember today the faith in the future you brought to so many,
both through your coming
and through your resurrection from the dead.
Lord Jesus, where faith has died and dreams have faded,
may hope flower again.

We remember how Mary and Joseph looked forward to the day of your birth,
how shepherds and magi caught their breath in wonder as they knelt before you,
how the hearts of Anna and Simeon leapt in anticipation,
and how your disciples and the crowds that flocked to hear you gave thanks,
convinced that you were the Messiah,
the one God had promised,
the long-awaited deliverer come to set them free.
Lord Jesus, where faith has died and dreams have faded,
may hope flower again.

We remember how that vision of the future was shattered by events to follow –
your pain, humiliation, suffering and death –
hope ebbing away as the lifeblood seeped from your body:
an end to their dreams,
an end to everything.
Lord Jesus, where faith has died and dreams have faded,
may hope flower again.

We remember how the news spread that the tomb was empty,
the stone rolled away,
your body gone,
and how,
despite it all,
your followers could scarcely bring themselves to hope –
afraid to take the risk of faith
in case they should face the heartache of losing you once more.
Lord Jesus, where faith has died and dreams have faded,
may hope flower again.

But we remember finally how you appeared,
in all your risen glory –
in the garden,
in the upstairs room,
on the Emmaus road,
by the Sea of Galilee –
and the dream was born again,
the smouldering embers of faith rekindled.
Lord Jesus, where faith has died and dreams have faded,
may hope flower again.

Lord Jesus Christ,
a world is waiting, hurting, longing,
searching for hope,
crying out for meaning,
hungry for some reason to believe in the future.
Come again in your living power,
and bring new life to all.
Lord Jesus, where faith has died and dreams have faded,
may hope flower again.
Amen.

92

Lord Jesus Christ,
into the darkness of our world,
may your resurrection continue to bring light.
Lord,
hear us.

Into the despair of our world,
may your resurrection continue to bring hope.
Lord,
hear us.

Into the emptiness of our world,
may your resurrection continue to bring meaning.
Lord,
hear us.

Into the enslavement of our world,
may your resurrection continue to bring liberty.
Lord,
hear us.

Into the sorrow of our world,
may your resurrection continue to bring joy.
Lord,
hear us.

Into the brokenness of our world,
may your resurrection continue to bring healing.
Lord,
hear us.

Risen Saviour,
in our world of need may love continue to conquer hatred,
good to defeat evil
and death to triumph over life.
Lord,
hear us.
Amen.

93

Lord Jesus Christ,
we remember today how you rose again,
bringing new beginnings out of what had seemed the end,
a new chapter in the life of your Church that is still being written today.
We recall how your resurrection changed life for the disciples,
calling them to let go of the past and embrace the future –
their role no longer simply to follow but to lead,
to go out in your risen power and proclaim the good news.
We know that life must change for us too,
but sometimes it is harder than we first anticipated,
moving on proving a painful business,
asking more of us than we feel able to give.
Take all that *has* been
and direct all that *shall* be.

Reach out to all who are finding endings hard to bear.
We think of those reeling from the termination of employment,
the breakdown of a relationship
or eviction from their homes.
Take all that *has* been
and direct all that *shall* be.

We think of those whose children are leaving home,
family and friends moving away from each other,
communities facing the upheaval of change.
Take all that *has* been
and direct all that *shall* be.

We think of those coming to terms with unfulfilled ambitions,
let down by broken promises,
or overcome by sudden catastrophe.
Take all that *has* been
and direct all that *shall* be.

We think of those disabled by disease,
mourning the loss of loved ones,
or suffering from terminal illness.
Take all that *has* been
and direct all that *shall* be.

Lord Jesus Christ,
remind all again today that endings can lead to new beginnings,
that from the old, new life can spring,
and may that confidence touch our lives
and bring hope to our troubled world.
Take all that *has* been
and open our hearts to all that *shall* be.
Amen.

94

Lord Jesus Christ,
it is hard to believe in you sometimes –
hard to believe in the message you preached,
the victory of love you proclaimed,
the way of sacrifice and self-denial you urged us to follow –
for so much in life challenges our faith,
speaking instead of the way of self,
of greed, evil, injustice and exploitation.
Yet you rose again from the tomb,
triumphant over the darkness.
Your love could not be defeated:
turn our doubt to faith.

We look at the course of human history,
and time after time it is the same –
a catalogue of hatred, violence, evil and oppression;
a world in which the strongest survive,
the wicked prosper
and the innocent are led like lambs to the slaughter.
Yet you rose again from the tomb,
triumphant over the darkness.
Your love could not be defeated:
turn our doubt to faith.

We look at the world today,
and nothing seems to change –
nations racked by division and war,
an economic order in which the few indulge their every craving
while the many are deprived of even their most basic needs;
an international system in which money outweighs principle;
a world of drugs, rape, vandalism, child abuse;
all this and so much more that scars the face of society.

Yet you rose again from the tomb,
triumphant over the darkness.
Your love could not be defeated:
turn our doubt to faith.

Lord Jesus Christ,
we know there are no easy answers to the harsh realities of life,
no glib explanations as to why suffering is allowed to continue,
evil go unchecked
and good be unrewarded.
But you have shown through your resurrection that,
whatever it may face,
love will not finally be extinguished,
and your purpose cannot be denied.
One day your will shall be done and your kingdom come.
Your love could not be defeated:
turn our doubt to faith.
Amen.

95

Lord Jesus Christ,
we praise you again in this joyful season for all that we celebrate:
the victory of love over hatred,
life over death.

We praise you for staying true to your chosen path,
despite all the malice thrown against you,
the repeated taunts to put yourself first,
and the very real temptation you must have felt to do just that.
Hear now our prayer for the world you gave your life for –
a world so racked by enmity and division
and so desperately in need of love.
Gracious Lord, wherever hatred seems to rule,
may love emerge victorious.

We pray for those whose personal relationships
have degenerated into hatred –
scarred by petty grievances and arguments,
undermined by verbal and physical abuse,
poisoned by coldness and indifference;
words spoken to wound rather than woo,

deeds designed to break down rather than build up,
all feeling and friendship long since forgotten.
Gracious Lord, wherever hatred seems to rule,
may love emerge victorious.

We pray for society at large
where hatred masquerades under a variety of guises –
prejudice, greed, selfishness, intolerance, ignorance –
so much that denies, divides and destroys,
creating a sense of 'them' and 'us',
the acceptable and the unacceptable.
Gracious Lord, wherever hatred seems to rule,
may love emerge victorious.

We pray for countries racked by inner tensions
and at odds with their neighbours –
torn apart by religious extremism,
by military dictatorships,
racial hatred,
civil war
and abuses of human rights –
lives wantonly destroyed,
families broken,
communities shattered,
nations decimated.
Gracious Lord, wherever hatred seems to rule,
may love emerge victorious.

Lord Jesus Christ,
we pray for our world in all its need –
a world of so much hatred,
yet one you loved so much you were willing to die for it,
and a world you will never abandon,
no matter how often your love is rejected.
Help us and all people to recognise the folly of our ways –
to understand that violence only breeds more violence,
vengeance more vengeance,
bitterness more bitterness
and hatred more hatred.

Give us faith and courage to try another way,
the way you revealed so powerfully through your life and your death –
the way of love.
Gracious Lord, wherever hatred seems to rule,
may love emerge victorious.
Amen.

96

Where life is dark,
may your presence bring light.
Lord, hear us,
graciously hear us.

Where evil is strong,
may good be stronger.
Lord, hear us,
graciously hear us.

Where suffering destroys,
may healing restore.
Lord, hear us,
graciously hear us.

Where sorrow bows down,
may joy lift up.
Lord, hear us,
graciously hear us.

Where doubt creeps in,
may faith hold out.
Lord, hear us,
graciously hear us.

Where deceit obscures,
may truth illuminate.
Lord, hear us,
graciously hear us.

Where hatred divides,
may love unite.
Lord, hear us,
graciously hear us.

Where war rages,
may peace reconcile.
Lord, hear us,
graciously hear us.

Where death casts its shadow,
may life shine afresh.
Lord, hear us,
graciously hear us.

Sovereign God,
may the victory we celebrate in Christ
transform not just this moment
but life itself.
Lord, hear us,
graciously hear us.
Amen.

97

Risen and victorious Christ,
you overcame evil,
defeated hatred,
scattered the darkness,
turning sorrow into joy,
despair into hope,
death into life.
So now we pray for all who struggle to make sense of their experiences of life –
those who are anxious,
fearful,
disillusioned,
depressed,
faced perhaps by inexplicable suffering, sorrow or evil,
or having lost their homes,
their employment,
their livelihoods,
their loved ones;
afflicted by disease, disability, disaster,
or exploited,
oppressed,
deprived of their basic human dignity.
God of the unexpected,
hear our prayer.

May the surprise of Easter burst afresh into the hearts of all,
revealing new possibilities to life
and a new dimension to your love,
giving new meaning to each day and every moment,
bringing new strength and opportunities,
offering new hope for the future
and renewed purpose in the present.
God of the unexpected,
hear our prayer.
Amen.

98

Almighty God,
thank you that our faith in life
and hope in the future
are based firmly on the wonder of your love
and miracle of your resurrection power
through which you are able to make all things new.
Giver of life,
hear our prayer.

Thank you that in the night-time experiences of life,
when everything can seem hopeless –
moments of sorrow,
suffering,
fear,
anxiety,
despair
and disillusionment,
even death itself –
you are able to bring a new dawn,
your light breaking into the darkness and shining brightly once more.
Giver of life,
hear our prayer.

Come now,
and shine afresh in our world,
in all its turmoil and need,
pain and injustice,
through your risen Son,
our Saviour,
Jesus Christ.
Giver of life,
hear our prayer.
Amen.

99

Almighty God,
we remember with awe the first Easter morning,
marvelling that, at a time when you seemed absent,
you were supremely at work,
and at a place where death seemed triumphant,
new life was coming to birth.
And so we pray:
take what *is* and fashion what *shall be.*

Remind us,
should we ever forget,
that you are a God of surprises,
a God who turns the expectations of this world upside down,
bringing hope out of despair,
laughter out of tears,
light out of darkness
and life out of death.
And so we pray:
take what *is* and fashion what *shall be.*

Work afresh now in our world of pain and need,
and show to all that no situation,
however bleak or hopeless it may seem,
is finally outside the scope of your love and transforming power –
able to make us and all things new.
And so we pray:
take what *is* and fashion what *shall be.*
Amen.

100

Living God,
we look at the world and at our lives
and we are dismayed sometimes at how little seems to change.
May your grace bring hope;
your love bring new beginnings.

We go on making the same mistakes we've always made,
and all around us there seems to be as much sorrow
suffering,
hatred
and evil
as there has ever been.
May your grace bring hope;
your love bring new beginnings.

Help us to hold on to the conviction that life can change;
to remember how,
in the resurrection of Christ,
you overcame the power of sin and death.
May your grace bring hope;
your love bring new beginnings.

Help us to remember that
though everything may seem to conspire against you,
you have won the victory through him –
a victory that nothing can ever undo –
and so may we trust in your ability to transform and renew all things.
May your grace bring hope;
your love bring new beginnings.
Amen.

101

Lord Jesus Christ,
it was not just *you* who was broken on a cross –
it was your disciples too,
their hearts broken just as surely,
their dreams and hopes snuffed out,
their faith cut from beneath them and laid to rest.
Where the future seems bleak and empty,
may hope flower again.

It was not just *you* who rose again –
it was your disciples too,
their hearts beating once more with joyful anticipation,
their vision for the future reborn,
their faith rekindled, bursting into unquenchable flame.
Where the future seems bleak and empty,
may hope flower again.

Come to us now where *we* are broken –
wherever love had died,
hope has faded,
faith grown cold.
Reach out and touch us in body, mind and spirit,
and help all to walk in the newness of life that you alone can bring.
Where the future seems bleak and empty,
may hope flower again.
Amen.

102

Lord Jesus Christ,
in a world where so much questions faith,
denies love
and threatens commitment,
may your resurrection life bring hope,
convincing all of your eternal purpose:
the blessings you hold in store –
imperishable,
unfading,
kept in heaven –
and may that assurance sustain us now and always.
Amen.

103

Lord Jesus Christ,
wherever shadows darken lives
and light seems extinguished,
grant the assurance that you not only endured death
but also rose victorious;
that you experienced the full force of hatred
and conquered it with love;
that you took on the powers of evil
and worked through them for good.

Remind us all, then, that your light will always shine,
nothing in heaven or earth finally being able to overcome it.
Amen.

104

Renewing and life-giving God,
as we celebrate again your victory over death
and triumph over evil,
open our hearts today to the way you are able to change our lives
and transform our world.
Remind us of your resurrection power all around us,
bringing hope out of despair,
joy out of sorrow,
peace out of turmoil
and love out of hatred,
and in that faith may we live now and trust for the future,
assured that nothing can defeat your purpose
or deny the life you offer for all eternity,
through Jesus Christ our Lord.
Amen.

105

Risen Lord,
continue to change our lives,
continue to change your people,
continue to change the world,
through your resurrection power and love.
Amen.

Ascension Day

106

Lord Jesus Christ,
Ruler of all,
Servant of all,
we pray again for the kingdoms and rulers of this world,
that those in positions of authority
may use their power in the service of their people
and for the good of all.
Servant King,
may your love reign supreme.

We pray for those who take counsel together on behalf of nations;
all those who carry the responsibility of leadership.
Grant them wisdom in all their decisions,
humility to listen to the point of view of others,
courage to stand up for what is right,
and a determination to work for justice and peace.
Servant King,
may your love reign supreme.

We think of our own country,
and we pray for the royal family and especially our Queen,
thanking you for the example she has given,
the dedication to duty she has shown,
and the commitment to our nation she has displayed throughout her rule.
Grant to her,
and to her successor when the time comes,
your guidance, discernment, strength and inspiration.
Servant King,
may your love reign supreme.

We pray for our government and members of Parliament,
giving thanks once more for the service they give.
Guide them in their discussions and decisions,
and give them a proper sense of the responsibility entrusted to them.

Help them to work not just for personal or party interest
but for the good of all.
Servant King,
may your love reign supreme.

We pray for all who strive to build a fairer society
and a better world –
those who campaign against poverty, injustice and exploitation;
who work for peace and reconciliation;
who offer healing to body, mind or spirit;
who serve the needy.
Encourage them in their work,
support them in adversity,
provide the resources they need,
and make known your love through their ministry.
Servant King,
may your love reign supreme.

Lord Jesus Christ,
we pray that your kingdom may come,
despite everything that seems to fight against it;
a kingdom in which the first are last and the last first,
in which everything that frustrates your purpose
and denies your love is defeated,
and in which all can live together in justice and harmony.
Servant King,
may your love reign supreme.
Amen.

107

Lord Jesus Christ,
humble yet exalted,
servant yet sovereign,
teach us afresh today that through honouring others
we honour you,
and through serving them we serve you.
Through our life and love, Lord,
reach out to others in turn.

Awaken us to your presence all around us,
and to your call, especially, in the cry of the needy,
and in responding to the hungry,
the sick,
the lonely
and the oppressed,
may we respond also to you.
Through our life and love, Lord,
reach out to others in turn.

Reach out to us in mercy,
that we might reach out to you and to all in love.
Amen.

108

Lord Jesus Christ,
crowned with thorns yet crowned with glory,
lifted up on a cross yet exalted on high,
crucified as a criminal yet honoured as Lord,
sealed in a tomb yet triumphant over death,
remind us again today of your transforming power
and renewing love;
the way you overturn the wisdom of this world,
bringing victory out of defeat,
joy out of sorrow
and hope out of despair.
Teach us again, as we worship you,
that you are able to change our lives and our world,
bringing light into our darkness,
wholeness in our brokenness.
Reach out in love
and work your miracle of grace.
Amen.

109

Lord of lords and King of kings,
teach us to honour you through living by the values of your kingdom:
to serve you through *serving*,
love you through *loving*,
give to you through *giving*.
Come into our hearts,
our lives,
our world,
and rule among us.
Amen.

Pentecost

110

Holy Spirit,
coming as wind and fire,
free and irrepressible,
we pray today for all who long for change
and for all who fear it.

We think of the poor and the hungry,
the homeless and the refugee,
the sick and the unemployed,
the downtrodden and the oppressed –
these, and so many others, who yearn for a new beginning,
an opportunity to start afresh.
May their prayers be answered and their dreams realised.
As you came at Pentecost,
come again today.

We pray for those who see change as a threat:
a sweeping-away of everything that is tried and trusted;
the imposition of unknown challenges and an uncertain future.
May they rest secure in the knowledge that,
whatever else may change,
you will remain constant.
As you came at Pentecost,
come again today.

Holy Spirit,
coming gently as a dove,
we pray for all who long for peace,
and all who have lost sight of what peace really means.
We think of those in homes racked by tensions,
families split by petty disputes,
communities scarred by prejudice and intolerance,
and countries torn apart by war.
May dialogue triumph over confrontation,
and unity replace division.
As you came at Pentecost,
come again today.

We pray for those who fill their lives with noise or activity,
afraid of facing themselves in a time of quiet reflection,
attempting somehow to mask their sense of emptiness;
and we pray, too, for those who seek fulfilment in that which can never finally satisfy –
wealth, possessions, power, success.
May they discover the secret of true contentment,
the peace that passes understanding that only you can give.
As you came at Pentecost,
come again today.

Holy Spirit,
you changed the lives of the apostles
and of countless people through history,
just as you are changing our lives in turn,
each renewed through your sovereign power.
Come now and change our world in all its need,
so that it may enjoy hope and peace,
healing and harmony,
and so that all may come to a saving knowledge of Jesus Christ our Lord.
As you came at Pentecost,
come again today.
Amen.

Trinity Sunday

111

Father God,
your purpose is for all,
for you are the Lord of heaven and earth,
the Creator of humankind,
Ruler over history.
You are always at work,
always involved in our lives,
calling,
guiding,
speaking
and responding,
everyone being important to you, no matter who they are,
each having a place in your purpose.
So, then, we pray for all in our world who feel they are drifting,
all who search for meaning to their lives,
a sense of direction,
a goal to strive for.
May they find, in Jesus Christ, the way, the truth and the life.
In faith we lift them before you:
hear our prayer.

Son of God,
your love is for all,
for you lived and died for others,
reaching out to both rich and poor,
Jew and Gentile,
righteous and unrighteous,
nobody being outside your care,
no one beyond your grace.
You gave your all,
enduring death on a cross,
so that everyone willing to receive you
may share in the joy of your kingdom.
So we pray for all in our world today who long for love –
those who yearn for a meaningful relationship,
and those whose once-precious relationships have ended in tears;
those who have been abandoned or orphaned as children,
and those who cannot have children of their own;

those cut off from family and friends,
and those who face the trauma of bereavement.
May they discover in you a love that will never let them go.
In faith we lift them before you:
hear our prayer.

Spirit of God,
your peace is for all,
for you are at work in every heart,
seen or unseen,
recognised or unrecognised,
striving to break down the barriers that keep us from one another,
from ourselves
and from you.
We pray, then, for all in our world who hunger for peace –
all who are tormented by fear,
torn by doubt,
troubled by anxieties,
or tortured by guilt;
families separated by feuds,
communities racked by division,
and nations ravaged by war.
May they find, through you, peace in body, mind and spirit.
In faith we lift them before you:
hear our prayer.

Almighty God,
Father, Son and Holy Spirit,
we bring you our world,
thankful that it is also *your* world,
precious to you and shaped ultimately by your will.
Remake,
redeem,
renew it through your sovereign power.
May all people everywhere come to know your purpose,
experience your love
and receive your peace,
and may each rejoice in the new life you so yearn to give them.
In faith we lift them before you:
hear our prayer.
Amen.

All Saints' Day

112

We remember today all who have gone ahead of us in the journey of faith,
running the race set before them,
and holding firm to the end.
Loving God,
grant to them, to us and to all your people your eternal blessing.

We remember those you called to trust –
those like Abraham, Isaac and Jacob –
examples of faith who have been an inspiration to
generations since.
Loving God,
grant to them, to us and to all your people your eternal blessing.

We remember those you called to lead your people
through adversity –
those like Moses, Joshua, Gideon –
examples of commitment and determination against all odds.
Loving God,
grant to them, to us and to all your people your eternal blessing.

We remember those you called to speak your word –
those like Samuel, Elijah, Elisha –
examples of wisdom and insight into your will.
Loving God,
grant to them, to us and to all your people your eternal blessing.

We remember those you called to rule your chosen nation –
those like Saul, David, Solomon –
examples of human greatness and human fallibility.
Loving God,
grant to them, to us and to all your people your eternal blessing.

We remember those you called to proclaim judgement and renewal –
those like Isaiah, Ezekiel, Jeremiah –
examples of openness to your word
and courage in proclaiming it.
Loving God,
grant to them, to us and to all your people your eternal blessing.

We remember these and so many more who anticipated the coming of Christ,
and we remember also your servants who were a part of his ministry,
or a part of his Church.
Loving God,
grant to them, to us and to all your people your eternal blessing.

We remember John the Baptist, the voice in the wilderness,
Mary, the mother of Jesus,
the twelve apostles, his friends and confidantes,
the women at the empty tomb, looking in vain for his body,
and all those countless individuals who were touched by his earthly ministry.
Loving God,
grant to them, to us and to all your people your eternal blessing.

We remember Peter, the Rock of the Church,
Paul, apostle to the Gentiles,
and those who have followed in their footsteps,
saints known and unknown, near and far,
yet each a part of the great company of your people
in heaven and on earth.
Loving God,
grant to them, to us and to all your people your eternal blessing.

We remember those we have known,
those who have been part of our own church,
who have influenced our lives,
who have inspired and encouraged us through their commitment.
Loving God,
grant to them, to us and to all your people your eternal blessing.

We remember those around us,
the churches of our town,
Christians across the country,
fellow believers throughout the world.
Loving God,
grant to them, to us and to all your people your eternal blessing.

And we pray for those who will come after us,
all who will come to faith,
offer their service,
and live for Christ.
Loving God,
grant to them, to us and to all your people your eternal blessing.

Remembering today those who have gone before us in the journey of faith,
we ask Lord, for all your Church , help to run the race as they did,
holding firm to the end.
Loving God,
grant to them, to us and to all your people your eternal blessing.
Amen.

113

Sovereign God,
reminded of the wider fellowship that we share in Christ,
the great company of your people in heaven and on earth
to which we are privileged to belong,
so now we pray for those who seek, in turn, to follow you today.
Rock of ages,
hear our prayer.

We pray for those for whom commitment is costly –
those who face hostility,
discrimination,
repression
and persecution
for the cause of the gospel.
Give them strength and courage,
so that they may keep the faith.
Rock of ages,
hear our prayer.

We pray for those who are finding the journey of discipleship difficult –
troubled by doubts,
plagued by temptation,
or simply slipping back into old ways.
Give them support and reassurance,
so that they may walk with new confidence.
Rock of ages,
hear our prayer.

We pray for those expressing their faith in action –
individuals through personal acts of kindness,
and agencies like Christian Aid, CAFOD, Tearfund and Shelter,
together with so many others,
working, often against the odds,
to give expression to the love of Christ.
Give them love and compassion,
so that they may make Christ real for others.
Rock of ages,
hear our prayer.

We pray for all seeking to communicate their faith –
ministers, evangelists, missionaries, chaplains,
but also ordinary, everyday believers like us –
each telling in their own way what Jesus means to them.
Give them wisdom and inspiration,
so that they may speak your word with power.
Rock of ages,
hear our prayer.

Sovereign God,
we pray for Christians everywhere striving to live out their
faith today,
with all the pressures, challenges and demands that confront them.
Give them guidance and encouragement,
so that they may grow in grace.
Grant them humility to learn more of you each day
and the ability to share their experience simply and effectively
with others,
making Christ known through word and deed.
Rock of ages,
hear our prayer.
Amen.

114

Almighty God,
we come together as those you have called into fellowship,
to be your people
and to share in the rich inheritance of your saints.
In and through us, Lord,
build your kingdom.

We come to worship you,
not alone,
but as part of the worldwide family of the Church,
united with our brothers and sisters in Christ across countries and continents,
centuries and generations,
bound together by the same Lord and the same faith.
In and through us, Lord,
build your kingdom.

We come as part of the great company of your people in heaven and on earth,
following in the footsteps of past generations,
picking up the torch from those who have run the race before us
and who have kept the faith,
heirs of your age-old promises.
In and through us, Lord,
build your kingdom.

We come as those called to build for the future,
conscious of successive generations that will follow us,
and mindful of our responsibility to pass on to them the message we have received,
to offer them inspiration and encouragement through the example of our commitment.
In and through us, Lord,
build your kingdom.

We come then united with all your people of past, present and future,
of here, there and everywhere,
all those who call upon your name and offer you their service.
In and through us, Lord,
build your kingdom.
Amen.

The Church Year

Old Year/New Year

115

Gracious God,
as we come to you at this time of new beginnings,
we are reminded of those who feel the future holds no promise,
those who struggle with burdens to which they can see no solution.
Take all that *has* been
and direct what *shall* be.

We pray for those facing pressures of home –
relationships strained between husband and wife,
parent and child,
brother and sister –
patience stretched to breaking point.
Take all that *has* been
and direct what *shall* be.

We pray for those facing pressures of work –
overwhelmed by responsibilities,
caught up in office politics,
troubled by job insecurity,
or simply bored and unhappy in what they do.
Take all that *has* been
and direct what *shall* be.

We pray for those facing pressures of money –
struggling to make ends meet,
crippled by debt,
frustrated by poor pay,
or uncertain whether and when their next pay cheque will arrive.
Take all that *has* been
and direct what *shall* be.

We pray for those facing pressures of health –
waiting perhaps for a diagnosis,
crushed by depression,
wrestling with infirmity as the years go by,
or living with the knowledge of terminal illness.
Take all that *has* been
and direct what *shall* be.

We pray for those facing pressures of faith –
racked by doubts,
troubled by questions,
feeling themselves cut off from your love,
enduring the dark night of the soul.
Take all that *has* been
and direct what *shall* be.

Gracious God, as we step into another year,
may your love, compassion, strength and support
reach out to all who are hurting,
and may you bring to them a sense of hope –
the conviction that, however bleak it may seem,
the future is in your hands,
now, and for all eternity.
Take all that *has* been
and direct what *shall* be.
Amen.

116

Loving God,
at the dawn of another year
hear our prayer for those who long to start again –
all who recognise their faults,
acknowledge their mistakes
and seek in you new beginnings.
In mercy, hear us:
in love, respond.

Hear our prayer for those who despair of changing –
all who have come to faith but find the old self stronger than they imagined,
their weaknesses still leading them astray,
their failings just as real.
In mercy, hear us:
in love, respond.

Hear our prayer for those who refuse to change –
all who knowingly oppose your will,
taking the way of greed,
selfishness,
hatred
and violence.
In mercy, hear us:
in love, respond.

Hear our prayer for those who work for change –
all who proclaim your grace and minister your love in word and deed,
working to win hearts and transform lives.
In mercy, hear us:
in love, respond.

What *we* cannot change,
achieve through your renewing Spirit,
bringing a fresh chapter,
a clean slate,
a new dawn for all.
In mercy, hear us:
in love, respond.
Amen.

The Week of Prayer for Christian Unity

see also Poetic prayers: For the Church

117

Loving God,
we pray for those many churches –
far too many –
which have experienced divisions among themselves,
split apart over issues of doctrine, worship and authority.
For all that denies our unity in Christ,
forgive us, O Lord.

We pray for those whose faith has been undermined by such disputes,
who feel hurt and let down by what has taken place,
and we pray also for those left to pick up the pieces.
For all that denies our unity in Christ,
forgive us, O Lord.

We pray for those outside the Church who have witnessed such division,
those who have been put off by what they have seen,
seeing it as an argument against the truth of the gospel,
a contradiction of everything we proclaim about you.
For all that denies our unity in Christ,
forgive us, O Lord.

Loving God,
unite your Church in every place,
drawing together those of different denominations,
temperaments,
outlooks
and traditions.
May there be a respect between all,
a willingness to work together,
and a sense of unity that speaks beyond such differences.
For all that denies our unity in Christ,
forgive us, O Lord.
Amen.

118

Lord Jesus Christ
we pray today for your Church,
conscious of the issues that still divide us,
our failure to enjoy the oneness you desire.
Wherever your body is broken today,
make us one, Lord.

We pray for Christians who feel threatened by contrasting patterns of worship,
diverging expressions of faith,
and conflicting theological positions;
who reject those they do not agree with as unsound,
rather than risk engaging in genuine dialogue.
Give them openness to other points of view.
Wherever your body is broken today,
make us one, Lord.

We pray for fellowships that have been torn in two,
split by controversies over doctrine and churchmanship,
divided over issues of faith and worship,
or undermined by petty disputes.
Instil in them a spirit of healing and reconciliation.
Wherever your body is broken today,
make us one, Lord.

We pray for denominations involved in moves towards greater unity,
striving to overcome years of separation
but finding themselves tied down by procedure and practicalities,
frustrated by bureaucracy and tradition.
Grant wisdom and insight, so that obstacles may be overcome.
Wherever your body is broken today,
make us one, Lord.

Lord Jesus Christ,
reach out to your Church
and work in hearts everywhere,
to break down barriers,
to overcome prejudice,
and to bring people together in genuine love and understanding.
Wherever your body is broken today,
make us one, Lord.
Amen.

119

Lord Jesus Christ,
you call us to love one another;
forgive the ways that Christians across the centuries have done the opposite,
hating those who think differently than they do,
persecuting those whose interpretation of the Bible clashes with their own.
Lord, in your mercy,
hear our prayer.

You call us to be one;
forgive the fact that,
too often,
it has been our divisions rather than unity that has caught the eye,
speaking not of your grace and goodness
but of human weakness and intolerance.
Lord, in your mercy,
hear our prayer.

You call us to make you known;
forgive the way the Church has sometimes forced its faith upon others,
and in so doing has put across a false picture of who and what you are.
Forgive the countless evils that have been perpetrated in the name of religion;
evils that have besmirched your name
and led people away from rather than towards you.
Lord, in your mercy,
hear our prayer.

Teach us always to be open to you and to others,
and truly to walk the way of Christ,
so that the world may know we are Christians by the sincerity of our love.
Lord, in your mercy,
hear our prayer.
Amen.

120

Lord God our Father,
we thank you for the family to which you have called us,
for our fellowship here,
the denomination of which we are part,
and the great company of the Church,
past, present and future.
For all your people,
hear our prayer.

We pray for one another,
those of our fellowship who have moved away,
those who are confined to their homes through age and infirmity,
those who are unwell,
those who have become disillusioned
and those who have lost their faith.
For all your people,
hear our prayer.

We pray for the churches of our town,
striving through word and deed to make known the love of Christ.
We think especially of those in positions of leadership and oversight,
asking that you will give them the faith and wisdom that they need,
and we pray also for those in their charge,
that they will respond gladly to opportunities for service,
making vision become reality.
For all your people,
hear our prayer.

We pray for the wider family of the Church,
all those seeking to work out their faith in their own particular situations.
We think especially of those who are persecuted for their beliefs,
all for whom commitment to Christ is dangerous and costly.
Grant them courage in adversity,
and help them to stand up for their convictions against all the odds.
For all your people,
hear our prayer.

We pray for the unity of the Church,
for the breaking down of barriers
and a further growing together,
and we pray also for the witness of your people everywhere,
that through their life and service
your love will be made known,
your word proclaimed,
and your kingdom brought closer.
For all your people,
hear our prayer.
Amen.

121

Lord Jesus Christ,
reach out in love to this foolish, faithless world
and, by your grace, tend our wounds.
Come again to all who are hurting and hating,
and overcome the things that still keep us apart.
Amen.

Christian Aid Week

see also under Poetic prayers: For healing, justice and peace in our world; For ourselves, the Church and the world; For real and lasting change; For those who strive for social justice; For a world in need; *also* Themed prayers: Social justice

122

Living God,
you have taught us through Jesus
that our neighbours are not just those who live next door,
or those who live nearby,
but everyone, everywhere.
And so now, once again, we pray for our world,
our neighbours near and far.
Lord of heaven and earth,
hear our prayer.

We pray for victims of injustice –
those who live in poverty,
or face starvation,
or have no roof over their heads.
Lord of heaven and earth,
hear our prayer.

We pray for victims of natural disasters –
those whose lives have been overwhelmed by flood,
earthquake,
or other catastrophe.
Lord of heaven and earth,
hear our prayer.

We pray for victims of war:
those who mourn loved ones,
those maimed and wounded,
and those forced to flee as refugees,
leaving possessions,
livelihoods,
and everything they hold dear.
Lord of heaven and earth,
hear our prayer.

Living God,
teach us to respond –
to reach out to our troubled, divided world,
recognising the call of our neighbour in the cry of the needy;
to see that, whatever may divide us, more unites us,
that beyond our differences lies a common humanity.
Lord of heaven and earth,
hear our prayer.

Help us to ensure that love triumphs over hatred,
goodness over evil,
justice over corruption,
and peace over war.
Lord of heaven and earth,
hear our prayer.

May the time come when, as individuals and as nations,
we live together as neighbours –
members together of an extended family of humankind.
Lord of heaven and earth,
hear our prayer.
Amen.

123

Almighty and all-loving God,
you have provided for our needs in plenty –
not just our daily bread but far more besides.
such that we have little idea what it means to go hungry.
But we think now of the many people in our world
who are less fortunate than we are.
Reach out to hold.
Reach out to help.

We pray for those facing famine,
the homeless,
those overwhelmed by disease,
victims of war and genocide,
those with inadequate means to provide for themselves or improve their situation,
the weak,
the sick
and the oppressed.

Reach out to them in their need,
and give them courage and strength,
the conviction that someone cares,
a reason to look forward.
Reach out to hold.
Reach out to help.

Almighty and all-loving God,
grant your blessing on all who, like Christian Aid,
strive to help the needy,
all who campaign for their cause –
who supply food and clothing,
nursing and medicine,
education and training,
crops and machinery,
the will and the opportunity to help themselves.
Reach out to hold.
Reach out to help.

Grant that those who are hungry may find bread for life,
and teach us the part we must play in bringing that to pass,
working for your kingdom not just in heaven,
but here on earth.
Reach out to hold.
Reach out to help.
Amen.

124

Lord of all,
we pray for those in need throughout the world,
remembering that, in their cry, you are calling for help,
and that, in responding to them, we respond to you.
Your kingdom come,
on earth as it is in heaven.

We pray for those who have no food –
those for whom hunger is an ever-present experience,
who do not know where the next meal is coming from,
who each day face the prospect of starvation.
Your kingdom come,
on earth as it is in heaven.

We pray for those deprived of the resources we take for granted –
fresh water,
clothing,
housing,
education
and medical care –
countless millions who have so little
while the few of us have so much.
Your kingdom come,
on earth as it is in heaven.

We pray for those who work for change –
organising and transporting relief supplies,
offering resources and opportunities for self-help,
striving to overcome exploitation and oppression,
campaigning for peace and justice for all.
Your kingdom come,
on earth as it is in heaven.

Use these,
and all your people,
to show something of your love and compassion.
Reach out,
wherever there is hunger,
poverty,
homelessness
and disease,
and stir the hearts of individuals and nations to live more simply,
so that others may simply live.
Your kingdom come,
on earth as it is in heaven.
Amen.

125

Gracious God,
as we come to you on this Christian Aid Sunday,
we are conscious that we are the lucky ones –
those with food in our bellies and a roof over our heads,
with ample supplies of water and medicine,
with access to education and technology –
our lives brimming over with good things.
You have given us so much:
teach us to give generously in turn.

We pray for the millions less fortunate than us –
those for whom hunger is a daily reality,
a proper home a luxury,
fresh water, medical care and education a dream,
and the lifestyles we enjoy here in the West
a source of wonder and bewilderment.
You have given us so much:
teach us to give generously in turn.

We know we cannot change the world alone,
yet we know also that, with your help, nothing is impossible.
Challenge us, then, to give sacrificially,
to live more simply,
and to work for change;
to remember those in need in both our prayers and our actions,
so that we may truly make a difference.
You have given us so much:
teach us to give generously in turn.

Sovereign God,
forgive us that it takes a day like Christian Aid Sunday to turn our thoughts to the poor.
Help us to live for others throughout our lives,
to practise what we preach,
and to work towards the fulfilment of our prayers
through the things we do
and the people we are.
You have given us so much:
teach us to give generously in turn.
Amen.

126

Lord of all,
we pray today for all in our world who are ill-equipped to cope with what life brings them –
the poor, the hungry and the homeless;
the disabled, the sick and the suffering;
the oppressed, the weak, the persecuted.
Lord, in your mercy,
hear our prayer.

We pray for those denied their basic human rights –
a basic education,
employment,
freedom of speech and conscience,
or the proper reward for their labours.
Lord, in your mercy,
hear our prayer.

We pray for those living in lands racked by war,
victims of brutality and violence,
and we pray for refugees,
those with no country to call their own.
Lord, in your mercy,
hear our prayer.

Lord of all,
we thank you for those who have the courage to stand up for such people –
the resolve to stand out against injustice,
and the faith to believe something can be done about it –
organisations like Christian Aid that work tirelessly,
despite powerful opposition,
frequent misunderstanding,
and all kinds of obstacles,
to build a fairer world.
Lord, in your mercy,
hear our prayer.

Give them strength to continue their work,
and give us the will to support their cause,
not just once each year in Christian Aid week,
but every day,
through the lives we live,
the sacrifices we make,
and the faith we proclaim.
Lord, in your mercy,
hear our prayer.
Amen.

Harvest Festival

127

Lord of all,
as we thank you for our harvest
we remember those who do not celebrate –
those whose harvest is poor or non-existent,
those with insufficient resources to tend their land,
those denied a just reward for their labours,
those whose harvest has been destroyed in the chaos of war
or by natural disaster.
Lord, you have blessed us richly:
teach us to remember others.

Help us, as we celebrate our plenty,
to remember those who have so much less –
the poor and needy of our world,
driven by famine, disaster or civil war to the brink of starvation.
Help us to respond with love and concern,
offering whatever help we can.
Lord, you have blessed us richly:
teach us to remember others.

Lord of all,
speak to us at this harvest time,
so that our hearts may be stirred
and our consciences quickened.
Teach us to share our bounty with those who have nothing,
so that the time may one day come when all have enough
and none too much.
Lord, you have blessed us richly:
teach us to remember others.
Amen.

128

Creator God,
we pray for those to whom we owe our harvest,
all whose labour and dedication enables us enjoy the bounty of this world's resources.
Gracious Lord,
hear our prayer.

We pray for farmers at this time of difficulty for so many –
a time of so much change and complexity,
of increasing pressures and demands,
of growing challenges and problems.
Grant your help in overcoming adversity.
Gracious Lord,
hear our prayer.

We pray for farmers in other countries –
denied the resources they need to cultivate their land,
overwhelmed by drought, flood or other catastrophe,
oppressed by exploitative regimes or economic systems loaded against them –
both they and their people unable to enjoy the due fruits of their labours.
Grant them hope, help and justice.
Gracious Lord,
hear our prayer.

We pray for those who bring in the harvest of earth and sea –
minerals, oil, gas, fish –
a harvest often involving danger to life and limb.
Grant them skill, courage and protection.
Gracious Lord,
hear our prayer.

We pray for those who make possible the harvest of technology –
scientists, technicians, computer programmers and engineers –
their skills opening up new worlds and untold horizons,
capable of so much good yet so much evil.
Grant them wisdom, ingenuity and a due sense of responsibility.
Gracious Lord,
hear our prayer.

We pray for those who help to reap the harvest of minds –
teachers, students, researchers and scholars –
each striving to expand our knowledge and enlarge our understanding.
Give them patience, dedication and integrity.
Gracious Lord,
hear our prayer.

Creator God,
hear our prayer for all who harvest the innumerable and diverse riches of your creation.
Equip, inspire and guide them in their work,
so that they may steward your gifts wisely to the good of all.
Gracious Lord,
hear our prayer.
Amen.

One World Week

see also under Themed prayers: Social justice; World peace and harmony

129

Loving and living God,
we rejoice that this is your world,
created by your hand,
sustained by your power,
guided by your purpose.
So now we bring it to you,
seeking your blessing on all its affairs.
In mercy, hear us:
in love, respond.

We pray for peace,
that the leaders of all nations may work to reduce weaponry and promote dialogue.
We pray for justice,
that the abundance of this earth's resources may be distributed more evenly.
We pray for liberty,
that moves towards greater democracy and freedom may prosper.
We pray for harmony,
that everyone, irrespective of race, sex, or creed,
may be valued for what they are.
In mercy, hear us:
in love, respond.

We do not pray only for the big things in life
but also for the little,
rejoicing that all situations are important to you,
all people matter in your sight.
So we bring the business of each day,
small in the eyes of the world, but important to us:
the responsibilities of family life and parenthood;
the cost of buying and running a home;
the problems of earning a living and making ends meet;
the joys and sorrows of marriage and relationships;
the well-being of our loved ones;
our places of work and recreation, worship and relaxation.

We put these into your hands,
knowing that they matter to you as much as they matter to us.
In mercy, hear us:
in love, respond.

Loving and living God,
we rejoice that you are involved in our world,
and involved in our lives,
not distant or remote,
but seeking the good of everything you have made.
Gratefully we put our trust in you.
In mercy, hear us:
in love, respond.
Amen.

130

Loving God,
we come to you today as the family of your people,
those you have united in Christ,
and as we come, reminded of that great truth,
we give you thanks for all the families to which we belong.
Lord of all,
bind us together in love.

We think of the families among whom we have been raised –
those with whom we have shared so much,
to whom we are specially close,
and who will always be uniquely precious to us.
Lord of all,
bind us together in love.

We think of the family of this church –
the fellowship we find here,
the friends we have made,
and the encouragement we give to one another.
Lord of all,
bind us together in love.

We think of the family of the Church as a whole –
those across this country,
across the world,
across the centuries who are one with us in Christ.
Lord of all,
bind us together in love.

We think of the family of humankind,
the common bond that ties us together,
the variety of peoples and nations of which we form a part,
the rich diversity of cultures and customs.
Lord of all,
bind us together in love.

Loving God,
we thank you that we share something in common with all people,
near and far,
our lives being interwoven,
interrelated,
interdependent,
intertwined.
Help us, we pray, to recognise more fully what that means,
to appreciate the responsibilities it brings
and the opportunities it offers,
and so may we learn to love our neighbours as ourselves.
Lord of all,
bind us together in love.
Amen.

131

Sovereign God,
Lord of all,
we pray once more for our troubled and divided world,
so full of tension,
so full of need.
We pray for our world,
recognising that it is *your* world also,
and your world *first*.
Lord, in your mercy,
hear our prayer.

We pray for those who strive to bring liberty –
a world free from religious and political persecution,
from racial bigotry and ethnic cleansing,
from dictatorship and oppression.
Strengthen their resolve,
and may the evil that holds people captive be destroyed.
Lord, in your mercy,
hear our prayer.

We pray for those who strive to bring justice –
a world free from exploitation and corruption,
prejudice and discrimination,
debt and dependence.
Prosper them in their work,
and may the rights of all be respected.
Lord, in your mercy,
hear our prayer.

We pray for those who strive to bring peace –
the breaking down of barriers between nations,
the challenging of long-held prejudices,
and the promotion of dialogue and reconciliation.
Encourage them in their efforts,
and may the fears and suspicions that divide us be overcome.
Lord, in your mercy,
hear our prayer.

We pray for those who strive to bring answerability –
an awareness of our common humanity,
of our responsibility towards the environment,
and of the consequences of our actions.
Speak through their voice,
so that your creation may be passed on intact to future generations.
Lord, in your mercy,
hear our prayer.

Sovereign God,
come again to our broken world
and grant your healing.
Bring peace where there is war,
and love where there is hatred;
reconciliation where there is division,
and cooperation where there is conflict;

good where there is evil,
and wisdom where there is folly.
Instil in all a willingness to engage in dialogue rather than dispute,
in discussion rather than destruction,
and so may your world become the *one world* you long for it to be.
Lord, in your mercy,
hear our prayer.
Amen.

132

Lord of all,
overcome the barriers that keep us apart –
the walls of fear and hatred that separate person from person,
country from country
and continent from continent.
Though we are many,
make us one.

Overcome the causes of division:
greed,
injustice,
envy,
prejudice.
Though we are many,
make us one.

Reach out to people everywhere
and, whatever their colour, culture or creed,
draw them together and heal their wounds,
so that we may learn to live and work together as one people,
one world,
united in our common humanity.
Though we are many,
make us one.
Amen.

133

Help us, Lord, to realise that we don't live in isolation
but are part of a wider world
in which not just our words and deeds
but our very lifestyles
impact on others.
Open our hearts to you.
Open our lives to all.

Awaken us to the ways in which our pleasures may be secured at others' expense,
how our gain can be their loss.
Open our hearts to you.
Open our lives to all.

Give us sensitivity,
compassion
and generosity of spirit,
so that in whatever we do,
however innocent it may seem,
we may consider the effect it has on other people's lives,
and take steps,
where necessary,
to change.
Open our hearts to you.
Open our lives to all.
Amen.

134

Lord Jesus Christ,
bring healing to our broken and bleeding world,
and, in your mercy, bind up our wounds.
Reach out afresh into the hearts of all,
and overcome the causes of hurt and hatred,
sorrow and suffering –
whatever estranges person from person
and nation from nation.
Challenge whatever keeps us apart,
and make us one.
Amen.

135

Lord of the nations,
when we browse in the shops or fill our basket at the supermarket,
speak to us of justice and injustice,
trade and commerce,
toil and effort,
sweat and tears –
of the interdependence of humankind
and the complex web of life.
Remind us each day of what we owe to others,
near and far,
and the many ways they enrich our lives.
Remind us of the breadth and wonder of creation
and of our responsibilities towards all.
Amen.

136

Give us each day, Lord, a concern not just for our own welfare
or that of our loved ones
but for people everywhere;
a recognition that we are part of a vast family of humankind,
our lives intertwined and interdependent.
Amen.

137

Father God,
help us to see beyond what separates us from others,
to the common humanity,
and above all the same Lord,
that binds us together as one.
Amen.

Remembrance Day

138

Lord of all,
hear us now as we pray for the victims of war
and for peace in our world.

We pray for those who bear the scars of conflict –
the injured, maimed and mentally distressed,
those who have lost their limbs, their reason or their loved ones
through the horrors of war.
Lord, in your mercy,
hear our prayer.

We pray for those left homeless or as refugees,
those who have lost their livelihoods and security,
and those who still live in daily fear for their lives.
Lord, in your mercy,
hear our prayer.

We pray for children who have been orphaned,
parents who mourn their children,
husbands and wives who have lost their partners –
countless families whose lives will never be the same again.
Lord, in your mercy,
hear our prayer.

We pray for those in the armed forces,
charged with keeping the peace in countries across the world –
their work involving months away from family and friends,
and often danger to themselves.
Lord, in your mercy,
hear our prayer.

We pray for world leaders and rulers,
politicians and diplomats –
those whose decisions and negotiations affect the lives of so many,
and in whose hands peace ultimately lies.
Lord, in your mercy,
hear our prayer.

Lord of all,
give wisdom to all who work for peace,
so that a more secure future may be ensured for all.
Give courage to those who strive for justice,
so that the causes of conflict may be overcome.
Give strength to those who seek to break down barriers,
that divisions over race, colour, creed and culture may be ended.
Grant that wherever war, or the threat of war, continues to haunt lives,
a way of reconciliation may be found,
and harmony established between people and nations.
Lord, in your mercy,
hear our prayer.
Amen.

139

Living God,
we are here to remember –
to remember again the awful cost of war,
to remember the millions who gave their lives for the cause of freedom,
to remember the courage and heroism,
fear and pain,
tragedy and grief of so many.
At the going down of the sun, and in the morning,
we will remember them.

Living God,
we are here to remember all of this, and much more besides –
those who still mourn the loved ones they lost,
those whose lives even now are blighted by war,
those scarred in body, mind or spirit,
those for whom warfare has meant life can never be the same again.
At the going down of the sun, and in the morning,
we will remember them.

And we remember also those who strive to establish and maintain peace –
governments and world leaders,
United Nations' forces and diplomats,
pressure groups and ordinary people;
all who in different ways strive to promote harmony between nations,
giving victims of war the opportunity to live a normal life once more.
At the going down of the sun, and in the morning,
we will remember them.

Living God,
we remember today the cost of war,
and the price of peace.
Help us to go on remembering, tomorrow and every day,
and to do all in our power to work for your kingdom,
here on earth.
At the going down of the sun, and in the morning,
we will remember them.
Amen.

140

Loving God,
we remember today the awfulness of conflict,
the stark reality of war.
Come afresh to our broken world,
and by your grace bring healing.

We remember how countless lives were lost or shattered in two world wars,
yet also how evil, hatred and injustice were overcome
through courageous service and selfless sacrifice.
Come afresh to our broken world,
and by your grace bring healing.

And we remember all who continue to serve,
each day risking life and limb in the course of duty.
Come afresh to our broken world,
and by your grace bring healing.

Teach us to appreciate the freedom we enjoy
and never to forget what it cost so many.
Conscious of the debt we owe,
may we always cherish the things so many died for –
liberty, justice and peace –
so that their deaths will not have been in vain.
Come afresh to our broken world,
and by your grace bring healing.
Amen.

141

Remind us, Lord,
lest we forget,
of the debt we owe to so many:
the life made possible for us through their deaths.
Help us to cherish and nurture the things they died for –
liberty,
justice
and peace –
so that their sacrifice will help to build a better world
and not have been in vain.
Amen.

142

Loving God,
grant that the time may come when swords will be beaten into ploughshares
and spears into pruning hooks,
when nation will no longer take up sword against nation
or train for war any more.
Heal our divisions,
and grant enduring peace to our world.
Amen.

Special Services

Mothering Sunday

see also Special Services: Infant baptism/Dedication;
and under Themed Services: Health – Childbirth; Home and family

143

Gracious God,
on this Mothering Sunday we bring you our prayers
for all entrusted with the responsibility of motherhood.
Loving Lord,
hear our prayer.

We pray for mothers the world over,
recognising both the joys and demands they experience –
the privilege and pressures,
hopes and fears,
pleasure and pain that motherhood entails.
Equip them with the love, wisdom and strength they need.
Loving Lord,
hear our prayer.

We pray for single mothers,
bearing the responsibility of parenthood alone,
struggling sometimes to make ends meet,
and stigmatised by certain sections of society.
Grant them the emotional, physical and financial resources they need.
Loving Lord,
hear our prayer.

We pray for mothers who have experienced heartbreak –
their children stillborn or seriously disabled,
injured, maimed or killed through accident or assault,
struck down by debilitating disease or terminal illness.
Comfort them in their sorrow.
Loving Lord,
hear our prayer.

We pray for those denied the joy of motherhood –
enduring the trauma of infertility,
prevented on health grounds from risking a pregnancy,
or unable to establish a relationship into which children can be born.
Help them to come to terms with their pain.
Loving Lord,
hear our prayer.

We pray for those who foster or adopt children,
those who long to do so but who are denied the opportunity,
and those who for various reasons have given up their children
and who are haunted by the image of what might have been.
Grant them your strength and support.
Loving Lord,
hear our prayer.

We pray finally for those who long to discover their natural mothers,
those who have become estranged from them,
and those whose mothers have died –
all for whom Mothering Sunday brings pain rather than pleasure,
hurt rather than happiness.
May your love enfold them always.
Loving Lord,
hear our prayer.

Gracious God,
we pray for mothers and children everywhere.
May your blessing be upon them,
your hand guide them,
and your love enrich them all.
Loving Lord,
hear our prayer.
Amen.

144

Gracious God,
you know what it is to love your children –
to watch over them tenderly,
anxiously,
proudly
and constantly.

You know what this means,
for you have called us your children,
and you care for each of us as deeply as a mother cares for her child.
So now we pray for those entrusted with the responsibility of motherhood –
all who watch over their children in the same way,
with the same feelings and intensity.
Grant to each one your wisdom, guidance and strength.
Lord of love,
hear our prayer.

We pray especially for single mothers –
those faced with the challenge of raising a child or children on their own,
with no one else to share the demands or joys of parenthood.
Give to each of them patience, devotion and dedication.
Lord of love,
hear our prayer.

We pray for those who have lost their mothers
or never known them,
those orphaned as children or given up for adoption,
those whose mothers have died,
all for whom this day brings pain rather than pleasure.
Grant them your comfort,
your support
and the assurance of your love always with them.
Lord of love,
hear our prayer.

We pray finally for those who are separated from their children –
those whose young ones have moved far from home,
those who have suffered a miscarriage or been through an abortion,
those who have endured the agony of a child's death.
Give to them your help,
your solace,
and hope for the future.
Lord of love,
hear our prayer.

Gracious God,
you understand what mothers face,
what they give,
what they feel.

Accept our thanks for them this day,
and grant them your special blessing.
Lord of love,
hear our prayer.
Amen.

145

Gracious God,
thank you for your gift of children,
for the joy,
the laughter,
and the fun they bring in so many ways.
Thank you for their innate zest for life –
the interest, excitement and fascination they find in so much we count as ordinary.
Thank you for their special qualities –
their innocence,
trust,
enthusiasm,
energy,
and sheer hunger to learn.
We lift them now to you:
open your heart to all.

Gracious God,
we pray for children everywhere,
so precious to us,
so precious to you.
Watch over them,
protect them,
guide them
and bless them.
We lift them now to you:
open your heart to all.

And hear also our prayer for those who are childless,
or who long to conceive another child.
Reach out to them in their pain,
their frustration,
their disappointment,
their anger.

Help them not to lose hope until all hope is past,
and if that time finally comes
give them the comfort you alone can bring,
and courage to channel their love to those around them.
We lift them now to you:
open your heart to all.

Finally we pray for disadvantaged children –
those who are disabled, abused, orphaned,
undernourished, unloved, unwanted –
so many denied the start in life they deserve
and the care they need.
We lift them now to you:
open your heart to all.

Loving God,
in Christ you welcomed little children,
demonstrating their importance to you,
their special place in your heart.
Prosper the work of all who care for children today –
all who strive to give them a better life,
a brighter future,
a safer world in which to grow.
Use them, and us, to make real your care for all.
We lift them now to you:
open your heart to all.
Amen.

Father's Day

146

Gracious God,
you know the joy of fatherhood,
and also the pain,
for you witnessed the life and death of your Son,
and you see each day the triumphs and tragedies of us,
your children.
Lord God our Father,
reach out in love.

In Jesus you experienced the delight of being a father –
as you watched him grow and mature into adulthood,
as you saw him baptised in the Jordan,
as day by day he responded to your guidance,
faithful to the very last –
a beloved son with whom you were well pleased.
Yet also you experienced agony –
in the horror of the cross,
the pain,
the humiliation,
and the sorrow he endured for our sakes.
Lord God our Father,
reach out in love.

In each of us you find pleasure –
when we pursue what is good,
when we honour your commandments,
when we seek your will and respond to your guidance.
But we cause you also so much pain –
through our weakness,
our repeated disobedience,
our deafness to your call
and our rejection of your love.
Lord God our Father,
reach out in love.

Gracious God,
you know the joy and the pain of fatherhood,
and so now we pray for fathers everywhere.
Help them to appreciate both the privilege
and the responsibility they bear,
and teach them to give freely of themselves
so that they may discover the happiness,
the fulfilment,
and the inexpressible rewards that fatherhood brings.
Lord God our Father,
reach out in love.

Give fathers wisdom, patience and dedication,
and when children brings tears as well as laughter,
anxiety as well as hope,
pain as well as pleasure,
grant them guidance as to how to respond.
Lord God our Father,
reach out in love.

Reach out, we pray, to all fathers in such circumstances –
those who question their ability to cope,
or who fear they have failed;
those striving to offer support,
or who feel they have nothing left to give.
Lord God our Father,
reach out in love.

And, finally, hear our prayer for children who,
on this Father's Day,
feel pain instead of joy –
those whose fathers have died,
those orphaned as children,
those who have been mistreated, rejected, abused,
and those from broken homes who barely see or know their fathers.
Lord God our Father,
reach out in love.
Amen.

147

Father God,
we pray today for those entrusted with the responsibility of fatherhood,
all who have the duty and privilege of raising children,
fashioning their lives,
offering a stable and loving environment in which they can grow,
leading them along the exciting yet demanding path to adulthood.
Grant them love, insight and devotion.
Father of all,
hear our prayer.

We pray for fathers whose relationship with their partner has broken down;
separated from their children or seeing them only occasionally,
many having responsibilities for another family;
and we pray also for stepfathers who will fill the role that once was theirs.
Grant them commitment, dedication and sensitivity.
Father of all,
hear our prayer.

We pray for fathers with no sense of responsibility,
failing to make time for their children,
careless in offering support and guidance,
casual in providing discipline,
washing their hands of their role as parents.
Grant them forgiveness,
and the opportunity to make amends.
Father of all,
hear our prayer.

We pray for children of broken homes,
deprived of a father figure
or knowing first one, then another,
rarely able to establish a meaningful and lasting relationship.
Grant them stability,
support
and the knowledge that they are still loved.
Father of all,
hear our prayer.

We pray for children abused by their fathers,
emotionally scarred for life,
struggling to come to terms with their experience,
haunted by an image of fear rather than love.
Grant them healing, peace and courage to face the future.
Father of all,
hear our prayer.

Finally, we pray for those who have lost their fathers,
whether as children or as adults,
for some their father seeming little more than a name,
for others, a heart-wrenching memory,
but each carrying a sense of loss.
Grant your strength, your comfort and your hope.
Father of all,
hear our prayer.

Father God,
we lift before you today fathers and their children.
Enfold them in your love,
and surround them with your fatherly care,
today and every day.
Father of all,
hear our prayer.
Amen.

Songs of Praise/Music Service

148

Living God,
we have sung your praises,
offering to you our worship in joyful celebration,
but we know that there are some who have very different feelings at this time.
We remember how your people long ago cried out by the waters of Babylon:
'How can we sing the Lord's song in a strange land?' –
their lives overwhelmed by sudden catastrophe,
their hopes for the future crushed,
their faith in your purpose shaken.
So now we pray for those today who are facing sorrow and suffering,
all for whom life seems a burden rather than a blessing.
Reach out in love,
and put a song of joy into their hearts.

We pray for those whose song is one of despair –
the poor and weak,
oppressed and exploited,
hungry and homeless –
all those denied the opportunity to help themselves,
condemned to a lifetime of making do as best they can.
Reach out in love,
and put a song of joy into their hearts.

We pray for those whose song is one of fear –
those in lands torn by war,
in communities racked by violence,
in homes and relationships broken by abuse;
victims of racial discrimination and sexual harassment,
or religious intolerance and political persecution –
all whose safety is daily put in doubt.
Reach out in love,
and put a song of joy into their hearts.

We pray for those whose song is one of grief –
all who have lost loved ones,
or seen them broken by accident or sickness,
or whose relationships have ended in separation;
those who have been betrayed or otherwise let down,
who have been hurt by words or deeds,
whose hopes and dreams have come to nothing.
Reach out in love,
and put a song of joy into their hearts.

We pray for those whose song is one of pain –
the sick and suffering,
those wrestling with chronic disease,
coming to terms with disabling injury,
battling against terminal illness.
Reach out in love,
and put a song of joy into their hearts.

We pray for those whose song is one of confusion –
overwhelmed by the complexities of life,
unsure of their ability to cope,
burdened by daily demands and responsibilities,
uncertain as to the right way forward.
Reach out in love,
and put a song of joy into their hearts.

Living God,
we look forward to that day when every tongue will sing your praises,
and all will rejoice in the light of your presence.
Until that time,
may everyone for whom life is hard know your hand upon them,
and find in you the strength and the hope they need
to walk safely through the valley of tears and the shadow of suffering,
confident that night will give way to dawn.
Reach out in love,
and put a song of joy into their hearts.
Amen.

149

Loving God,
we have come to you in song,
expressing our praise and gratitude for all you have done
and everything you have given.
But we pray now for those in our world who feel they have nothing to sing about,
nothing to celebrate or rejoice over –
the poor, the sick and the hungry,
the homeless, the unemployed, the downtrodden,
the weak, the vulnerable and the oppressed,
the lonely, the unloved and the unwanted,
the sorrowful, the depressed and the despairing,
the sick, the diseased, the dying.
Lord, in your love, put a new song into their hearts –
a song of hope instead of despair.

We pray for those for whom life brings intolerable demands –
those facing famine,
fleeing as refugees,
suffering persecution,
enduring war,
struggling against injustice,
terrified of the future,
haunted by the past.
Lord, in your love, put a new song into their hearts –
a song of hope instead of despair.

Loving God,
reach out in compassion to all in such circumstances,
assuring them that, despite appearances, you are there,
sharing their pain,
anxious for their welfare,
hungry to bless.
May the day come when they, with us,
join in singing songs of praise,
Lord, in your love, put a new song into their hearts –
a song of hope instead of despair.
Amen.

Believer's Baptism/Confirmation

(Where text is italicised, insert name/select gender, as appropriate)

150

Living God,
we thank you for your call,
your gracious invitation to respond to your love
that goes on reaching out to us until we have turned to you
and accepted the gift of new life you so long to give us.
Lord, hear us,
graciously hear us.

We thank you for the way *A* has responded to that call,
publicly committing *his/her* life today to the service of Christ,
and we pray now for everything the future holds for *him/her.*
Lord, hear us,
graciously hear us.

Grant your guidance, strength and inspiration,
keep *his/her* faith strong
and *his/her* love for you burning bright,
and may your blessing enrich *his/her* life.
Lord, hear us,
graciously hear us.

We pray for all those who have committed their lives to you,
declaring Jesus Christ as their Lord and Saviour.
Equip them for service,
unite them in love,
empower them through your Spirit,
and bless them with peace.
Lord, hear us,
graciously hear us.

We pray for those who resist your call,
afraid of what commitment might entail.
Conquer their doubts,
overcome their hesitation,
and may they discover the blessing they have been missing.
Lord, hear us,
graciously hear us.

We pray for those who are unmoved by your call,
untouched by the message of the gospel.
Speak your word,
stir their hearts,
and touch their lives with your blessing.
Lord, hear us,
graciously hear us.

We pray for those who have responded to your call
and then gone back,
the faith they once professed grown cold.
Rekindle the flame,
restore their vision
and may your blessing thrill them once more.
Lord, hear us,
graciously hear us.

Living God,
may your word reach out with power,
creating, sustaining and renewing faith.
May your call touch our lives, today and always,
and may we respond with heartfelt devotion
and faithful service.
Lord, hear us,
graciously hear us.
Amen.

Infant Baptism/Dedication

see also Special Services: Mothering Sunday

(Where text is italicised, insert name/select gender, as appropriate)

151

Creator God,
we worship you today for the gift of a new life.
We come with joy in our hearts,
to thank you for this child,
to praise you for all *his/her* birth means to us,
and all it means to you.
Enfold them in love
and grant your blessing.

We thank you for the love that has brought *A* into being,
the care that surrounds *him/her,*
the excitement *his/her* arrival has brought,
and the happiness that *he/she* has given
to those around *him/her.*
Enfold them in love
and grant your blessing.

Watch over *A*.
Guide *his/her* footsteps.
Protect *him/her* from danger.
Bless *him/her* with health.
Fill *him/her* with joy.
And in the fullness of your time
may *he/she* come to know your love,
and respond to you in faith,
discovering the joy and peace
that you alone can offer.
Enfold them in love
and grant your blessing.

Creator God,
we pray also for *C* and *D*,
whom you have entrusted
with the responsibilities of parenthood –
give them wisdom,

patience,
devotion,
and dedication.
Enfold them in love
and grant your blessing.

May *A* enrich their lives in immeasurable ways,
and may they in turn offer *A* the security of a loving, caring home in which to grow.
Help them, through their words and actions,
to sow the seeds of your love in *A*'s heart,
and then to give *him/her* space to make *his/her* response
in *his/her* own time
and own way.
Enfold them in love
and grant your blessing.

Creator God,
we thank you for this day,
this child,
and this family.
And we thank you for your love that surrounds all,
this day and always.
Enfold them in love
and grant your blessing.
Amen.

152

Gracious God,
we pray for *AB* in whatever the future may hold for *him/her.*
May your hand be there to lead,
and your love be there to bless.

Grant help to *A* in times of learning,
so that *he/she* may grow in wisdom and understanding,
in knowledge, skill and ability,
and in experience and character,
equipped to make the most of life's possibilities.
May your hand be there to lead,
and your love be there to bless.

Grant *A* your strength in times of testing –
the ability to overcome difficulties,
withstand trials,
and conquer temptation,
staying true to *his/her* convictions
and emerging stronger out of adversity.
May your hand be there to lead,
and your love be there to bless.

Grant your guidance in times of uncertainty –
discernment as to the right way forward,
patience in coming to a decision,
and confidence that a door will open,
your will ultimately becoming apparent.
May your hand be there to lead,
and your love be there to bless.

Grant your peace in times of turmoil –
the knowledge that, whatever may happen, you are there,
nothing ever being able to separate us from your love,
and so may *A* be able to meet changing circumstances of life with equanimity,
assured of your ultimate purpose.
May your hand be there to lead,
and your love be there to bless.

Grant your blessing in times of opportunity,
so that *A* may discover lasting love,
enduring joy,
and fulfilment in work, faith and life.
May your hand be there to lead,
and your love be there to bless.

Gracious God,
put your hand upon *A*,
watch over *him/her*,
direct *his/her* footsteps
and make known to them your love,
so that *he/she* may respond freely to you
and know you as fully as you know them.
May your hand be there to lead,
and your love be there to bless.
Amen.

153

Gracious God,
you have brought this child into being –
go with *him/her* now in their journey of life.
Be there to hold;
be there to lead.

May *he/she* know joy,
health,
and peace.
Be there to hold;
be there to lead.

May *he/she* grow in love,
wisdom,
and faith.
Be there to hold;
be there to lead.

Direct *his/her* steps,
keep *him/her* from evil,
and help *him/her* to live life in all its fullness,
this day and always.
Amen.

Church Anniversary/Rededication

154

Loving God,
at this time of rededication,
we pray for ourselves and for others.

We pray for those who feel they have failed you –
burdened by a sense of guilt,
ashamed of their faithlessness,
and convinced that their mistakes can never be forgiven.
Assure them of your mercy,
your constant willingness to help us start again.
Lord, in your mercy,
hear our prayer.

We pray for those who have lost their faith –
those who once professed faith in Christ,
but who have drifted away,
losing their first flush of enthusiasm,
and abandoning the commitment they once made.
Stir their hearts,
and rekindle faith within them.
Lord, in your mercy,
hear our prayer.

We pray for those unsure of what you would have them do;
certain that you have called them,
yet unclear as to the way you would use their gifts,
or which avenue of service you want them to pursue.
Speak your word,
and help them to hear your voice.
Lord, in your mercy,
hear our prayer.

We pray for one another –
the future stretching before us,
rich in promise,
full of possibilities for worship, fellowship and service.
Help us to respond in faith,
and to make the most of all the opportunities life brings us.
Lord, in your mercy,
hear our prayer.

Loving God,
may those who do not know you hear your call,
those who knew you once come to know you again.
and those who long to know you better receive your guidance.
Come now, and draw us closer to you,
to the glory of your name.
Lord, in your mercy,
hear our prayer.
Amen.

The Lord's Supper

155

Living God,
we are reminded as we share this supper of how,
before he died,
Jesus prayed for unity –
not just in the Church and among Christians
but in the world as a whole;
between individuals and nations,
creeds and cultures.
So now we pray for harmony and peace,
an end to all that divides.
In a broken world,
may all be one through Christ.

We pray for those places scarred by violence and conflict,
sectarian tension or ethnic unrest,
warfare, terrorism or genocide.
In a broken world,
may all be one through Christ.

We pray for victims of intolerance and prejudice,
hatred and persecution;
all whose lives are blighted by division and discord,
religious extremism or political ideology.
In a broken world,
may all be one through Christ.

We pray for those who ferment division,
inflaming passions and inciting violence,
resorting to the bomb or bullet in pursuit of their goals,
maiming or killing the innocent with no compunction or remorse.
Stir their consciences and bring an end to the cycle of violence.
In a broken world,
may all be one through Christ.

We pray finally for the Church,
asking forgiveness for its history of disunity
and praying for an ever-deepening spirit of togetherness,
so that, instead of denying your purpose,
it may testify to your reconciling love;
a love that breaks down all that keeps us apart.
In a broken world,
may all be one through Christ.
Amen.

156

Gracious Lord,
reminded of all you suffered for our sakes,
we bring before you the pain and sorrow so many endure.
We pray for reconciliation in a world of so much division –
an overcoming of the barriers of fear, hatred and suspicion
that overshadow so many lives.
Lord Jesus Christ, suffering to bring us life,
hear our prayer.

We pray for justice in a world of haves and have-nots –
an end to greed, corruption and exploitation;
to persecution and oppression;
to violence and terror;
to all that denies dignity of life and opportunity for the future.
Lord Jesus Christ, suffering to bring us life,
hear our prayer.

We pray for unity in the Church –
a spirit of trust and harmony,
love and acceptance,
so that, respecting our differences,
we may work together as one people
with one goal.
Lord Jesus Christ, suffering to bring us life,
hear our prayer.

We pray for those of all faiths, philosophies, creeds and convictions –
that there may be dialogue rather than confrontation,
and respect rather than dismissal.
Lord Jesus Christ, suffering to bring us life,
hear our prayer.

We pray finally for those, known and unknown to us,
stretched to breaking point by their experiences of life –
the disheartened and disillusioned,
the depressed, lonely, afraid and anxious,
the sick and terminally ill,
those who mourn loved ones;
all for whom the future seems bleak or the present hopeless.
Lord Jesus Christ, suffering to bring us life,
hear our prayer.
Amen.

157

Jesus Christ,
Light of the World,
wherever life seems dark, bleak, hopeless,
may your love bring a new dawn.
Lord of life,
hear our prayer.

Jesus Christ,
Shepherd of the Sheep,
wherever people feel lost,
searching for guidance and direction,
may your love lead them forward.
Lord of life,
hear our prayer.

Jesus Christ,
Bread of Life,
wherever people hunger for meaning and purpose,
something to give shape to their lives,
may your love nourish them deep within.
Lord of life,
hear our prayer.

Jesus Christ,
Living Water,
where life has lost its sparkle
and laughter seems a thing of the past,
may your love rekindle joy.
Lord of life,
hear our prayer.

Jesus Christ,
the True Vine,
wherever your people strive to serve you,
working for your kingdom,
may your love flow in, through and from them.
Lord of life,
hear our prayer.

Jesus Christ,
Prince of Peace,
wherever there is war and division,
hatred and violence,
may your love bring lasting reconciliation.
Lord of life,
hear our prayer.

Jesus Christ,
Lamb of the World,
wherever there is hurt and suffering
may your love bring healing.
Lord of life,
hear our prayer.

Jesus Christ,
Man of Sorrows,
wherever there is heartache and heartbreak
may your love bring comfort.
Lord of life,
hear our prayer.

Jesus Christ,
the Resurrection and the Life,
wherever death casts its shadow
may your love bring the promise of eternal blessing.
Lord of life,
hear our prayer.

Jesus Christ,
Lord of all,
to you be praise and glory,
honour and worship,
now and always.
Amen.

158

Lord Jesus Christ,
as you put your faith in God's future,
trusting that you would drink again of the fruit of the vine in your Father's kingdom,
so we pray for new beginnings in our world today.
Saviour of all,
hear us.

May peace replace war,
dialogue replace confrontation,
and unity replace division.
Saviour of all,
hear us.

May those who grieve find joy,
those who despair find hope,
and those who suffer find relief.
Saviour of all,
hear us.

May the homeless receive refuge,
the hungry receive food,
and the oppressed receive justice.
Saviour of all,
hear us.

May truth conquer falsehood,
love conquer hatred,
and good conquer evil.
Saviour of all,
hear us.

Help all to put their trust in you,
confident that grace will triumph over law,
right over wrong,
and life over death.
Saviour of all,
hear us.
Amen.

159

Lord Jesus Christ,
broken for all,
risen for all,
we bring before you
the broken people of our world.

We pray for the broken in body:
victims of disease, hunger or neglect,
of torture and violence,
of disaster or accident.
Loving Lord,
bring healing.

We pray for the broken in mind:
those oppressed by fears and phobias,
alcohol or drug abuse,
depression or other clinical disorders.
Loving Lord,
bring healing.

We pray for the broken in spirit:
those whose hopes have been shattered,
trust betrayed,
faith destroyed,
or resilience tested beyond the limit.
Loving Lord,
bring healing.

Lord Jesus Christ,
broken for all,
risen for all,
grant, we pray, renewed life for all.
Loving Lord,
bring healing.
Amen.

160

Lord Jesus Christ,
we remember that, before you died,
you prayed not for yourself but for others,
and not simply for your followers,
but for all people, everywhere.
You offered your life not just for the chosen few
but for the whole world,
your desire being that everyone should come to know your love for themselves.
So now we pray for our world of so much good yet so much evil,
so much joy yet so much sorrow,
so much beauty yet so much ugliness.
Come among us,
and establish your kingdom.

We pray for those who have plenty
and those who have little,
those for whom life brings pleasure
and those for whom it brings pain.
We remember all who celebrate
and all who mourn,
all who look forward with confidence
and all who view the future with dread.
Come among us,
and establish your kingdom.

We pray for those who know you
and those who don't;
those of other faiths
and those of none.
We remember those who look for truth
and those who feel they can never find it;
those who seek purpose
and those who believe life is devoid of meaning.
Come among us,
and establish your kingdom.

We remember the rich and the poor,
the healthy and the sick,
the well-fed and hungry,
the employed and unemployed,
the free and the oppressed,
the comfortably housed and the homeless.
Come among us,
and establish your kingdom.

Lord Jesus Christ,
we pray for our world in all its contrasts,
and for the situations people face in all their complexity.
Teach us that everyone, everywhere, matters to us
because they matter to you,
and so help us to respond wherever we are able,
in the name of Christ.
Come among us
and establish your kingdom.
Amen.

161

Lord Jesus Christ,
you wrestled in Gethsemane with a turmoil of emotions.
Hear our prayer for all today who wrestle in turn,
struggling to make sense of life,
unsure of their ability to get through.
May your grace bring hope;
your love bring help.

After sharing supper you faced betrayal and denial.
Hear our prayer for all today who feel let down by loved ones,
abandoned by those they looked up to,
forsaken by people they trusted.
May your grace bring hope;
your love bring help.

You endured mockery and humiliation before Pilate.
Hear our prayer for all today who are misrepresented,
misjudged and mistreated,
their humanity belittled,
their basic rights denied.
May your grace bring hope;
your love bring help.

You suffered unspeakable agony on the cross.
Hear our prayer for victims of violence and torture,
and for those whose bodies are broken by injury or disease.
May your grace bring hope;
your love bring help.

You entered into the darkness of death and coldness of the tomb.
Hear our prayer for those coping with terminal illness,
for those we have loved and lost,
for all who have died.
May your grace bring hope;
your love bring help.

Lord Jesus Christ,
you rose again,
overcoming all that would deny life and destroy good,
doing away with it,
defeating evil.
Grant new beginnings in our world today,
victory over everything that frustrates your purpose,
and the assurance of your kingdom,
where sorrow, sickness and suffering will be no more.
May your grace bring hope;
your love bring help.

Until then we pray,
reach out in love,
reach out to bless.
May your grace bring hope;
your love bring help.
Amen.

Themed Prayers

The anxious and fearful

see also under Themed prayers: Health; Trouble, those facing

162

Living God,
we pray for those who face the future with uncertainty or anxiety –
those who fear it,
who despair of it
or who feel they have no future.
In your mercy Lord,
give guidance, peace and confidence.

We pray for those in the troubled places of our world –
those who long for peace,
an end to conflict and a time of harmony,
but who in their hearts have given up hoping.
In your mercy Lord,
give guidance, peace and confidence.

We pray for those who face trauma and upheaval in their lives –
what seemed secure swept from under them,
what they had hoped for denied them,
what they had trusted in proven false.
In your mercy Lord,
give guidance, peace and confidence.

We pray for those who doubt their ability to cope with what life may bring –
those overwhelmed by pressures,
paralysed by fears,
crushed by sorrows.
In your mercy Lord,
give guidance, peace and confidence.

We pray for those faced with difficult decisions –
circumstances beyond their control,
unexpected dangers,
awkward choices.
In your mercy Lord,
give guidance, peace and confidence.

Living God,
reach out to all for whom the future seems uncertain or unwelcome,
and bring the assurance that even in the darkest moments,
the greatest challenges,
the most worrying times,
you are there working out your purpose;
able to bring light out of darkness,
hope out of despair,
joy out of sorrow
and good out of evil.
In your mercy Lord,
give guidance, peace and confidence.

Grant the assurance that there is nothing in heaven or earth,
in life or death,
in the present or the future,
that is finally able to separate us from your love,
through Jesus Christ our Lord.
Amen.

163

Living God,
we pray for all those who are weighed down by the stresses and strains of daily life –
those who long for peace of mind,
who crave rest for their souls,
but cannot find it.
Lord, in your mercy,
hear our prayer.

We pray for those oppressed by worry,
unable to throw off their anxieties,
held captive by a multitude of secret fears.
Lord, in your mercy,
hear our prayer.

We pray for those who cannot let go,
those who find it impossible to relax or unwind,
always fretting over this or that.
Lord, in your mercy,
hear our prayer.

We pray for those who lose themselves in busyness,
masking their true feelings
and running from their emptiness,
hoping that keeping active might bring them happiness.
Lord, in your mercy,
hear our prayer.

We pray for those who have lost time for you,
allowing the pressures and demands of each day to shut you out,
putting off any thought of you until tomorrow.
Lord, in your mercy,
hear our prayer.

We pray for those who have no time for you,
no interest in anything other than their daily routine,
no awareness of their spiritual needs.
Lord, in your mercy,
hear our prayer.

Living God,
speak to each one in your still small voice,
and grant them your peace that passes understanding,
the quiet confidence that only you can bring,
and so may their burdens be lifted
and their souls refreshed.
Lord, in your mercy,
hear our prayer.
Amen.

164

Lord of all,
we pray for all who are searching for peace in their lives –
those burdened with anxiety,
either about themselves or their loved ones,
facing difficulties and problems to which they can see no solutions.
God of peace,
reach out and still the storm.

We pray for those wrestling with inner fears and phobias,
torn apart by emotional and psychological pressures.
God of peace,
reach out and still the storm.

We pray for those living among change and upheaval,
especially all who are threatened by violence and warfare.
God of peace,
reach out and still the storm.

To all those in chaos and turmoil,
all who are restless and troubled,
grant your calm,
your tranquillity,
your quietness,
your peace beyond that of this world.
God of peace,
reach out and still the storm.
Amen.

165

Loving God,
we pray for all who are bearing heavy burdens –
those facing difficulties and problems to which they can see no solutions,
wrestling with inner fears and phobias,
racked by anxiety for themselves or loved ones,
troubled about money, health, work or relationships –
all who crave rest for their souls but cannot find it.
In your mercy,
hear our prayer.

We pray for those who feel crushed under a weight of care,
and for those who in seek to minister to them,
sharing their burden,
offering hope and encouragement,
comforting and supporting,
simply being there for them in their time of need.
In your mercy,
hear our prayer.

Work through them, Lord, to offer love and guidance,
help and inspiration,
and, above all, speak in your still small voice,
granting the peace and quiet confidence that only you can bring;
so that anxieties may be lifted and troubles overcome.
In your mercy,
hear our prayer.
Amen.

The armed forces

see also The Church Year: Remembrance Day

166

Sovereign God,
bless those who serve in our armed forces.
Equip them with the reserves and resources they need to fulfil their missions,
not seeking war or glorifying violence,
but fighting evil where necessary,
confronting oppression,
combating terror
and working for just and lasting peace.
Protect from danger,
and give help in adversity,
courage in moments of fear,
and coolness in times of crisis,
enfolding them and their loved ones in your gracious care,
now and always.
Amen.

167

Hear our prayer, Lord, for those who serve in the armed forces,
and especially today for chaplains within the various services.
In peace or conflict,
routine manoeuvres or active service,
help them to reflect Christ's love,
making him known through their life and ministry.
Equip them to inspire and uplift,
comfort and reassure,
nourish and nurture,
challenge and enrich,
so that, in the harsh realities and tensions of this world,
they may offer a glimpse of something deeper –
a sense of purpose worth living for,
and, if necessary, worth dying for.
Amen.

The bereaved

see also Poetic prayers: For those under the shadow of death

Those who mourn

168

Loving God,
you have promised that those who mourn shall be comforted.
So now we pray for all facing sorrow at this time.
Reach out to hold.
Reach out to help.

We pray for those who grieve for loved ones,
struggling to come to terms with personal tragedy.
Cradle them in your everlasting arms.
Reach out to hold.
Reach out to help.

Loving God,
hold on to all who walk through the valley of tears.
Minister to them,
and grant them the knowledge that you are with them,
sharing their pain and moved by their sorrow.
Reach out to hold.
Reach out to help.

Minister the consolation that you alone can offer,
and give them the assurance
that those who mourn shall be comforted;
those who weep will laugh,
those who despair will hope once more.
Reach out to hold.
Reach out to help.
Amen.

169

Loving God,
you have promised your special blessing to those who mourn,
your comfort to those overwhelmed by grief,
your joy to those enduring sorrow.

So now we pray for those facing sadness,
those burdened by misery,
those weighed down by despair,
those who have lost loved ones
and who are striving to come to terms with the emptiness and heartbreak they feel.
Lord, hear us,
graciously hear us.

We pray for those known to us who are facing such times,
all those among family, friends and colleagues,
all those among our own fellowship,
and all in the wider world.
Lord, hear us,
graciously hear us.

Loving God,
grant to those who grieve your special blessing.
May they know that your hand is upon them,
your arms encircling them,
and your heart reaching out to them.
Lord, hear us,
graciously hear us.

May all who mourn discover the comfort you have promised,
and find strength to face tomorrow,
until that time comes when light shall dawn again,
and hope be born anew.
Lord, hear us,
graciously hear us.
Amen.

170

Loving God,
hear our prayer for all who mourn,
all who have lost loved ones.
Into the darkness,
shed your light.

Reach out to them in their shock,
grief,
sorrow
and loneliness,

and grant them the comfort you promise,
the assurance that death is not the end but the gateway to new life.
Into the darkness,
shed your light.

May that truth support them as they struggle to come to terms with their loss,
helping to soften the sense of emptiness and separation that threatens to overwhelm them.
Into the darkness,
shed your light.

Give to all a similar confidence in your eternal purpose:
a sure and certain faith in your love that has defeated the last enemy,
that has triumphed over the grave and will never let us go.
Into the darkness,
shed your light.

Death has been swallowed up by victory!
May that knowledge support and sustain us,
this and every day.
Into the darkness,
shed your light.
Amen.

171

Loving God,
we remember today all who mourn,
their hearts broken by tragedy,
tears a constant companion,
laughter and happiness seeming a distant memory.
May your grace bring hope;
your love bring healing.

Reach out into their pain, heartache and sadness,
and give them the knowledge that you understand their hurt
and share their sorrow.
May your grace bring hope;
your love bring healing.

May your arms enfold them,
your love bring comfort,
and your light scatter the shadows,
so that they may know joy once more
and celebrate life in all its fullness.
May your grace bring hope;
your love bring healing.
Amen.

172

Gracious God,
reach out to our broken and bleeding world,
and bind up its wounds.
Minister to those who are sorrowful and hurting,
and bring solace deep within.
Comfort all who walk through the valley of tears
and bring the assurance that those who mourn will one day laugh –
that, by your grace,
tears will give way to laughter,
and despair to delight.
Amen.

173

Caring God,
thank you for the assurance that in times of sorrow you will be there to comfort –
ready to mend our broken hearts
and bring us joy once more.
Amen.

174

Eternal God,
in the ugliness of death
speak of life born again,
and in the apparent finality of the grave
point to new beginnings.
To all who mourn
give the assurance that the close of one chapter
is the opening of another;
that this world is the gateway to your eternal kingdom.
Amen.

175

Everlasting God,
remind us that even in the darkest days of life
and the bleak chill of death,
you are there,
bringing new beginnings.
For your life-giving power,
beyond containment,
receive our praise.
Amen.

176

God of all comfort,
when we despair,
life bringing hurt and sorrow,
give us strength to continue,
until light dawns,
hope returns
and tears are wiped away.
Amen.

177

Gracious God,
we need to grieve when we lose loved ones,
for the sorrow is real,
the pain hard to bear;
but we also need to rejoice,
for with you death is not the end but a new beginning.
The shell is empty
but has nurtured life;
the casket is bare
but its treasure is safe in your hands;
the person we knew we will know again,
for they are truly at home,
secure in your everlasting arms,
alive with all your people, for evermore.
May that truth comfort and strengthen those who mourn,
giving them the assurance that nothing finally can separate us from your love
in Christ.
Amen.

178

Living God,
thank you for the awesome truth that, in Christ,
you entered the darkness of death itself –
the cold finality of the grave.
May that knowledge sustain and inspire us
and all who wrestle with the prospect of death,
together with those who mourn loved ones
or face the prospect of bereavement.
Remind us that through experiencing death you have defeated it,
not just once but for evermore,
not just for Jesus but for us too.
Amen.

179

Remind us, Lord, that Jesus truly died,
not just playing a part
or going through the motions,
but enduring the darkness of death itself.
Yet remind us also that he rose again,
greeting his disciples in the upper room,
meeting them on the road,
restoring faith, hope, joy and purpose.
So then, to all facing the agony of bereavement,
the trauma and despair of loss,
give the assurance that beyond the grave lie new beginnings;
that from dust and ashes you will bring new life,
now and always.
Amen.

180

Lord Jesus Christ,
thank you for your promise of comfort.
Reach out to all who mourn,
and turn their sorrow to joy,
their tears to laughter
and their despair to hope.
Amen.

At a funeral

(Where text is italicised, insert name of the deceased/relatives, as appropriate)

181

Loving God,
as we wrestle now with our grief,
we are reminded of all who have lost loved ones,
whose lives have been touched by tragedy,
and who are overwhelmed by sorrow.
Lord, in your mercy,
hear our prayer.

We pray for them in their shock, hurt and bewilderment.
We lift before you their sense of desolation and despair,
their feelings of numbness and emptiness,
their aching hearts that see just a blank void where so much joy used to be.
Lord, in your mercy,
hear our prayer.

We pray for each of us here today
and especially for those closest to *A*;
for *(enter names as appropriate)*.
Reach out and encircle them in your loving arms.
Grant them the comfort you have promised to all who mourn,
your peace that passes understanding,
your light that reaches into the darkest places of life
and beyond into the darkness of death.
Lord, in your mercy,
hear our prayer.

Loving God,
may the hope of the gospel,
the experience of your love,
and the support of family and friends
bring the help that is needed at this time;
the strength to endure sorrow in all its intensity
and to face death in all its apparent finality,
yet ultimately to look forward in faith,
knowing that, in Christ, nothing can finally separate us from you
or from those we love.
Lord, in your mercy,
hear our prayer.
Amen.

182

Loving God,
you have promised that those who mourn shall be comforted.
So we pray now for each of us here today,
bringing before you the sorrow we all feel at this moment.
Lord, in your mercy,
hear our prayer.

We pray especially for *A*'s family,
in their shock and grief,
their pain and loneliness,
the turmoil of emotions that death inevitably brings to those left behind.
Lord, in your mercy,
hear our prayer.

We pray for all those who counted *A* as a friend,
those in this church,
those who worked with *A*,
who lived near to *him/her*,
who shared *his/her* hobbies and interests –
all those whose lives were, in different ways, touched by *A*'s presence.
Lord, in your mercy,
hear our prayer.

Loving God,
we bring before you now our sense of emptiness, separation and sorrow.
Give us your support as we struggle to come to terms with our loss.
Give strength to face the days ahead,
courage when life seems dark
and hope when the future seems without purpose.
Lord, in your mercy,
hear our prayer.

Help us to know that your love for *A* and for us continues beyond death,
that you are with us in this moment and always,
and may that knowledge bring comfort and hope today and in the days ahead.
Lord, in your mercy,
hear our prayer.
In the name of Christ.
Amen.

183

Loving God,
you tell us to look forward to a day when your kingdom shall come
and your will be done;
a new age when there will be no more suffering, sorrow or death;
a place where there will be an end to mourning and weeping,
every tear wiped away from our eyes.
Support us by your grace
and comfort us through your love.

We thank you for that promise,
and we look forward to that time,
but we pray also for your help now,
for today our grief is all too painful,
and the fact of death an all too stark reality.
Support us by your grace
and comfort us through your love.

So we ask you to reach out to us
and to all whose lives have been enriched by *A*'s presence –
family,
friends,
neighbours,
colleagues –
each so much the poorer for *A*'s passing.
Support us by your grace
and comfort us through your love.

Loving God,
reach out now into the darkness of this moment,
the blackness of our sorrow,
and grant your light that nothing can overcome,
your peace that defies understanding,
and your hope that will never be extinguished.
Support us by your grace
and comfort us through your love.
Amen.

The bruised and broken

see also Themed prayers: Trouble, those facing

184

Loving God,
we pray for those whose dreams have been destroyed,
who no longer have the heart to look forward,
who have lost their vision for the future.
So many people, known and unknown,
whose happiness and hopes have been dashed by tragedy,
whose faith in loved ones has been betrayed,
who face poverty, unemployment, homelessness, disease, starvation –
even death –
their trust in you having been tested beyond the limit.
God of hope,
light a new flame in their hearts.

We pray for all who plod wearily through life with no sense of purpose –
those who feel the future is empty,
bereft of promise,
and those who live only for today,
fearful of tomorrow.
God of hope,
light a new flame in their hearts.

Touch their hearts, we pray,
stir their imagination,
rekindle their faith,
renew their hope.
And so may new dreams and new visions be born in the most broken of lives.
God of hope,
light a new flame in their hearts.
Amen.

185

Gracious God,
reach out into our bruised and bleeding world,
fractured by prejudice,
shattered by hate
and torn by fear.
Bring help.
Bring hope.

Where lives are broken,
mend them.
Where they are ravaged by sickness and disease,
heal them.
Where they are troubled,
calm them.
Where they are hurting,
relieve them.
Where they are sorrowful,
comfort them.
Bring help.
Bring hope.

Pick up the pieces,
and, through your healing touch,
bring renewal and wholeness deep within.
Amen.

186

Lord Jesus Christ,
reach out to our world,
just as you did to so many during your earthly ministry.
Minister to us in our brokenness:
our inner yearning for meaning,
our sense of guilt and shame,
our struggle to love you and others,
our weakness of will,
our hurts and fears,
our pride, envy, greed and stubbornness –
so much that undermines life and devalues our humanity.
May your grace bring hope;
your love bring healing.

Minister to all who are broken:
the sick and suffering,
the physically and mentally disabled,
the terminally ill;
victims of war,
the homeless and dispossessed;
the oppressed and exploited,
vulnerable and poor;
so many crying out for help,
strength
and support.
May your grace bring hope;
your love bring healing.

Lord Jesus,
bring healing to us and to all,
and show us how we,
in turn,
can reach out in your name,
seeking to share your wholeness
and make known your love.
Amen.

187

Loving God,
hear our prayer for all who are worn down by the daily grind of life –
crushed by the demands, pressures, fears and difficulties that each day can bring.
Reach out to hold.
Reach out to help.

Minister to those who have had just about as much as they can take –
their nerves stretched,
their tempers frayed,
their self-belief eroded,
their faith in the future hanging by a thread –
and restore their strength.
Reach out to hold.
Reach out to help.

Grant the peace that you alone can give,
inner reserves that they never knew they had.
And, should something snap,
give those around them patience,
compassion,
gentleness
and, above all, love,
to enfold them until they are mended.
Reach out to hold.
Reach out to help.
Amen.

188

Loving God,
reach out to those who have lost the will to live,
all who are broken in body, mind or spirit,
seeing no hope,
no future,
no reason to continue.
Lift their despair,
and may they find in you a life that satisfies,
now and always.
Amen.

189

Be present, Lord, in this broken world,
to bind up its wounds.
Reach out to all who are hurting,
and minister your love,
your grace,
your peace
and your hope.
Amen.

190

Loving God,
when hearts are broken,
lives wrecked by sickness, fear, hurt and sorrow,
we know that people can break down completely,
the business of repair being a long and uncertain business.

Reach out to all who feel they cannot carry on,
and give them strength not just to resume their journey
but to embark on it with confidence renewed
and anticipation restored,
able to see it safely through until they reach the end.
Amen.

191

Merciful God,
thank you for the knowledge that you are always there,
ready to carry us when we cannot continue,
to tend our wounds when we lie bruised and broken,
to provide healing and renewal in body, mind and spirit.
Teach us to minister to life's casualties in turn,
reaching out with supportive hands and caring touch,
in your name.
Amen.

192

Mighty God,
we believe you are a God of love and compassion,
yet sometimes we look at the world and find it hard to keep faith,
for so many lives are shattered by tragedy.
We see millions dying of starvation or overwhelmed by natural disaster,
thousands more crushed by war, disease and deprivation,
others, again, facing heartbreak and hurt,
the damage often seeming too great to mend.
Reach out, we pray, into fragmented lives,
broken communities
and our shattered world,
bringing healing,
hope,
renewal
and restoration,
until that day when your kingdom comes
and all is finally made whole.
Amen.

193

Renewing God,
touch the lives of those crushed by the loss of a loved one,
broken by accident or injury,
shattered by the onset of disease
or overwhelmed by the breakdown of relationships.
Though to us the damage may seem too great to mend,
help to put the pieces back together again,
gently and lovingly restoring them through your grace.
Reach out into hurting hearts,
bringing healing and hope,
until that day when your kingdom comes,
and all is made whole.
Amen.

194

Saviour Christ,
so many in life are worn to breaking point,
ground down by sickness, hurt, worry and fear,
by the ravages of time,
and uncertain how much longer they can cope.
Reach out to strengthen and restore,
from the tangled threads of their lives weaving cords that will not be broken.
Amen.

195

To all whose minds are troubled, Lord,
who wrestle with fear,
worry,
depression
or mental illness,
bring help and healing.
Speak your word of peace,
and may they find in you acceptance and understanding,
quietness of mind
and rest for their souls.
Amen.

196

Where lives are broken, Lord,
mend them.
Where there is sickness and disease,
bring healing.
Where minds are disturbed,
give peace.
Where there is pain and suffering,
grant relief.
Where there is yearning for meaning,
offer guidance.
Through your healing touch,
grant true wholeness deep within.
Amen.

Changed lives

197

Lord Jesus Christ,
thank you for your ability to change lives,
to transform even the most unlikely of people,
turning them upside down and inside out.
Continue to work in our world,
and bring new beginnings to all.

Thank you for having changed *our* lives,
filling them with hope,
joy,
peace
and purpose.
Continue to work in our world,
and bring new beginnings to all.

Reach out in love,
and wherever there is pain,
sorrow,
evil
and injustice
accomplish real and lasting change.
Continue to work in our world,
and bring new beginnings to all.
Amen.

198

Loving God,
for the countless ways you've transformed people's lives,
restoring and renewing,
we praise you.
Lord, hear us,
graciously hear us.

For giving strength to the weak,
hope to the oppressed,
freedom to those held captive
and healing to the sick,
we worship you.
Lord, hear us,
graciously hear us.

For bringing joy to the sorrowful,
peace to the troubled,
and light to those in darkness,
we thank you.
Lord, hear us,
graciously hear us.

For conquering evil with good,
hatred with love
and death with life,
we honour and acclaim you.
Lord, hear us,
graciously hear us.

Work in our world through your Spirit,
and finish among us your new creation.
Lord, hear us,
graciously hear us.
Amen.

199

Loving God,
in a world where hopes are so often shattered,
ideals ground into the dust until they seem little more than empty delusion,
give us courage to continue dreaming dreams,
not as a wistful means of escapism,
but as a natural expression of our faith in your purpose,
and of your ability to work in ways beyond our understanding or expectation.
Where faith has died and vision has faded,
may hope flower again.

Help us to keep hold of a sense of everything you are able to do
and all that life can become;
to recognise that, despite the way things may sometimes appear,
you are able to change lives and transform situations in ways beyond our imagining.
Where faith has died and vision has faded,
may hope flower again.

Work in the Church,
in this nation,
in this world
to raise up people of faith and courage;
people who believe that,
however hopeless life may seem,
things can be different.
Where faith has died and vision has faded,
may hope flower again.

Grant to our hurting disillusioned world a vision of the future,
and confidence that you can turn dreams into reality.
Amen.

200

Loving God,
we lose sight sometimes of what,
through Christ,
you can do within us,
the way you can change who and what we are,
transforming us and making us new.
Rekindle faith.
Restore hope.

We lose sight of how you can change others,
fashioning the most unlikely people into something different,
not just on the outside but deep within.
Rekindle faith.
Restore hope.

We lose sight of the way you can change the world;
of how –
despite the sorrow, suffering, hatred, violence, evil and injustice that continue to scar it –
you are able to revitalise communities,
combat exploitation,
restore hope,
rekindle life.
Rekindle faith.
Restore hope.

Teach us to look beyond the obvious and apparent;
to recognise more fully what you are able to do,
and to trust in your renewing power;
your ability to transform all.
Rekindle faith.
Restore hope.
Amen.

Disaster and tragedy

201

Almighty God,
why do you let people suffer?
Why have you created a world in which so many have to endure pain,
brokenness,
heartache
and despair?
In your mercy, Lord,
hear our cry.

We look for answers but find none,
strive to make sense of it all,
but are left clutching at straws,
confused and troubled.
In your mercy, Lord,
hear our cry.

Help us to understand that somehow,
in ways we don't understand,
you share with us in whatever we go through;
that, though it often may not seem like it,
your are moved by our pain,
seeking to heal,
comfort,
support
and strengthen.
In your mercy, Lord,
hear our cry.

Enfold all who suffer in your loving arms
until that time when we enter your kingdom,
and hurt and pain will finally be no more.
Amen.

202

Another disaster,
another tragedy,
another tale of sorrow and suffering.
Where were you, Lord, when it happened?
What were you thinking of?
How could you let it be?
Lord, hear us,
graciously hear us.

We look for answers,
yet search in vain,
the attempt raising more questions than it solves,
but if one thing is clear,
it's that here,
in each time of crisis,
we need you more than ever.
Lord, hear us,
graciously hear us.

Come to our broken, bleeding world
and bind up its wounds.
Assure us, despite how things seem,
that hope is mightier than fear,
right stronger than wrong,
and love greater than all.
Lord, hear us,
graciously hear us.
Amen.

203

(Give relevant details where text is italicised)
Loving Father,
as we think of ourselves
we think also of those for whom recent days have brought disaster and tragedy.
Especially we pray for those in *(name of country/region)*
their lives thrown into turmoil by the events that have ravaged their land.
Lord, in your mercy,
hear our prayer.

We pray for the families of those who have lost their lives.
Give them comfort,
support
and the knowledge of your eternal love.
Lord, in your mercy,
hear our prayer.

We pray for those injured or maimed;
those who will face the rest of their days coming to terms with physical scars
or with deeper mental and spiritual wounds.
Grant healing and help to each one.
Lord, in your mercy,
hear our prayer.

We pray for all who are striving to give support amid the devastation,
whether to body, mind or soul.
Equip them with compassion,
wisdom
and skill in all their work.
Lord, in your mercy,
hear our prayer.

We pray for those still searching among the chaos
as hope runs out for any last survivors –
their homes lost,
their *town/city* destroyed,
their country left in shock.
Give them encouragement to persevere.
Lord, in your mercy,
hear our prayer.

Living God,
we believe you grieve and suffer wherever people are in need.
Reach out then to these in their sorrow and despair,
and grant them help to rebuild their shattered lives and hopes.
Lord, in your mercy,
hear our prayer.
Amen.

204

Mighty God,
you have created so awesome a world,
and yet one that can also be so awful,
cursed by sorrow as well as joy,
suffering as well as health,
hatred as well as love,
death as well as life.
In a world of so much darkness, Lord,
may your love somehow still shine.

We can make sense of it to a point,
for many of our ills are down to humankind,
but many are not,
and we cannot help but wonder why you let such things happen.
In a world of so much darkness, Lord,
may your love somehow still shine.

We search for answers yet seek in vain,
the horror, agony, misery and trauma that so many endure
seeming to deny your love and contradict your purpose.
Yet, in Christ, broken for all,
we see you sharing human suffering,
telling us that you can use it for good –
out of the deepest night-time bringing light,
life,
joy
and hope.
In a world of so much darkness, Lord,
may your love somehow still shine.

Strengthen all who suffer
and comfort them with the knowledge of your presence,
though so much seems to obscure it.
Be there to help,
to hold
and to heal.
In a world of so much darkness, Lord,
may your love somehow still shine.
Amen.

205

We want to believe, Lord,
to trust in your purpose,
but we find it hard sometimes,
for so much seems to deny your love.
Reach out to hold.
Reach out to help.

We see people broken by sickness, violence and disaster;
lives blighted by poverty and hunger;
a world scarred by greed, injustice and war;
and we wonder why you let it be.
Reach out to hold.
Reach out to help.

Teach us that you not only feel our pain but long to answer it;
that, however hard it is to see,
you are always at work,
seeking to bring good out of evil,
hope out of despair,
life out of death.
Reach out to hold.
Reach out to help.

Help us, then,
however hard it may be,
to keep faith,
trusting that in the fullness of time
your will shall be done and your kingdom come.
Amen.

Doubt and questions

see also under Themed Prayers: Disaster and Tragedy, *and* Poetic prayers: For those struggling to come to terms with questions of faith; For a world in which God seems absent

206

Living God,
we pray for those wrestling with difficult and demanding questions –
those facing complex matters of conscience,
those struggling with confusing moral decisions,
those wrestling with controversial social issues,
those coping with challenging theological concerns.
Grant to all in such situations your wisdom,
and help them to find the right way forward.
Lord, in your mercy,
hear our prayer.

We pray for those who are faced with awkward yet important choices:
between good and evil,
right and wrong,
truth and falsehood,
love and hate;
between the way of the world and the way of Christ,
the way of self and the way of service.
Give to all faced with such choices
the courage to take your way.
Lord, in your mercy,
hear our prayer.

We pray for your Church.
Save it from naive fundamentalism,
from judgemental attitudes,
from dogmatically believing it has the answers to every situation.
Grant to your people everywhere
the humility to recognise that asking questions is part of faith.
Lord, in your mercy,
hear our prayer.

Living God,
we pray for ourselves as, day by day,
we are confronted with the need to choose.
Sometimes we find the choice clear,
sometimes confusing,
sometimes easy,
sometimes hard,
sometimes mattering little,
sometimes much.
But help us, whatever the case,
to gladly accept the responsibility of choosing,
recognising that it is a privilege of being human.
Lord, in your mercy,
hear our prayer.

Help us to decide wisely,
seeking your will and responding to your guidance.
Help us to admit our error when we choose wrongly
and to be ready to change our decisions when necessary.
And help us to remember, when we go astray,
that you are always there to help us start again.
Lord, in your mercy,
hear our prayer,
Amen.

207

Living God,
there are times when you seem silent,
when, listen though we might, we cannot hear your voice.
So we pray now for those who cry for help
but who feel their prayers are unanswered.
Lord, in your mercy, hear us,
and all who call to you.

We think of those known to us facing difficult times –
battling with illness,
wrestling with depression,
anxious about the future,
grieving for loved ones –
those for whom life seems a puzzle,

even a burden,
and who long to find hope,
to make some sense out of their confusion.
Lord, in your mercy, hear us,
and all who call to you.

We think of those who feel far from you –
burdened by doubt,
overwhelmed by temptation,
crushed by failure –
those who long to know you better
but who find it hard to get close;
who seek to serve you
but who are weighed down by a sense of their weaknesses,
their lack of faith
and their repeated mistakes.
Lord, in your mercy, hear us,
and all who call to you.

We think of those who seek guidance –
who feel unsure of the way ahead,
uncertain of their ability to face the future,
unclear as to what you want from them –
all who ask you to lead the way forward
yet who have no clear sense of their particular calling.
Lord, in your mercy, hear us,
and all who call to you.

We think of the poor and weak,
the vulnerable and disadvantaged in society –
those denied their rights,
their dignity,
their freedom,
their livelihoods –
all who long for a time when justice will be established
but who have given up believing it will ever happen.
Lord, in your mercy, hear us,
and all who call to you.

Living God,
we are conscious that so many in our world cry to you
yet seem to receive no answer –
some because they do not expect to receive any,
some because they are not ready or willing to listen,
some because they do not understand what you are saying,
but many genuinely and urgently longing to hear your voice,
yearning for some response.
Speak to them, we pray.
Do not keep silent,
but reach out into their pain and hurt,
their need and hopelessness,
and bring your word of comfort,
of peace,
of healing, love and renewal.
Lord, in your mercy, hear us,
and all who call to you.
Amen.

208

Lord Jesus Christ, the way, the truth and life,
we pray today for those who seek truth –
the truth about themselves,
about others,
about this world we live in,
about you.
Lord, in your mercy,
hear our prayer.

We pray for those who study and research into the workings of our universe,
the deep mysteries of life,
the complexities of this world,
the mechanics of science.
Give them insight and humility,
patience and understanding.
Lord, in your mercy,
hear our prayer.

We pray for those in the mass media –
journalists, reporters, photographers, cameramen,
editors of news bulletins and newspapers,
presenters and programme-makers,
authors and script-writers –
all who in different ways have the power to shape public opinion.
Give them honesty and integrity,
courage and perception.
Lord, in your mercy,
hear our prayer.

We pray for theologians,
preachers,
evangelists
and teachers –
all who seek to understand more about the reality of God
and to communicate it to others,
leading them to a greater knowledge of your love.
Give them vision and dedication,
vision and open-mindedness.
Lord, in your mercy,
hear our prayer.

We pray for those who cannot face the truth,
who find it too challenging,
too depressing,
too frustrating
or too frightening to contemplate.
Give them courage and help,
hope and perseverance.
Lord, in your mercy,
hear our prayer.

We pray for those who deny the truth,
twisting and distorting it,
leading others astray,
blind to right and wrong.
Give them honesty to recognise their mistakes,
and grace to amend them.
Lord, in your mercy,
hear our prayer.

We pray finally for those who work to help people come to terms with truth:
counsellors,
psychiatrists,
doctors,
ministers,
writers,
philosophers.
Give them compassion and sensitivity,
understanding and inspiration.
Lord, in your mercy,
hear our prayer.
Amen.

209

Living God,
we pray for all those who find faith difficult or impossible –
those beset by doubt,
troubled by questions to which they can find no answer,
unable to take the leap of faith,
yet seeking, searching and thirsting for truth.
Lord, in your mercy,
hear our prayer.

We think of those unable to reconcile their own situations with the claims of the gospel –
those whose dreams have been shattered,
their love betrayed,
their trust abused,
and their best efforts gone unrewarded.
Lord, in your mercy,
hear our prayer.

We think of those for whom events in the world at large seem to deny your love –
those confronted by natural disaster,
sickened by war and violence,
bemused by sickness, suffering and disease,
perplexed by the apparent victory in so many places of evil over good.
Lord, in your mercy,
hear our prayer.

We pray also for those confirmed in their unbelief,
unwilling to consider further the claims of the gospel,
unmoved and unchallenged by the love of Christ.
Lord, in your mercy,
hear our prayer.

Living God,
break through the barriers of doubt and unbelief.
Open the hearts and minds of all who are troubled and confused,
and all who are closed to your presence.
Meet with those who find it hard to meet with you,
and lead them to a living, life-giving faith.
Lord, in your mercy,
hear our prayer.
Amen.

210

Living God,
we pray for those who find faith hard,
those who want to believe but cannot get past their doubts.
Lord, hear us,
graciously hear us.

We pray for those whose faith is wavering,
undermined by the pressures and temptations of life.
Lord, hear us,
graciously hear us.

We pray for those who have lost their faith,
the fire that once burned within them extinguished.
Lord, hear us,
graciously hear us.

We pray for ourselves,
conscious that for us too faith can sometimes lose its spark.
Lord, hear us,
graciously hear us.

For all those whose faith is faltering we pray:
'Lord, we do believe,
help us overcome our unbelief.'
Lord, hear us,
graciously hear us.
Amen.

211

Living God,
in a world where so many search for meaning,
where people feel lost and hopeless,
confused about who they are,
why they are here
or what they should do,
give guidance.
Prompt and challenge through your Holy Spirit,
so that all who long for answers may find in Christ an end to their seeking –
their questions resolved
and their lives fulfilled.
Amen.

212

Loving God,
hear our prayer for those who seek fulfilment in what fails to satisfy;
those who surround themselves with material possessions
yet are uneasily aware that all is not as it should be.
Reach out to all who,
for all their striving,
feel that something is missing from their lives,
and help them to find what they seek:
inner peace and fulfilment that satisfies their inner hunger,
and gives meaning to all.
Amen.

213

Mighty and mysterious God,
we pray for those for whom life feels like an incomplete jigsaw –
frustrating,
disappointing,
infuriating;
those who,
for all their striving,
feel unfulfilled,
as if a component is missing that they cannot quite find.
Draw near to them,
and reveal to them the elusive final piece to complete the picture:
the one who satisfies their deepest yearning
and answers their innermost needs.
Amen.

214

Sovereign God,
help us to live with the mysteries of faith and conundrums of life,
trusting always in you for help and guidance.
Keep us open to your searching voice,
ready to recognise your challenge and respond.
Keep us eager to seek and hungry to learn more
rather than closing our minds to what might stretch them.
Be with those who struggle with questions,
or who run from them,
and lead us all into a living knowledge of your gracious purpose,
through Jesus Christ our Lord.
Amen.

215

Loving God,
we pray for those who seek to serve you,
but who find faith threatened:
those who face pain and suffering,
those overwhelmed by sudden calamity,
those confused by apparent injustice,
and those whose convictions have been undermined by the experiences of life.
Assure them of your continuing purpose,
your enduring love,
and your final triumph.
Amen.

Education

Learning difficulties

216

Loving God,
we pray for children and young people with learning difficulties.
Grant them the care, encouragement and provision they need to realise their full potential.
Through the devotion of parents and family,
the support of friends
and the dedication of teachers,
instil self-belief,
enthusiasm,
resilience
and resourcefulness,
equipping them to meet whatever challenges they may face,
and to triumph over them.
Amen.

Crèches and nursery schools

217

Lord Jesus Christ,
remembering how you welcomed children to your side,
we pray for crèches and nurseries.
Give guidance to those who work within them,
that they may wisely and ably guide those in their care,
helping them to learn,
to grow
and to flourish as individuals.
Grant your blessing on all the babies, toddlers and parents who pass through them,
and surround each with your love and care,
this day and always.
Amen.

Schools, colleges and universities

Those starting school

218

Hear our prayer, Lord, for children who are starting school.
May they find pleasure in learning,
enrichment through friendships
and fun through shared activities,
their education helping them to grow
not only in knowledge but also as people.
Protect them from harm,
equip them with wisdom
and enfold them in love,
granting them joy now
and fulfilment in the years to come.
Amen.

Those starting at university/college

219

Hear our prayer, Lord, for those starting college or university.
At what is an exciting yet daunting time –
one for embracing the new and moving on from the old –
grant the sure and certain knowledge of your presence,
your guidance,
and your love that, come what may, will not fail.
Grant the ability to work
but also to rest,
to study
but also to socialise,
to embrace new insights
but also to respect the lessons of the past,
to welcome all that is good in student life
but also to resist whatever is bad,
knowing when to say yes, and when to say no.
Equip and enable them for all the challenges and opportunities that lie ahead,
so that they may find true fulfilment,
now and in the years ahead.
Amen.

Staff and students

220

Loving God,
we pray today for those involved in the difficult and often unappreciated task of education.
We pray for teachers with all the pressures they face –
expectations from parents,
demands from governments and politicians,
a growing burden of administration,
and mounting problems of discipline,
sometimes involving even a threat to their own safety.
Grant your wisdom to guide,
and your hand to bless.

We pray for schools and colleges in an increasingly competitive world –
struggling to balance budgets,
short of staff and resources,
disheartened by performances in league tables,
some even facing the prospect of closure through lack of numbers.
Grant your wisdom to guide,
and your hand to bless.

We pray for staff who feel unable to cope with the demands made upon them –
worn down by stress,
confused by change,
frustrated by bureaucracy,
exhausted by unruly pupils.
Grant your wisdom to guide,
and your hand to bless.

We pray also for students who feel similarly overwhelmed,
though by different pressures –
crushed by a weight of expectations,
broken by bullying,
wrestling with learning difficulties,
fearful of examinations.
Grant your wisdom to guide,
and your hand to bless.

And we pray finally for governors,
local education authorities,
politicians and planners,
as they seek to respond to changing circumstances,
juggling the practical, financial and electoral issues involved.
Grant your wisdom to guide,
and your hand to bless.

Loving God,
we pray for all involved in the task of education,
whether it be those at the forefront of delivery,
those behind the scenes,
or students and scholars directly involved in the pursuit of knowledge.
Reach out in love,
and grant to each your guidance, strength and support.
Grant your wisdom to guide,
and your hand to bless.
Amen.

221

Loving God,
hear our prayer for schools,
and those within them.
Lord, hear us,
graciously hear us.

Give guidance to teachers,
support staff,
children
and parents alike.
Lord, hear us,
graciously hear us.

Promote an eagerness to learn,
a desire to give of one's best,
a respect for all,
and a sense of community and togetherness.
Lord, hear us,
graciously hear us.

Instruct,
enable,
enthuse,
encourage
and enfold all in your constant love.
Lord, hear us,
graciously hear us.
Amen.

222

Sovereign God,
we prayer for the schools of our town and country.
Gracious Lord,
hear our prayer.

Encircle them with your love,
touch them with your presence,
surround them with your protection
and endow all within them with your wisdom.
Gracious Lord,
hear our prayer.

Equip teachers with the skills they need,
dedication to develop them
and sensitivity in applying them,
so that those in their charge may find inspiration,
encouragement,
insight
and guidance.
Gracious Lord,
hear our prayer.

Grant that, as well as being places of learning,
our schools and colleges may offer an environment where friendships grow,
confidence is built,
characters are fashioned
and skills are learnt for daily life.
Gracious Lord,
hear our prayer.
Amen.

223

Living God,
hear our prayer for all involved in the task of education.
In your love, Lord,
hear us.

Grant them wisdom to teach,
sensitivity to encourage,
skill to enthuse,
strength to discipline,
and patience to persevere.
In your love, Lord,
hear us.

Keep their vision fresh,
their minds hungry
and their motivation strong,
enabling them to capture the imagination of those they teach,
getting the best from them
and helping each to realise their full potential.
In your love, Lord,
hear us.

Grant them joy and fulfilment in their work,
that through it they may be a blessing and inspiration to all in their care.
In your love, Lord,
hear us.
Amen.

224

Father God,
we pray for all those responsible for offering instruction.
Especially we pray for teachers in our schools,
faced in recent years by so many changes,
so many extra demands,
so much that is new and unfamiliar,
so much added responsibility,
and all too often with so little resources or support.
Equip them with the wisdom and enthusiasm they need to equip others for life.
Lord, in your mercy,
hear our prayer.

We pray for those whose morale is low,
who question their ability to adapt,
who find the pressures too demanding,
who feel themselves to be undervalued and overworked.
Guide,
inspire,
equip
and enable them.
Lord, in your mercy,
hear our prayer.

Grant, we pray, that the importance of education in our society will be fully appreciated,
that the contribution of all who teach,
whether in schools, colleges or universities,
by profession or as volunteers,
will be properly recognised and rewarded.
Lord, in your mercy,
hear our prayer.

And grant to all teachers everywhere
the wisdom they need,
the dedication, commitment, skill and sensitivity required,
to nurture those in their care,
develop their gifts,
and prepare them for life ahead.
Lord, in your mercy,
hear our prayer.
Amen.

Those taking exams

225

Father God,
we pray for young people sitting exams around this time of year.
At what is a stressful time for many of them,
grant composure of mind and serenity of spirit,
so that the long hours of work, study and revision may bear fruit,
bringing due reward.
Help them to give of their best,
knowing that no one could ask for more.
Amen.

University/college chaplains

226

Loving God,
grant your blessing on chaplains in our universities, schools and colleges.
Equip them, by your grace, to reach out in love,
offering insight and understanding to those seeking knowledge;
a glimpse of Christ,
the way, the truth and the life.
Grant them a wise tongue,
a listening ear,
a loving heart
and a sensitive spirit,
so that they may help lead young people into a deeper awareness of your love,
for them
and for all.
Amen.

The elderly

see also Poetic prayers: For the elderly and infirm

227

Living God,
save us from pigeonholing the elderly;
from accepting negative stereotypes that depict them as infirm,
senile,
redundant.
Father of all,
hear our prayer.

Thank you that people today are able to remain fit and active in later life as never before,
continuing to contribute not just to family and friends,
but to wider society,
through their wisdom and experience gained across the years.
Grant that they will be respected and valued for who and what they are.
Father of all,
hear our prayer.

Reach out to those for whom advancing years *does* bring a decline in body or mind,
and give them,
their loved ones
and their carers
strength and support to alleviate their suffering and maintain their dignity.
Father of all,
hear our prayer.

Grant to all,
young and old,
the knowledge that your love is always with us,
throughout our lives
and beyond.
Father of all,
hear our prayer.
Amen.

228

Eternal God,
hear our prayer for those in their twilight years,
the sun beginning to set though yet not gone down.
Though the energy of youth is long past
and aspirations of middle years seem distant,
may this time of life bring joys of its own:
an inner tranquillity and contentment in the light of all that has gone before,
coupled with confident trust in what is yet to come –
the new dawn that, by your grace, will surely follow the night.
Amen.

229

Gracious God,
to all whose strength is failing and faculties diminishing,
advancing years taking their toll,
grant the assurance that your love daily encircles them
and that, in the fullness of time, you will bring new beginnings,
life that will never fade.
Amen.

230

Eternal God,
reach out in love,
and support those for whom advancing years bring trials.
Though health may fade and faculties fail,
strength decline and vigour wane,
grant the assurance that your grace is the same
yesterday, today and tomorrow,
a fixed point in a world of change.
So, then, in your mercy,
grant help and strength,
comfort and joy,
and, above all, confidence in your enduring purpose –
the knowledge that,
come what may,
your love will never let us go.
Amen.

Employment

Factories and industry

231

Sovereign God,
we pray for factories and those within them.
May they provide lasting jobs,
security for families now and in years to come.
May they be wisely managed,
upholding standards of health and safety,
quality and service,
fair trade,
environmental responsibility
and employee relations.
And may their products contribute to the well-being of others,
promoting economic growth and benefiting consumers,
while wisely stewarding the resources you have given.
Amen.

Factory workers

232

Living God,
recognising that you are as much Lord of daily life as of Sunday worship,
as much involved in the mundane as the 'sacred',
we pray for those who work in our factories.
Reach out, then, to those on production lines and the shop floor,
supervisors and managers,
accounts, sales and marketing teams,
drivers, engineers and technicians,
office and support staff –
all who contribute towards the viability of their company
and the jobs it makes possible.
Seen or unseen,
acknowledged or unacknowledged,
work, through your Spirit, in labour relations,
in banter and camaraderie,
in health and safety,
in work honestly done and honestly rewarded,
to the good of all.
Amen.

Industrial chaplains

233

Living God,
reach out through those who serve as industrial chaplains.
Minister, by your grace, in the noise and bustle of the workplace:
the routine and repetition,
automation and technology,
tensions and camaraderie,
decline and change,
research and development –
showing that in this world of work
you are at work as well.
Amen.

Farmers

234

Loving God,
we pray for farmers and all who work the land.
Give vigour to their crops and contentment to their animals,
conditions that promote strong and healthy growth.
Give skill and sensitivity in husbandry,
the quest for productivity balanced by respect for your creation.
Give guidance in managing natural resources,
the ability to steward them wisely for the good of all.
Provide,
protect,
equip
and encourage,
bringing joy in times of fruitfulness
and support when days are hard.
Amen.

Fishermen

235

Lord of all,
hear our prayer for those in peril on the sea,
and in particular for fishermen, in the constant dangers they face.
Watch over their vessels,
quieten their seas,
prosper their work,
and embrace their loved ones.
In rain or sunshine,
calm or storm,
be with them and those they cherish,
guiding,
prospering
and protecting.
Amen.

Office work

236

Living Lord,
we pray for office workers,
here and across the world.
In the bustle of commerce,
amid the telephone calls, faxes, emails and letters,
the piles of paperwork,
the endless tasks of filing, assessing, analysing and decision making,
reach out to the people behind it all –
the human faces of workers, colleagues, contacts
and all those behind the records, forms, orders and correspondence.
Grant that,
however intense the pressures of work,
tedium of routine,
demand for profit
or pull of personal ambition,
there will always be time for others,
a recognition that each employee and 'client' is not just a name or number
but an individual,
a person in their own right,
valued by you
and so to be valued by all.
Amen.

237

Hear our prayer, Lord, for the offices of our town and country,
and those who work in them.
In the tasks done there –
decisions taken,
plans made,
business implemented;
in the people employed there –
management,
personnel
auxiliaries;
in the lives influenced there –
customers,
clients
or claimants;
be present, Lord,
to guide, bless and prosper,
through Jesus Christ our Lord.
Amen.

Shop work

238

Grant your blessing, Lord, on those who work in our shops.
Help them in the work they do,
so that, in the service they offer,
camaraderie share,
people meet
and money earn
they may find interest, enjoyment and satisfaction.
Give them a sense of consideration towards their customers,
and may their employers and customers likewise show consideration towards them.
Amen.

Small businesses and the self-employed

239

Sovereign God,
hear our prayer for those who work in small businesses
or who are self-employed.
Give wisdom to make right decisions,
ability to cultivate necessary skills,
and health to cope with the workload.
Give encouragement when business is slow
and equanimity in times of disappointment;
the vision needed to grasp opportunities,
but also integrity when it is tempting to cut corners.
Above all, give discipline to do whatever must be done
yet the ability also to switch off,
recognising that there must be time for rest and recreation,
for friends and loved ones.
Amen.

Those starting a new job

240

Hear our prayer, Lord, for those starting new employment.
In their anxiety yet anticipation,
uncertainty yet eagerness,
grant them the assurance that whatever their new job might bring,
and whatever the future may hold,
you will be there in it,
guiding,
equipping,
supplying
and sustaining.
Through work done,
friendships made,
challenges faced
and goals realised
may they find lasting fulfilment and blessing.
Amen.

The environment

241

Eternal God,
thank you for the place you have given humankind in creation,
fashioning us in your image
and giving us the ability to shape and control our environment.
Save us, though, from valuing ourselves too much
and the rest of creation too little;
from failing to treat our environment with the care and respect you expect.
Through honouring your creation,
may we also honour you.

Forgive the wanton destruction of habitats
and mindless slaughter of endangered species for commercial gain;
the putting of human interests before all others.
Through honouring your creation,
may we also honour you.

Forgive the way humankind has impoverished our countryside,
our world
and our lives
through our failure to steward this planet's resources as wisely as we should.
Through honouring your creation,
may we also honour you.

Teach us to recognise the beauty, wonder and diversity of the natural world
and to fulfil our responsibilities towards it,
understanding that it is not ours to use and abuse at will
but is held in trust for future generations to enjoy in turn.
Through honouring your creation,
may we also honour you.
Amen.

242

Living God,
forgive the self-centredness of humankind,
our acting sometimes as though only *we* matter to you
and nothing else in the natural world is really important.

Remind us that you created *all* things –
the vast variety of creatures that populate
or once lived
in this astonishing world you have given.
Teach us and everyone to recognise that this is not *our* world but yours,
fashioned by your hand and precious to you,
and so may we learn to treat it with the reverence it deserves,
conscious that your horizons extend far beyond our own.
Amen.

243

Lord of heaven and earth,
you've honoured us,
each and every one,
placing in our care not just land or money
but the world itself,
an asset beyond price.
Forgive humankind's squandering of its resources,
living today with no thought of tomorrow.
Forgive our betrayal of your trust,
giving little thought for present and future generations.
Teach all to live wisely,
mindful of your creation,
and, above all, mindful of you.
Amen.

244

Loving God,
teach us that this is not *our* world but yours,
and therefore that caring for it is not an optional extra
but integral to faith,
part of our responsibility towards you.
Help all people everywhere to discharge that calling faithfully.
Amen.

245

Sovereign God,
teach us that the skills and ingenuity you have given humankind
can either sustain your creation or destroy it.
Remind us that the fate of the planet is in our hands,
each of us having a part to play.
Help us to do our bit faithfully,
and grant that others may do the same.
Amen.

246

Merciful God,
we've made progress,
but not much,
each of us still being part of a wasteful culture,
a society that consumes resources with little thought of tomorrow
and still less for others.
Give us a greater sense of responsibility to future generations
and to you;
an appreciation of the countless blessings we have received
and the duty we have to use them wisely,
so that others may enjoy them in turn.
Amen.

Freedom, those denied

247

Sovereign God,
we pray for all who are denied freedom –
freedom to worship,
to express their opinions,
to vote,
to determine their own affairs.
Help them to make their voice heard
and to secure the justice they seek.
Set at liberty those held captive,
and may the oppressed go free.

We pray for all denied the opportunity to live life to the full –
the mentally and physically disabled,
victims of accidents and illness,
the depressed and broken-hearted.
Help each to conquer that which can so easily enslave them.
Set at liberty those held captive,
and may the oppressed go free.

We pray for those whose freedom has been justly taken away from them –
those who have knowingly broken the law,
who have caused injury and hurt to others,
who are a danger to themselves and society.
May your love help them to find new life in Christ,
and deliverance from their past ways.
Set at liberty those held captive,
and may the oppressed go free.

We pray for those whose spirits are held captive –
poisoned by greed, envy, pride and selfishness,
trapped in a vicious circle of hatred and bitterness,
crushed by fear and anxiety,
led astray by empty hopes and vain ambitions,
false gods and superstition.
May they find in Jesus the way, the truth and the life.
Set at liberty those held captive,
and may the oppressed go free.

Sovereign God,
break through everything that denies your love and frustrates your will.
Reach out to your world in which so many are held hostage to fortune,
and, by the power of your Spirit,
grant release from all that imprisons.
Set at liberty those held captive,
and may the oppressed go free.
Amen.

248

Lord Jesus Christ,
you came into our world
and lived and died among us
in order to set us free from everything that holds us captive.
Your kingdom come,
your will be done.

Thank you for that glorious freedom,
and thank you for those who, in turn,
work – or laboured in times past –
to bring freedom for others from whatever denies, destroys or negates life.
Your kingdom come,
your will be done.

Especially we thank you for those who, in your name,
strove to overcome and outlaw the evil of slavery,
determined that all should enjoy the liberty and dignity they deserve.
Your kingdom come,
your will be done.

Help us to learn from the mistakes of the past
and to build on the achievements,
so that we, in some small way,
may contribute to building a better world
and to bringing nearer the fulfilment of your eternal purpose.
Your kingdom come,
your will be done.
Amen.

249

Hear our prayer, Lord, for those denied their freedom –
those who are forced to work without pay,
subjected to threats and violence,
sold for sex,
trafficked as objects,
tortured, abused, exploited, oppressed:
a host of people for whom slavery is not some abstract memory
but a horrific daily reality.
Support and strengthen all organisations,
protest groups
and campaigners
who work to bring this evil to the attention of nations and governments,
and stir the hearts of people everywhere to do all in their power to bring it to an end.
Grant release to the enslaved,
this and every day.
Amen.

250

Redeemer God,
reach out to those who feel trapped,
imprisoned by circumstances,
held captive by past mistakes, present worries or future prospects.
Give to them and to all the liberty that you alone can give:
your truth that sets us free.
Amen.

251

Loving God,
hear our prayer for all those wrongly held captive:
for victims of miscarriages of justice,
for people held hostage,
for those who have been abducted –
all who are denied their freedom
and who live each day in frustration,
despair,
fear
or desperation.

Reach out and bring hope,
help,
strength
and support;
the knowledge that they are not forgotten;
and the prospect, finally, of release.
Amen.

Health

AIDS sufferers

252

Lord of all,
hear our prayers today for those whose lives are overshadowed by AIDS,
its spectre haunting their existence.
We pray for those struck down by the disease
and struggling to come to terms with its implications:
living with its repercussions in terms of their relationships,
their work,
their friendships,
their future;
knowing they are judged by some,
rejected by others
and feared by many;
and grappling always with the knowledge that though their life can be prolonged,
it will almost certainly finally be ended by this cruel disease.
Reach out into their turmoil and despair,
and bring strength and hope.
Lord, hear us by your grace,
and in your love, respond.

We pray for those who carry the virus –
not yet under its sentence,
perhaps never becoming so,
yet facing much the same prejudice and fear,
coupled with the knowledge that their closest relationships are clouded,
or perhaps coloured forever,
by the fear, or reality, of passing the disease on.
Reach out into their anxiety and isolation,
and bring comfort and support.
Lord, hear us by your grace,
and in your love, respond.

We pray for children who have been born HIV positive,
their prospects in life blighted from the start,
their future uncertain or all too certain,
many destined never to reach adulthood,
many wrestling with ill-health from the moment of their birth.

Reach out into their bewilderment and suffering,
and bring courage and relief.
Lord, hear us by your grace,
and in your love, respond.

We pray for those exposed to HIV through contaminated blood transfusions,
infected surgical appliances,
or other medical procedures,
their lives suddenly and unexpectedly turned upside down.
Reach out into their anger and devastation,
and bring help and consolation.
Lord, hear us by your grace,
and in your love, respond.

We pray for those who –
either through ignorance,
necessity,
addiction
or a moment of madness –
put their lives or those of others at risk,
contracting or passing on AIDS through unprotected sex
or the sharing of used needles.
Reach out into their regrets or recriminations,
and bring guidance and resolve.
Lord, hear us by your grace,
and in your love, respond.

We pray for the many millions across the world suffering from the AIDS virus
but having, as yet, no benefit from medical advances –
their bodies wasting away,
their future bleak,
their despair total –
lacking the resources to pay for help.
We think especially of the continent of Africa
where so many needlessly die each day,
but we think also of those in every part of our world
deprived of the treatment that others now take for granted.
Reach out into their poverty and need,
and bring resources and help.
Lord, hear us by your grace,
and in your love, respond.

We pray finally for all who seek a cure for AIDS,
all who nurse sufferers,
all who offer support and counselling,
and all who minister to the dying.
Reach out into their hearts and minds,
and grant them wisdom, perseverance, patience and compassion,
the ability to recognise the wholeness and worth you see in every person,
and to channel your love through word or deed.
Through them may healing of body, mind or spirit be offered,
until the time come when this illness is conquered,
its scourge lifted once and for all.
Lord, hear us by your grace,
and in your love, respond.
Amen.

253

Caring and compassionate God,
support those who are facing the trauma and turmoil of AIDS.
Bring help.
Bring hope.

When terror suffocates,
grant your peace.
When despair overwhelms,
renew hope.
When vigour wanes,
bring healing.
When rejection isolates,
draw close.
Bring help.
Bring hope.

Give help to wrestle with this disease,
and still feel whole;
to meet with fear and suspicion,
yet still to love;
to confront the spectre of death,
yet still to celebrate life.
Bring help.
Bring hope.

Support,
equip
and bless,
this day and always,
in Christ's name.
Amen.

254

Loving God,
we pray today for all who, through disease or the fear of infection,
find themselves ostracised by society,
and especially we think of those who suffer from AIDS,
for so many still having a stigma attached,
and creating a sense of despair and hopelessness.
Lord, in your mercy,
hear our prayer

Support those who fear they may be at risk,
those who are anxious that they may unknowingly carry the virus,
those who know they have the disease,
those who are terminally ill,
and those who have lost hope in the future.
Lord, in your mercy,
hear our prayer.

Give wisdom and inspiration to those who strive to find a cure.
Equip them with the skill, patience, diligence and resources they need to persevere.
Lord, in your mercy,
hear our prayer.

Strengthen all who minister to sufferers,
who labour to bring relief,
who seek to show something of your love and compassion.
Lord, in your mercy,
hear our prayer.

Grant to each your wisdom and guidance,
and work through them,
so that those who suffer may find strength to face life or death with dignity, hope and peace.
Lord, in your mercy,
hear our prayer.
Amen.

Ambulance staff and paramedics

255

God of love and compassion,
grant your blessing on all involved in ambulance cover –
paramedics,
support staff,
drivers,
mechanics
and technicians –
all those whose dedication and skills are vital in providing a service
that we so much take for granted.
Enthuse,
equip
and enable them in all they do,
providing them with the resources they need –
physical, emotional and spiritual –
to continue their ministry of healing, support and comfort.
Work through them to express your loving care,
through Jesus Christ our Lord.
Amen.

Blood donors

256

Lord Jesus Christ,
who shed your blood for all,
thank you for those who donate theirs to others in turn,
from so simple an offering
coming so special a gift
to so great a multitude.
Inspire us, if we are able, to do the same.
Amen.

Carers

257

Here our prayer, Lord, for those who serve as carers for loved ones.
Support them in their demanding ministry,
and through your blessing may they in turn be a blessing to those they care for.
When exhaustion overwhelms them,
renew their vigour.
When patience is tested,
grant fortitude.
When all seems bleak,
shed light.
When tears flow,
bring comfort.
May they and their loved one experience your peace, strength and love
surrounding and supporting them always,
through Jesus Christ our Lord.
Amen.

258

Living God,
hear our prayer for carers,
those who devote so much of their lives to looking after loved ones –
parents,
partners,
children,
friends –
often at immense personal cost.
Strengthen them,
that they may find the reserves to continue.
Minister to them,
so that they may minister in turn.
In all they do,
may they be sustained by the knowledge that they too are loved,
they too are cared for –
above all by you.
Amen.

Childbirth

see also Special Services: Mothering Sunday; Themed prayers; Home and family

The birth of a premature child

259

Lord Jesus Christ,
born as a baby into a hostile and dangerous world,
watch over those children who are born prematurely,
so vulnerable yet so precious,
so tiny yet carrying such hopes
and inspiring such enormous love.
Cherish, protect, support and strengthen them,
so that they may grow in health and strength,
wisdom and maturity,
experiencing joy
and bringing it to others.
Amen.

Those whose child has been stillborn

260

Loving God,
hear our prayer for those whose child has been stillborn.
In the heartbreak of broken dreams and shattered expectations,
the numbness of shock and disbelief,
the ache of grief and despair,
the pain of loss and bereavement,
may your love somehow bring strength,
support,
courage
and comfort.
Receive their little one into your eternal care,
and assure them of your purpose beyond death itself,
through Jesus Christ our Lord.
Amen.

Those who have suffered a miscarriage

261

Loving God,
we pray for parents whose child has miscarried,
taken from them before love could fully be expressed,
relationships built
or dreams fulfilled.
Support them through this time
in their sorrow, pain and confusion,
and help them somehow to deal with their loss
and to find strength and hope to face the future.
Take their little one,
and grant them joy, peace and blessing in your eternal kingdom,
through Jesus Christ our Lord.
Amen.

The disabled

262

Loving God,
reach out to those born with disabilities.
Watch over them,
and grant them the care, support, love and provision they need,
not just now but throughout their lives.
Give wisdom, dedication, help and strength to all who will assist them,
so that, through loving nurture, they will find inner happiness,
peace,
security
and inner contentment.
Amen.

263

Loving God,
reach out to the incapacitated –
those injured through accident,
wounded in war,
maimed through illness,
or deformed at birth.

Equip them to face the challenges life brings,
and to see themselves always,
however disfigured they may be,
as whole people,
precious in your sight.
Amen.

264

Almighty God,
hear our prayer for the physically disabled,
whether through birth, accident or illness.
Though they will face challenges,
give them strength to overcome them,
and to live life still to the full.
Grant them patience,
courage,
resilience
and determination,
and, above all, the knowledge that,
whatever their disability,
they are whole people with as much to contribute as anyone.
Amen.

265

Living God,
when limitations or disabilities make life hard,
teach us that you love and value us,
not for what we do,
but for who we are,
and may that knowledge teach us to appreciate and respect the worth of everyone we meet.
Amen.

Drug and alcohol abusers

266

Lord Jesus Christ,
reach out to all who,
seeking freedom and fulfilment,
abuse their bodies to escape them;
all who, in their search for happiness,
are vulnerable to unscrupulous predators.

Help them to get a buzz out of life not through artificial means,
chemically induced elation,
but through experiencing the thrill of your presence,
and tasting the inner ecstasy that you alone can bring.
Amen.

267

Loving God,
reach out to all who are searching for fulfilment in their lives,
especially those who abuse their bodies in its pursuit,
striving to numb their senses to fill the void within.
Speak to them of the life you want them to enjoy –
abundant,
overflowing,
satisfying beyond measure.
Teach them where true happiness lies,
and help them to receive the contentment,
meaning,
hope
and freedom
you offer to all in Christ.
Amen.

268

Father God,
hear our prayer for all who abuse alcohol;
who feel that in order to have a good time,
they need to get drunk.
Minister to those who resort to drink as a way of coping with boredom,
loneliness,
fear,
sorrow
or anxiety,
inexorably being drawn in to an ever-greater sense of dependency.
Reach out to alcoholics,
those who feel they cannot get through the day without another 'fix' to see them through.
Grant to everyone held in alcohol's thrall help and strength to escape from it,
and teach all to use it wisely,
enjoying it in moderation but avoiding excess.
Amen.

269

Living God,
to all who seek pleasure through intoxication,
blotting out perception to fill their inner emptiness,
grant genuine fulfilment.
Pour into their hearts the sparkling wine of your love
that they may find true life,
their cup spilling over,
full to overflowing.
Amen.

GPs

270

Grant your blessing, Lord, on all who serve as GPs in our communities.
In their work of examining and diagnosis,
give them wisdom.
In their task of prescribing and treating,
give them skill.
In their ministry of listening and counselling,
give them insight.
In everything they do,
work through them,
to heal and help,
relieve and reassure,
safeguard and support,
bringing them motivation, joy and fulfilment in their calling,
through Jesus Christ our Lord.
Amen.

The healing ministry

271

Loving God,
thank you for those who care about their fellow human beings;
those who are ready to give of their time, energy, skills or money
to reach out to them in their need
and to offer a ministry of love and healing.

Thank you for those,
both within and beyond the Church,
who strive to bring strength,
solace,
support
and succour to all battling with ill-health.
Inspire us through their example to care more about others in turn
and to respond practically to their needs.
Help us to live more fully as your people,
in a way that truly brings honour to you
and blessing to others.
Amen.

272

Lord Jesus Christ,
as you reached out to the sick and suffering
throughout your earthly ministry,
bringing wholeness and healing to so many,
reach out now through all who minister to body, mind and spirit,
and through them grant your renewing, restoring touch.
Amen.

Hospices and the terminally ill

273

Eternal God,
hear our prayer for hospices and those who work in them.
Amid the death, trauma and sorrow that will inevitably touch them,
may there also be a celebration of what each day brings,
an imparting of joy, love and peace,
and the bringing of hope,
both now and in life to come.
Shine now.
Shine always.

Equip all who exercise their special ministry there
with the emotional, physical and spiritual reserves they need,
and through them bring relief from pain,
reassurance to the fearful,
respite to carers
and comfort to all who grieve.
Shine now.
Shine always.

Grant through the therapy administered,
the compassion shown,
and the support offered,
that all who spend their last days there
may find quality in life
and dignity in death.
Shine now.
Shine always.
Amen.

274

Reach out in love, Lord, to those who are terminally ill.
Help them to face the prospect of death,
yet still celebrate life;
to wrestle with despair,
yet still hold on to hope;
to cope with sorrow,
yet still find joy;
to bear pain,
yet still embrace pleasure;
to experience fear,
yet still know peace;
to be broken,
yet still be whole;
to face endings,
yet still look forward to new beginnings,
trusting that nothing can finally separate them from your love,
through Jesus Christ our Lord.
Amen.

275

Christ our Saviour,
reach out to the terminally ill.
Christ of Gethsemane,
strengthen those crushed by fear and sorrow at the prospect of death.
Christ of the cross,
minister to those enduring pain in body, mind and spirit.
Christ of the tomb,
support the dying and bring comfort to those who mourn.

Christ of the resurrection
bring light in darkness,
hope in despair,
peace in confusion
and life out of death.
Amen.

276

Eternal God,
to all wrestling with terminal illness,
give the assurance that you will always value them for who they are;
and help their families, friends and colleagues,
as they struggle to come to terms with their feelings,
to do the same,
seeing not the illness but the individual underneath.
Whatever else may be lost,
may that continue,
to the end and beyond.
Amen.

277

Eternal God,
we pray for those faced by the prospect of death,
whether wrestling with terminal illness
or coming to terms with failing health and advancing years.
In the fear and sorrow they may feel,
give the assurance that not even death itself can separate them from your love
and that you hold in store for them things more wonderful than they can yet imagine,
through Jesus Christ our Lord.
Amen.

278

Hear our prayer, Lord, for those who are dying.
May Christ who wrestled with the prospect of suffering and death
support them in facing sorrow.
May Christ who endured the agony of crucifixion
strengthen them in bearing pain.
May Christ who surrendered his spirit, and breathed his last,
accompany them in the shadow of death.

May Christ who rose again, triumphant over the grave,
lead them into his eternal kingdom.
May Christ bless and keep them as they journey with him,
and *to* him,
their final destination.
Amen.

Hospitals

Those facing an operation

279

Loving God,
we pray for those in hospital facing an operation.
Soothe their spirit,
calm their fears,
and grant them strength, support and healing.
Guide the surgeons and teams who will be operating upon them,
the nurses caring for them
and the support staff providing for their needs.
Work through all to fulfil your purpose
and to bring health and wholeness in body, mind and spirit.
Amen.

Hospital chaplains

280

Christ the healer,
reach out through the service and ministry of hospital chaplains,
bringing courage where there is fear,
hope where there is despair,
comfort where there is sorrow,
strength where there is suffering,
peace where there is turmoil
and faith where there is doubt.
May your grace go with them,
your light shine in them,
your love flow from them
and your power work through them.
Amen.

Nurses

281

Living God,
we thank you for the work of nurses in our hospitals and local communities,
and ask your blessing upon their work.
Through care given,
treatment administered,
reassurance offered
and understanding shown,
reach out to those in their trust,
bringing healing and wholeness,
renewal in body, mind and spirit.
Give skill, diligence, patience and compassion in all they do,
through their ministry giving expression to your love for all.
Amen.

Patients and staff

282

Compassionate God,
hear our prayer for hospitals.
Equip, encourage and enable those who work within them –
from consultants, clinicians, nurses and chaplains
to cleaners, caterers, porters and support staff –
that all may contribute in bringing healing and wholeness in body, mind and spirit.
Reach out to hold.
Reach out to heal.

Minister to patients,
and, in your love, reach out into the contrasting circumstances they will face –
the joy of childbirth and heartbreak of bereavement,
the delight of recovery and shock of bleak diagnoses,
the exhilaration of an all-clear and trauma of surgery –
so much hope and despair,
faith and fear,
so many joys and sorrows,
beginnings and endings.
Reach out to hold.
Reach out to heal.

Be present in it all, Lord,
to strengthen and support,
granting in sickness or in health,
life or death,
the knowledge that you will be there, come what may.
Reach out to hold.
Reach out to heal.
Amen.

283

God of grace and mercy,
reach out to all in hospital:
the sick and frail;
those waiting for an operation,
fearful about the procedure or the future;
those recovering from major surgery,
wrestling with chronic disease
or struggling with pain;
those coming to terms with terminal illness.
Work through nurses, doctors, surgeons and support staff,
through counsellors, ministers, friends and family,
and through your Holy Spirit,
to bring comfort,
strength,
relief
and healing.
Through your love
and that of others,
grant to all facing ill-health the knowledge that they are not alone.
Amen.

284

Lord Jesus Christ,
hear our prayer for those in our hospitals:
for patients and their loved ones,
but, above all, for those who staff them –
those with the courage to face,
day after day,
the sheer intensity of it all,
striving with such dedication to nurture wholeness in body, mind and spirit.

Thank you for their skill and compassion;
the renewal they bring,
life they make possible,
understanding they show
and comfort they extend.
Thank you for their willingness to care for others.
Amen.

285

Living God,
hear our prayer for the sick,
especially those in hospital.
Reach out to those awaiting a diagnosis or surgery,
those wrestling with chronic or terminal illness,
those troubled in the present or fearful of the future.
Minister to the broken in body, mind or spirit,
and enfold them in the knowledge of your eternal love.
Strengthen not just patients and their loved ones
but also nurses,
doctors,
surgeons,
consultants,
administrators
and the countless support staff integral to patient care.
Uphold them in their work,
and through their care and compassion bring comfort,
relief,
hope
and healing –
inner renewal and wholeness.
Amen.

Leprosy sufferers

286

Loving God,
we bring before you today the sick and suffering of our world,
and especially we pray for those who suffer from the disease of leprosy,
so horrible in its effects
and yet potentially so easy to cure and prevent.
Lord, in your mercy,
hear our prayer.

Forgive us that so many people continue to endure the pain,
the disfigurement,
and the stigma associated with leprosy,
when in real terms it would cost so little to wipe this disease out for ever.
Lord, in your mercy,
hear our prayer.

Prosper the work of all those who, like Leprosy Mission,
strive to bring help and healing.
Give them the words to get their message across,
the resources to treat sufferers wherever they find them,
and support in their drive to make leprosy a thing of the past.
Lord, in your mercy,
hear our prayer.
Amen.

Medical workers

287

Through the work, Lord, of those in our doctors' surgeries,
health centres,
hospitals,
nursing homes,
hospices,
and other places of care and compassion,
may those who face illness or infirmity know the touch of your hand upon them,
your healing love
and sustaining grace.
Amen.

Nursing/residential care homes

288

Eternal God,
hear our prayer for the work of nursing and residential care homes.
Though residents may be in their twilight years,
many wrestling with physical or mental decline,
may there nonetheless be a celebration of life in such places,
an appreciation of all that continues to be good and special,
an atmosphere of community
and a respect for the dignity and worth of all.

Work through the staff,
whatever their role may be,
filling them with gentleness,
compassion,
sensitivity
and understanding,
that in giving they may receive,
and in serving others they may serve you.
Amen.

Psychiatric hospitals

289

Be present, O Lord, in our psychiatric hospitals,
and, through the ministry they offer,
grant peace to those in turmoil.
Protect and equip all who work in them,
in their demanding and sometimes dangerous work,
and give them skill, patience, wisdom and compassion,
as they strive to bring relief to the disturbed and deranged,
those whose sanity has been undermined or destroyed by illness,
drug abuse,
personality disorder,
depression
or psychological trauma.
Though so much seems to deny love and question faith,
grant yet your help to calm the storm in broken lives and minds.
Amen.

The sick and suffering

290

Loving God,
we bring before you the sick and suffering of our world,
all those wrestling with illness in body, mind or spirit.
Lord, in your mercy,
hear our prayer.

We pray for those afflicted in body –
enduring physical pain,
overwhelmed by disabling disease,
waiting for an operation or further treatment
and fearful of what the future may hold,
or living with the knowledge of a terminal illness.
Lord, in your mercy,
hear our prayer.

We pray for those disturbed or troubled in mind –
those whose confidence has broken down,
those unable to cope with the pressures of daily life,
those oppressed by false terrors of the imagination,
those facing the dark despair of clinical depression.
Lord, in your mercy,
hear our prayer.

We pray for those afflicted in spirit –
those who feel their lives to be empty,
or whose beliefs are threatened
or who have lost their faith,
or who worship gods of their own making with no power to satisfy,
or whose hearts have become bitter and twisted,
and their minds dark.
Lord, in your mercy,
hear our prayer.

Living God,
we thank you for all who work to bring help, wholeness and healing to the sick –
doctors and nurses,
surgeons and medical staff,
psychiatrists, counsellors,
clergy and therapists.
Support and strengthen all those who share in the work of healing,
all who strive to bring relief,
all who minister to others.
Lord, in your mercy,
hear our prayer.

Grant them your wisdom and guidance,
your care and compassion,
your strength and support.

Equip them in all they do,
and bring wholeness through them.
Lord, in your mercy,
hear our prayer.

Finally we pray for your Church
in the healing ministry you have called it to exercise:
an inner healing of body, mind and soul that only you can offer.
Grant that your people everywhere may be so filled with your Holy Spirit,
and so touched by the grace of Christ,
that they may share effectively in the wider work of healing,
through their life and witness bringing wholeness to broken people
and a broken world.
Lord, in your mercy,
hear our prayer.
Amen.

291

Father God,
reach out to all who are unwell and minister your love.
Bring help.
Bring healing.

Grant relief from pain,
comfort in sorrow,
hope in despair,
and reassurance in moments of fear and anxiety.
Bring help.
Bring healing.

Bless those who work to bring healing,
those who offer counsel and consolation,
those involved in research seeking new cures and treatments,
those who must make diagnoses,
those who care for loved ones,
and those whose lives have been overturned by disease,
whether of themselves or those dear to them.
Bring help.
Bring healing.

Grant a sense of wholeness even in the throes of illness
and, by your grace, make well.
Amen.

292

Lord Jesus Christ,
you speak of coming among us to make us whole –
whole in body, mind and spirit.
Thank you for the gift of health –
of being truly well in every part of our being –
and help us to understand more fully what that means.
May your grace bring hope;
your love bring healing.

Hear our prayer also for those who do not enjoy good health –
the sick,
injured,
disabled,
chronically or terminally ill.
May your grace bring hope;
your love bring healing.

And hear our prayer also for all those who seek to minister to their needs –
doctors,
nurses,
consultants,
surgeons,
counsellors
therapists
and medical staff of all kinds.
May your grace bring hope;
your love bring healing.

Thank you for the ministry all these perform
and inspire us in our turn to care more meaningfully for others,
offering what support and compassion we can.
May your grace bring hope;
your love bring healing.
Amen.

293

Reach out, Lord, to those who are sick.
May the compassion of Christ enfold them,
the arms of Christ support them,
the peace of Christ engulf them,
the grace of Christ sustain them,
the Spirit of Christ renew them,
and the power of Christ make them whole.
Amen.

294

Compassionate God,
forgive us, for we forget those who live in constant pain,
longing for release yet finding no end to their suffering,
each day blighted by its stranglehold.
Give them strength not just to get through
but also to find joy and fulfilment in life,
and grant the assurance that, just as you shared our sufferings in Christ,
so, through him, we will all finally enter a brighter kingdom
in which pain and sorrow will be at an end.
Amen.

295

Gracious God,
it's easy to extol your love when health is good,
but when life is overshadowed by pain and discomfort,
sapping our strength and eroding our happiness,
it's much harder to trust you and to offer our praise.
Though, for some, such pain is temporary,
brought about by illness or injury,
we know that for others, wrestling with chronic or terminal conditions,
it is an ever-present reality,
each day bringing more of the same.
Help us through expressing *our* love and concern for them
to express also *yours*.
Amen.

296

Healing God,
hear our prayer for the sick –
all who are in pain,
waiting for or recovering from surgery,
undergoing long-term treatment,
battling against disease,
anxious about the future.
Support them through family and friends,
through the skill and dedication of medical staff,
and, above all, through the knowledge of your love.
Minister your healing touch,
and grant them the peace and strength they need to find wholeness in you.
Amen.

297

Lord Jesus Christ,
as you touched those with leprosy,
restored sight to the blind,
brought peace to the disturbed
and enabled the lame to walk,
come now to all who are sick in body, mind and spirit,
bringing again your healing touch and renewing grace.
Amen.

298

Lord Jesus Christ,
hear our prayer for the sick –
all who are in pain,
waiting for or recovering from surgery,
undergoing treatment
or coming to terms with terminal illness.
Give help and strength to any whose health is failing,
and to all who tend them.
Amen.

299

Lord Jesus Christ,
we remember today how, throughout your ministry,
you looked to bring healing and wholeness.
We remember how you touched the lepers,
restored sight to the blind,
cured the sick,
and helped the lame to walk;
how you brought hope to the broken-hearted
and those crushed in spirit,
peace of mind to those who were troubled,
and forgiveness to those burdened by guilt or failure.
Lord Jesus Christ,
we bring before you all in any kind of need,
praying again for your healing and renewing touch
in body, mind and spirit,
this and every day.
Restore and make whole,
by your grace.
Amen.

300

Loving God,
for those troubled about their health,
and those with the responsibility of ministering to them,
grant your help,
guidance
and love.
Amen.

301

To all under the weather, Lord –
all who are sick or suffering –
give strength,
help,
love
and healing.
Amen.

302

To all who wrestle with pain, Lord,
grant help and hope;
above all, the assurance that the time will come
when there will be no more suffering and sorrow,
and they will rejoice in the light of your love for evermore.
Amen.

Home and family

see also Special Services: Mothering Sunday;
Themed Prayers: Health – Childbirth

Babies and toddlers

303

Father God,
hear our prayer for babies and toddlers.
Provide for and protect them,
granting them health,
wisdom,
peace
and joy.
Guide their footsteps,
and equip them for their journey through life,
wherever it might lead.
Be with those who love them,
and those whom they will love in turn,
that together they will taste your goodness
and celebrate the life you offer in all its fullness,
through Jesus Christ our Lord.
Amen.

Children leaving home

304

Grant your blessing and guidance, Lord,
on children leaving home.
As they travel from the old to the new,
go with them,
wherever they may be and whatever life might bring –
a light to their path
and companion along their way.
May your hand guide and arms embrace them,
bringing the knowledge that they are as close to your heart
as they will always be to those of their parents,
families
and loved ones.
Amen.

Grandparents

305

Father God,
thank you for grandparents and all that they do.
Thank you for the many ways they give a helping hand –
the practical support they offer,
the time they give up,
the skills they use,
the things they make possible.
Helper of all,
hear our prayer.

Thank you for grandchildren –
the pleasure they give,
the fun they share,
the appreciation they show,
and the fulfilment they bring.
Helper of all,
hear our prayer.

We ask your blessing on grandparents,
and think especially of those who have lost their partner,
those wrestling with poor health,
those worried about making ends meet,
those who feel forgotten;
and we pray also for those whose hopes of becoming a grandparent have never been realised.
Helper of all,
hear our prayer.

We think finally of those who mourn a grandparent,
those whose grandparents are unwell
and those who have become their carer.
Helper of all,
hear our prayer.

Father God,
you who offer help beyond all others,
we bring you these our prayers,
in gratitude and in love,
through Jesus Christ our Lord.
Amen.

306

Father God,
we thank you for all we can learn from others,
and especially today from the wisdom and experience of grandparents.
We celebrate the insights they can share and advice give,
borne from long years of life.
In your love,
work through them.

We pray for those who bring up grandchildren,
attempting to fill the void where, for some reason,
parents are unable to look after children themselves.
In your love,
work through them.

We pray for those anxious about grandchildren,
wanting to guide or counsel
yet feeling unable or prohibited from doing so.
In your love,
work through them.

We pray for those who feel rejected by grandchildren,
their concern misunderstood,
suggestions spurned
and approaches dismissed,
In your love,
work through them.

We pray for older grandparents whose memories or faculties or failing,
advancing years bringing them anxiety and frustration,
and especially we think of victims of dementia,
no longer seeming the people they once were.
In your love,
work through them.

We thank you for grandparents we have loved and lost,
those who helped shape what we are
and whose memory we will always cherish in our hearts.
In your love,
work through them.
Amen.

Homes

307

Be present, Lord, in the homes of all
and fill them with laughter, love, peace and pleasure.
May they be places of harmony, happiness, warmth and welcome,
bringing contentment, security and lasting memories.
Protect,
nurture,
guide
and provide,
so that each may be not just a house
but, above all, a home –
touched by your presence and sanctified by your grace.
Amen.

Those moving house

308

Loving God,
be with those who are moving house.
At what for them is a time of excitement yet apprehension,
hopes for the future mingled with memories of the past,
grant them the knowledge that wherever they may go,
and whatever life may bring,
you will always be with them,
looking to guide, strengthen and bless.
May their old homes be remembered with thanksgiving and affection,
but may their move prove a stepping stone into a new chapter,
bringing joy,
peace
and fulfilment –
each day illumined by the light of your grace
and the radiance of your love.
Amen.

New parents

309

Hear our prayer, Lord, for new parents.
May the delight they feel in their baby
continue to fill and thrill them in the years ahead,
the privilege of nurturing a young life –
supporting, guiding, protecting and providing –
being a constant source of joy.
In the demands and duties of daily life,
may there always be time to listen,
share,
encourage
and enjoy –
time to appreciate the unique and priceless treasure of parenthood.
Bless them and their little ones,
this and every day.
Amen.

Those whose children are leaving home

310

Loving God,
be with those whose children are leaving home and moving on to new things.
At this time of change and contrasting emotions –
pride . . .
yet pain;
love . . .
yet loss –
help them to let go . . .
yet also stay close;
to keep in contact . . .
yet also leave space;
to be there when needed . . .
yet also to let their loved one make their own decisions.
Open up to them new avenues for their service,
new uses for their time,
and new directions in their life.
Amen.

The lonely and estranged

311

Almighty God,
hear our prayer for those who feel lonely,
unloved,
unwanted.

We pray for those whose relationships have been broken,
whether through separation, divorce or bereavement;
and we pray for those deprived of the relationships they might have had:
children unwanted by their parents,
parents alienated from children,
family members estranged from one another.
Lord, in your mercy,
reach out in love.

We pray for individuals who feel rejected by society –
those who have no confidence in their abilities,
no place where they feel accepted,
no sense of their own worth.
Lord, in your mercy,
reach out in love.

We pray for communities divided by prejudice, race or religion,
for churches where there is disagreement, tension and disharmony,
and for nations broken by war and violence.
Lord, in your mercy,
reach out in love.

Almighty God,
bring friendship to the lonely,
reconciliation to the estranged,
harmony to the divided,
and comfort to the bereaved.
Lord in your mercy,
reach out in love.

In our homes and our families,
our schools and our places of work,
our country and our world,
may your love be shared among us,
bringing hope and healing.
Lord in your mercy,
reach out in love.
Amen.

312

Gracious God,
lover of the poor,
the weak,
the vulnerable
and the oppressed,
we pray for those who feel they have no roots,
no identity,
no sense of belonging.
Friend of the friendless,
hear our prayer.

We pray for those who live as refugees in strange lands,
driven from their own homes and country by civil war,
oppression,
famine,
natural disaster.
Friend of the friendless,
hear our prayer.

We pray for those who have been orphaned as children;
those who have been adopted
and who long to discover their true parents;
those who come from broken homes
and who are scarred by the trauma of bitter separation;
those who have been abused;
those who feel unloved and unwanted.
Friend of the friendless,
hear our prayer.

We pray too for those who are lonely,
deprived through age or infirmity of human companionship,
or separated from others even when they are with them
through fear,
shyness,
mistrust,
or prejudice.
Friend of the friendless,
hear our prayer.

We pray for our society in which a sense of community has been lost,
where ties that once bound families together have been broken,
where values, customs and convictions that gave stability have been flouted,
all too many today living only for themselves.
Friend of the friendless,
hear our prayer.

We pray for churches that have become divided,
tragically allowing the things that separate them to become more important than the faith that unites,
denying through their intolerance the unity that Christ desires for all his people,
and so experiencing the pain of discord and division.
Friend of the friendless,
hear our prayer.

Lord of our world,
give to all a recognition of the humanity that binds us together,
transcending our differences.
Give us a sense of your love for everyone;
the purpose you have for each person
no matter what their race or culture,
background or circumstances.
Friend of the friendless,
hear our prayer.

Help your Church to offer a place of acceptance,
welcome,
and belonging.
And help all who feel isolated to find in you the true source of their being
and the root of their lives.
Friend of the friendless,
hear our prayer.
Amen.

313

Gracious God,
we thank you that you value each of us,
that we are all important in your eyes.
We thank you that everyone matters to you,
none more than others and none less.
Hear now our prayers
for those who have lost that sense of perspective.
Lord of all,
hear our prayer.

We pray for those who fall into the error of pride,
thinking of themselves more highly than they should,
looking down on others,
trusting in themselves rather than in you.
Help them to recognise their weaknesses as well as their strengths,
their need to receive as well as to give.
Lord of all,
hear our prayer.

We pray for those who have no sense of worth,
who feel they are unimportant, unvalued, or unloved –
victims of broken homes and broken relationships,
the powerless and the poor,
homeless and refugees,
shy and depressed,
lonely and rejected.
Grant them the assurance that, whatever their circumstances,
they are precious to you,
each one your unique creation.
Lord of all,
hear our prayer.

Gracious God,
give to all a proper sense of their own value,
a true appreciation of the worth of others,
and, above all, an understanding of your greatness,
beside which we are nothing
yet through which you count us as your children.
Lord of all,
hear our prayer.
Amen.

314

God of love,
we pray for those many people in our world who have been deprived of love,
who feel unloved,
or for whom love has been painful.
Through your presence,
touch their hearts.

We pray for those for whom love has involved pain –
those who have faced the trauma of breakdown in their marriage,
or experienced the collapse of friendships or romantic engagements;
those who have come from broken homes,
or who have become estranged from family and friends;
those whose children have moved away to begin new lives of their own,
or whose parents have become frail, confused and infirm;
those whose loved ones have been taken from them by death,
or those who have been forced to leave those they count most dear.
May the knowledge of your unending love
be a constant source of comfort and inspiration.
Through your presence,
touch their hearts.

We pray for those who find it hard to love –
those whose love has been betrayed,
those who are scarred by bitter and painful experience,
those who have been subjected to abuse,
those afraid of showing their true feelings,
those oppressed by mental illness.
Through your presence,
touch their hearts.

Loving God,
we bring before you the complex world of human relationships,
capable of bringing such joy but such sorrow,
so much pleasure yet also so much pain.
We thank you for your gift of love
and all the love that surrounds us,
but help us never to forget those who have lost love
or been hurt through it.
Restore their faith in what love can do,
and help them both to find love and share it.
Through your presence,
touch their hearts.

Grant to us all the knowledge
that your love will never fail,
and never let us go.
Amen.

315

Father God,
we pray today for all who are lonely.
Minister to those starved of company,
confined by illness or infirmity to their homes
and longing simply for someone to talk to.
Creator of us all,
hear our prayer.

Comfort those who feel unloved or unvalued;
all who struggle to build meaningful relationships,
feeling isolated even when they're with others.
Creator of us all,
hear our prayer.

Give them the assurance that they are never completely on their own;
that, however much it may sometimes seem otherwise,
you are always by their sides,
a constant friend and companion in the journey of life.
Creator of us all,
hear our prayer.

Help them, and all, to recognise your love reaching out,
each moment of every day,
through Jesus Christ our Lord.
Creator of us all,
hear our prayer.
Amen.

316

Living God,
hear our prayer for those who feel themselves to be alone
in a cold and impersonal universe,
having no sense of your love reaching out to them,
of your care and compassion for all.
Reach out to hold.
Reach out to help.

Hear our prayer for those who feel lost in a faceless and uncaring society,
believing themselves to be of little concern to anyone.
Reach out to hold.
Reach out to help.

Hear our prayer for those who question their self-worth,
crushed by guilt, anxiety, shyness or fear.
Reach out to hold.
Reach out to help.

Hear our prayer for those unfulfilled in their work or lives,
those for whom each day seems empty of meaning.
Reach out to hold.
Reach out to help.

Hear our prayer for all who wonder how they can possibly matter;
how you can conceivably be interested in lives as small as theirs.
Reach out to hold.
Reach out to help.

Remind us that you care infinitely for each person you have made,
and may everyone,
everywhere,
come to understand just how much they mean,
and will always mean,
to you.
Reach out to hold.
Reach out to help.
Amen.

317

Living God,
reach out to the helpless and hopeless,
those who feel themselves to be unimportant,
unvalued
or unloved.
Friend of the friendless,
hear our prayer.

Reach out to all who question their own worth,
who feel they have nothing to contribute,
who believe they have no future,
who regard themselves as weak,
foolish,
despised,
forgotten.
Friend of the friendless,
hear our prayer.

However hopeless they may feel,
however disheartened, disillusioned or despondent,
assure them of the place they have in your heart,
of the infinite value you place upon each and every individual,
and in that knowledge may they hold their heads up high.
Friend of the friendless,
hear our prayer.
Amen.

318

God of grace,
thank you for the company of others,
all who enrich each day simply by being there.
Reach out to those who have no one,
and in their loneliness be there for *them*.
Amen.

319

Living God,
we feel trapped sometimes,
imprisoned in our own small world.
Reach out to all who feel separated from others
and from you;
come and set them free.
Amen.

320

Loving God,
we pray for all who are lonely:
those whose relationships have been broken
or who have never enjoyed the relationships they might have had;
those who feel rejected by society and unsure of their worth;
those who spend day after day alone
and those who feel hopelessly isolated even when they are in company.
Give to each the knowledge that you are with them always,
and enrich their lives with companionship and friendship.
Amen.

321

Saviour Christ,
reach out to the lonely,
those who wait in vain for a knock at the door,
a friendly face,
a moment of company.
However isolated they may be,
teach them that you are by their side.
Amen.

322

Lord Jesus Christ,
may all those who feel isolated and unloved
find in you a friend they can depend on and,
through realising how much you value them,
may they discover a sense of worth
that leads to and informs their relationships with others.
Amen.

Prejudice

Breaking down barriers

323

God of all,
we like to think that we're open to others,
free from prejudice, pettiness or partiality,
but we're not.
Open our heart to you,
and so to others.

In reality, we erect all kinds of barriers,
some reflecting our preconceptions,
others being the result of disagreement,
perceived injustice
or simply innate antipathy.
Open our heart to you,
and so to others.

We shut people out of our lives
or keep them at arm's length,
afraid of or unwilling to risk genuine encounter.
Open our heart to you,
and so to others.

We pigeonhole those who challenge or unsettle us,
and hide behind labels in order to dismiss them and keep our distance.
Open our heart to you,
and so to others.

Forgive us,
and break down the walls we erect –
the barriers of prejudice,
fear,
pride
and suspicion –
so that our lives may reflect the love and openness to all
that you so powerfully demonstrated in Christ.
Open our heart to you,
and so to others.
Amen.

324

Jesus Christ,
throughout your ministry you reached out to those who were seen as beyond the pale:
the diseased,
the sinful,
the outcasts,
the despised.
As you have loved us,
help us to love others.

Even when it involved risk and rejection,
you put love first,
consistently showing compassion and acceptance, come what may.
Forgive the way we keep our distance from people,
afraid of somehow becoming contaminated or put in danger.
As you have loved us,
help us to love others.

Forgive our lack of love,
our inability to care,
our innate prejudice and mistrust.
As you have loved us,
help us to love others.

Help us, as you did, to see beneath the surface to individuals,
with all their hurts and needs,
and, like you once more,
may we lovingly respond.
As you have loved us,
help us to love others.
Amen.

325

Gracious God,
teach us to look behind the labels,
especially when it comes to people,
recognising that the terms so often used –
East,
West,
black,
white,

Christian,
Muslim,
liberal,
extremist –
can only tell part of the story,
never the whole.
Help everyone in their dealings with others,
to see the person first
and the label second.
Amen.

326

Lord Jesus Christ,
as you touched the untouchables throughout your ministry,
so you reach out still,
seeing not the affliction but the person underneath.
Forgive the feebleness of our love,
and teach us to do the same.
Amen.

327

Loving God,
help us to put ourselves into the shoes of others;
to look beyond our limited horizons and unconscious prejudices
and to recognise the problems they face
and the circumstances that shape them.
Help us to identify as much as we can with their situations,
seeking to understand and empathise
rather than making snap judgements
or allowing narrow preconceptions to dictate our attitudes.
Just as you see the best in us rather than the worst,
the good instead of the bad,
give us the openness and generosity of spirit we need
to do the same in all our dealings with others.
Amen.

328

Mighty God,
we like to consider ourselves open,
approachable,
unbiased,
but in reality we know that we can be as close-minded as any,
swift to put up the shutters when our beliefs are questioned.
Speak through those around us,
and help us to listen.

Forgive us for closing our ears to what challenges our assumptions,
for automatically rejecting ideas that seem to question or threaten our own.
Speak through those around us,
and help us to listen.

Teach us to open our minds to others,
recognising that you can guide through their perspective,
instruct through their questions
and enrich through their insights.
Speak through those around us,
and help us to listen.
Amen.

329

From everything, Lord, that closes our mind to other people
and stops us from recognising them as our neighbour,
deliver us.
Amen.

Homophobia

330

Father God,
open our eyes to the prejudice that lurks within us,
within society
and within the Church –
prejudice that too easily in the past,
and even still today in the present,
has dismissed as 'perverted',
'sick'

'abnormal'
or 'sinful'
those whose sexuality differs from the 'norm'.
Lord of all,
hear us.

Help us to focus instead on encouraging loving relationships
in which trust and commitment can flourish;
relationships consecrated to you that are able to stand the test of time.
Lord of all,
hear us.

Forgive the way that so many not considered 'straight' have,
across the years,
endured mockery, suspicion, hostility and persecution,
driving many to the edge of despair
and some of them beyond.
Lord of all,
hear us.

Help us and your people everywhere to be truly welcoming of all,
following together in the footsteps of Christ.
Lord of all,
hear us.
Amen.

Racism

331

Lord of all,
you have made us in your image,
each the work of your hands,
a unique and precious creation,
and we praise you for it.
Yet we remember also how, across the centuries and still today,
so many have endured prejudice and discrimination,
rejected because of the colour of their skin,
persecuted due to their creed or culture.
Reach out in love,
and heal our divisions.

Forgive the racism that still exists in our society –
the automatic attaching of labels,
the taunting and snide remarks,
the denial of opportunities,
the unconscious negative attitudes.
Break down the barriers that divide our world,
the ignorance and suspicion that inflict such pain on so many.
Reach out in love,
and heal our divisions.

Forgive the racism that exists within ourselves,
recognised or unrecognised –
the naïve assumptions and hidden biases –
and forgive us those times we have remained silent when we should have spoken up,
when we have ignored prejudice because *we* are personally unaffected.
Help us to see each individual in their own right,
and to appreciate their true worth.
Reach out in love,
and heal our divisions.

We pray for all who experience racism –
victims of verbal abuse or physical assault,
of social exclusion, deprivation and discrimination.
Give them courage to hold their heads high,
perseverance in standing up for their rights,
and support in times of adversity.
Reach out in love,
and heal our divisions.

We pray finally for those who work for change –
campaigning for equality of opportunity,
striving to break down preconceptions,
building bridges across divided communities.
Encourage them in their efforts,
and grant that through bringing people together
prejudices may be overcome.
Reach out in love,
and heal our divisions.

Lord of all,
you have made us in your image,
each one the work of your hands,
a unique and precious creation.
Break down everything that comes between us,
and grant unity to our divided world,
and a proper respect for all.
Reach out in love,
and heal our divisions.
Amen.

332

Loving God,
forgive the racism that has scarred our world across the centuries –
the hatred it has engendered,
persecution it has led to,
injustices and misery it has caused,
violence, murder and genocide it has been used to justify.
Break down the barriers, Lord,
and make us one.

Forgive the racism that has scarred the Church over the years:
persecution of Jews and Muslims,
the iniquity of apartheid,
innate white elitism,
rank prejudice and discrimination.
Break down the barriers, Lord,
and make us one.

Reach out to those who continue to be victims of racism today,
being intimidated,
discriminated against,
victimised,
abused,
suffering on account of the colour of their skin or place of origin.
Break down the barriers, Lord,
and make us one.

Prosper, we pray, the work of all those who work to combat racism,
and break down the barriers of prejudice that keep people apart,
so that everyone,
everywhere,
may learn to recognise, respect and value the common humanity we share.
Break down the barriers, Lord,
and make us one.
Amen.

Sexism

333

Loving God,
thank you for creating humankind in your image,
male and female;
for making us one in Christ,
each having an equal share in the work of your kingdom.
Lord, hear us,
graciously hear us.

Thank you for the immeasurable contribution women have made across the years,
in countless ways,
to the life of the world and of your people –
for the gifts they have brought to bear,
the sacrifices they have made,
the vision, dedication and perseverance they have shown.
Lord, hear us,
graciously hear us.

Forgive the ways women have all too often been discriminated against,
marginalised not only in society
but also in in the life of the Church,
their talents undervalued,
their creativity stifled,
their contribution overlooked,
Lord, hear us,
graciously hear us.

Defend the cause of women everywhere,
and prosper those who work in positions of authority
and responsibility,
both outside and within the Church.
Lord, hear us,
graciously hear us.
Amen.

334

Living God,
thank you for making us different,
men and women,
each having particular gifts,
particular characteristics,
particular instincts,
particular qualities.
Lord of all,
hear our prayer.

But thank you also that, overriding everything that sets us apart,
we are bound by a common humanity,
male and female having as much to contribute,
as much right to lead,
as much potential as the other.
Lord of all,
hear our prayer.

Teach us more of what that means,
and help us to recognise some of the injustices women have faced across the centuries,
including those that continue to this day.
Lord of all,
hear our prayer.

Help us, within the Church,
to allow for the views of those who think differently than we do,
but also to do all that we can to put right what we consider to be wrongs,
so that the legacy we leave to those who come after us may be one that both they,
and we,
can truly be proud of.
Lord of all,
hear our prayer.
Amen.

Relationships

see also Themed prayers: Prejudice

Anger

335

Lord Jesus Christ,
teach us that we should simmer with rage about some things in life –
injustice,
exploitation,
greed,
hatred
and violence –
but remind us also how easily anger can spill over into rage,
destroying and wounding,
adding to rather than alleviating the world's misery.
Show us when it's right to be angry,
but help us always to channel it,
so that it will be a tool for good instead of evil.
Amen.

Betrayal, hurt of

336

Lord Jesus Christ,
when love brings hurt,
the pain of rejection, betrayal or loss,
may *your* love bring comfort,
and help to heal the wounds.
Amen.

337

Loving God,
just as you came in Christ to reconcile the world to yourself,
come again now and reach out to all whose relationships are broken,
undermined by mistakes and misunderstanding,
and, through your healing touch,
rekindle love.
Put an end to our petty divisions,
and bring back together those whom life has pushed apart.
Amen.

Engagement

338

Gracious God,
bless those who have become engaged to one another,
publicly witnessing to the love they feel,
joy they have found,
commitment they have made,
and hopes, plans and dreams they share.
May their love continue to flourish,
their joy be deepened and enriched,
their commitment hold firm in the changing fortunes of life
and their dreams be realised,
through Jesus Christ our Lord.
Amen.

Judging and finding fault

339

Forgive, Lord, our knee-jerk reactions to those who we feel have wronged us;
our instinctive desire to extract an eye for an eye
and a tooth for a tooth.
Forgive us for failing to see in ourselves the wrongs we see in others;
for expecting allowances to be made for our faults
yet refusing to make them in turn.
Help us truly to do to others what we'd have done to us,
giving though we do not receive,
loving though no love is returned.
Teach us always to remember that for us who deserve so little
you gave so much.
Amen.

340

It's easy to tear down, Lord –
we do it all the time.
Through a harsh word or critical look
we rip the ground from beneath people's feet,
undermining their confidence and demolishing their self-esteem.

Forgive us for finding fault,
magnifying weaknesses and dwelling on mistakes,
and instead of putting people down,
help us to build them up –
constructive in all we do, think and say.
Amen.

Our need of others

341

Living God,
we need the company of others to remove rough edges,
the experience of rubbing shoulders with people of different backgrounds,
ideas
and experiences
if we're to become fully rounded.
Open our hearts to others
and, through our bouncing off them,
shape our lives, and theirs, for good.
Amen.

342

Lord of all,
teach us that we need others –
that you created us not to exist in isolation
but to enjoy company,
interacting with those around us.
Cement, then, the ties of friendship,
and build up the relationships we share,
reminding us that, so often,
it is through these that you give shape and purpose to life.
Amen.

Sensitivity towards others

343

Father God,
forgive us,
for all too often we live carelessly,
having little thought for you or for others.
As we would be done by,
so may we do, in turn.

We speak without thinking,
act with little thought of the consequences,
and then wonder why our mistakes return to haunt us.
As we would be done by,
so may we do, in turn.

Instead of joy we bring sorrow;
instead of harmony, discord;
instead of help, hindrance;
instead of encouragement, dismay.
As we would be done by,
so may we do, in turn.

Teach us that we reap what we sow,
for good or ill,
and so, in everything we do,
help us to be more caring,
more considerate,
more supportive,
more wise,
so that the harvest of our lives may be pleasing to you.
As we would be done by,
so may we do, in turn.
Amen.

344

Father God,
if you were to deal with us as we deserve we'd be in a sorry state,
for we fail you time and again,
ignoring your guidance,
wandering from your way,
failing to love you and others as we should.
Teach us your way,
and help us to follow.

Yet, instead, you deal with us graciously,
constantly reaching out in love to heal the broken relationship between us.
Teach us your way,
and help us to follow.

Help us to show a similar generosity of spirit in our dealings with others,
to act kindly towards them irrespective of their actions towards us.
Teach us your way,
and help us to follow.

Teach us to love though we are not loved in return,
to give though we do not receive,
to forgive though we are not forgiven,
to care though we are not cared for.
Teach us your way,
and help us to follow.

Help us truly to do to others as we'd have them do to us.
Amen.

345

Father God,
too often we're clumsy in our dealings with others,
coming down forcefully on little things when a quiet word would suffice,
hopelessly heavy-handed when a light touch is all that's needed.
Teach us, if we would foster rather than shatter the spirit,
to think fairly,
love deeply
and deal gently in all we do.
Amen.

346

Almighty God,
so much in this world can be used for good or evil,
to bring blessing or harm,
joy or sorrow.
Give us wisdom and sensitivity,
so that we might use rather than misuse the blessings you have given,
enjoying them in healthy moderation rather than indulging to excess.
Remind us that some things must be treated with caution
and enjoyed responsibly
if *we* are to consume them rather than them *us*.
Help us, above all, to consider the effect our actions may have upon those around us,
and to do everything possible to avoid leading them astray.
Give us love and courage to put the good of others before our own.
Amen.

347

Give us sensitivity, Lord, in our dealings with others,
and wisdom to look beyond appearances to what lies deeper.
Remind us that what people allow us to see is rarely the whole story;
that beneath the surface they wrestle with their own secret fears,
problems,
hurts
and uncertainties –
tossed about,
just as we are,
in the maelstrom of life.
Teach us that behind the public face each of us wears for the world
lies a private person,
and help us in all our dealings to allow for both.
Amen.

348

Gracious God,
in many things,
more than we realise,
our pleasure comes at the expense of others,
what brings us joy causing them pain.
Teach us, in all we do,
however innocent it may seem,
to consider its impact on those around us,
and, where necessary, to put their wishes before our own.
Amen.

349

Teach us, Lord, to be as gentle and considerate towards others
as you are towards all.
Amen.

350

Whatever our troubles, Lord,
whatever our problems or worries,
may we never be so wrapped up in ourselves
that we've no time to comfort another.
Amen.

Wedding anniversary

351

We thank you, Lord, for the gift of marriage,
and especially for those celebrating another year together.
For their mutual commitment,
working, sharing and building together through good times and bad,
hopes and fears,
joys and sorrows,
we give glad and heartfelt thanks.
May their love,
their bond,
their closeness
bless and enrich them as surely in the days to come
as it has done in years gone by,
and may your own great love continue to watch over them,
now and always.
Amen.

Retirement

352

Living God,
hear our prayer for those who are retired.
Grant that what is in one sense a time of endings
may also be one of new beginnings,
of exploring new horizons and discovering fresh joys.
May it bring opportunities for well-earned rest and relaxation,
but equally for using gifts and skills in different ways –
the chance to do things long dreamt of, which,
up to now,
time or circumstances have made impossible.
May memories of the past bring pleasure
and hopes for the future bring anticipation,
years of experience being complemented by a youthful spirit,
a mind that is ever young at heart.
In all that is yet to come,
bring happiness, peace, love and fulfilment,
through Jesus Christ our Lord.
Amen.

Scientists and researchers

353

Almighty God,
thank you for human intelligence,
for the ability to explore and unravel the mysteries of life.
Grant wisdom.
Grant understanding.

Thank you for those who,
in a host of disciplines,
conduct ground-breaking studies
and open up horizons that past generations could only have dreamt of.
Grant wisdom.
Grant understanding.

Thank you for medical breakthroughs,
labour-saving devices,
technological gadgets,
mind-boggling discoveries –
so much that broadens our minds and enhances our lives.
Grant wisdom.
Grant understanding.

Give wisdom to all at the forefront of research,
and help them to recognise the dangers as well as the possibilities inherent within it,
the abuse as well as the use that it may involve.
Grant wisdom.
Grant understanding.

Guide them and those who debate,
fund,
legislate
or profit from their efforts,
so that the intellect and abilities you have given may be used for the good of all,
for the enhancement and enrichment of life.
Grant wisdom.
Grant understanding.
Amen.

354

Creator God,
the powers of modern science scare but excite us,
for they have potential for both good and evil,
being able to enrich life or undermine it,
to transform yet destroy.
Give wisdom to all scientists and researchers,
and to those who set laws regulating their activities,
so that the skills you have given may be used responsibly and for the good of all.
Amen.

Serving others

see also Themed prayers: Social justice

355

Lord Jesus Christ,
we pray, week in, week out, that your kingdom will come
and your will be done.
It's easy to say the words,
far harder to mean them,
for they are concerned finally not just with you but with us.
Help us to understand that your kingdom is not just in the future,
but something that begins within us, here and now,
and so help us to recognise our role in bringing it nearer,
through the love we show,
the care we display
and the service we offer.
Your kingdom come, your will be done,
on earth as it is in heaven.

So now we pray for our world
and for an end to all that frustrates your purpose.
We think of those in countries racked by conflict,
famine, disease and poverty;
of those who face repression and discrimination,
persecuted for what they believe or for who they are;
and of those who are victims of crime, violence and war.
Your kingdom come, your will be done,
on earth as it is in heaven.

We pray for the unemployed and homeless,
the sick and suffering,
the lonely and unloved,
the disabled and disadvantaged.
Your kingdom come, your will be done,
on earth as it is in heaven.

We pray for those who work to build a more just and loving world,
all who strive to bring help and healing to those in need –
pastors, preachers, missionaries and evangelists,
doctors, nurses, psychiatrists, counsellors.
Your kingdom come, your will be done,
on earth as it is in heaven.

We think, too, of aid agencies,
pressure groups,
charities,
churches,
politicians,
police
and members of the armed forces –
these and so many others who, in different ways,
contribute to the fulfilment of your purpose.
Your kingdom come, your will be done,
on earth as it is in heaven.

Lord Jesus Christ,
we look forward to that day when you will rule in splendour,
when you will establish justice between the nations
and there will be an end to sorrow,
suffering,
darkness
and death.
Until then,
help us to commit ourselves to your service
and to work for your glory,
so that we may honestly say and truly mean:
Your kingdom come, your will be done,
on earth as it is in heaven.
Amen.

356

God of love,
we pray for all those in our society who minister to the needs of others.
We think of those in our hospitals,
the caring professions,
and the emergency services –
doctors, surgeons, nurses and ancillary staff,
paramedics, firemen, police,
psychiatrists, therapists, counsellors,
hospice, nursing-home and special-needs workers –
these, and so many others,
upon whose skill, compassion and dedication we depend in time of need.
Support them in their work,
and show your love through their ministry.

We think of caring organisations –
those like Oxfam, Christian Aid and UNICEF that work overseas,
like Shelter, Barnardo's and Sue Ryder homes that work in our own country –
a host of aid and relief agencies that bring hope to the poor,
support to the sick,
help to the homeless,
and comfort to the dying,
working in different ways to support those facing times of crisis.
Support them in their work,
and show your love through their ministry.

We think of individual carers –
those who offer their time and energy as volunteers,
who look after elderly parents, disabled children or terminally ill loved ones at home,
who each day perform small but vital acts of kindness for friends and family,
neighbour and stranger –
their acts unnoticed except by a few
yet so valuable to those they care for.
Support them in their work,
and show your love through their ministry.

We think finally of the family of the Church –
of those entrusted with full-time pastoral responsibility;
of chaplains in hospitals and hospices,
industry and commerce,
prisons and the armed forces,
sport and education;
of missionaries offering their skills abroad;
and of individual believers seeking to express their faith through caring words and deeds.
Support them in their work,
and show your love through their ministry.

God of love,
we thank you for all who minister to the needs of others.
Inspire us through their example,
equip them in their continuing efforts,
and enrich the lives of many through the service they offer.
Amen.

357

Lord of all,
we pray for those who in different ways spend much of their lives in the service of others,
those whose work offers us the care, security and support we take for granted in society.
In all their work,
Lord, uphold them.

We think of those in hospitals or hospices,
in the police, the armed forces or the emergency services,
in voluntary services and charities,
in social and community work,
in schools, colleges and universities,
in the Church or mission field,
in local, national and international government.
In all their work,
Lord, uphold them.

Strengthen and encourage them in their efforts,
give them the support, inspiration and resources they need,
and work through them to express your love for the world.
In all their work,
Lord, uphold them.
Amen.

358

Gracious God,
thank you for those who offer service to others,
especially those who do it without any thought of reward.
Lord of love,
hear us.

Thank you for those in the caring professions,
ministering to body, mind and soul;
for unsung carers who devote themselves to looking after partners,
children,
parents
or other loved ones,
sacrificing so much of their time and energy for their well-being;
for volunteers working for charities and good causes,
without whose efforts so much important work could not continue.
Lord of love,
hear us.

Teach us to appreciate what such people contribute,
and to be ready to make our own contribution in turn.
Remind us that though we need to focus on spiritual things,
it is possible to be too heavenly minded to be of any earthly use;
that though daily devotion is important
so also is rolling our sleeves up and practising what we preach.
Lord of love,
hear us.

Help us, then, to get the balance right
and to be ready to serve whenever you call.
Amen.

359

Gracious God,
thank you that you didn't just talk about love
but showed it in action,
entering our world in Christ
and enduring suffering and death to bring us life.
Through our service and witness, Lord,
reach out to others in turn.

Thank you that, through him,
you strengthened the weak,
healed the sick,
comforted the sorrowful
and redeemed the lost,
bringing good news to the poor,
hope to the oppressed
and acceptance to the outcast.
Through our service and witness, Lord,
reach out to others in turn.

Help us, in turn, to live in such a way that our deeds and words are one –
that what we profess with our lips we express in our lives.
Teach us your way,
and help us to follow.
Through our service and witness, Lord,
reach out to others in turn.
Amen.

360

Gracious God,
we know that a problem shared is a problem halved,
and we know also, from personal experience,
just how much it means when someone offers help in times of need,
yet we can be slow sometimes to respond in our turn.
If we would serve you, Lord.
teach us to serve others.

Alert us to opportunities to help bear the burdens of others;
to any way,
no matter how small,
that we might help to lighten their load.
If we would serve you, Lord.
teach us to serve others.

Give us truly caring hearts,
an ability to put ourselves in the shoes of others
and to look to their interests and needs rather than our own.
If we would serve you, Lord.
teach us to serve others.

Though we may only be able to do a little,
help us to do what we can,
lovingly and faithfully.
Amen.

361

Gracious God,
we pray for all who have offered their service to you:
those who have taken on new positions of responsibility –
equip them to fulfil their duties wisely and faithfully;
those undertaking long-term projects –
give them renewed inspiration and vigour in their work;
those who have stood down from positions of office –
may they know their labours have been appreciated
and find new ways to be of service;
and finally those who have not yet found an avenue for their labour –
may they not feel undervalued or rejected
but find opportunities to use their gifts.
Lord, hear us,
graciously hear us.

Loving God,
help us, in turn, to respond to the needs of others,
remembering that your love is not just for the Church
but for the world.
Show us where you would have us serve you,
and give us the vision to hear and respond –
to put our words into action,
to show our faith through our deeds,
to proclaim the gospel through demonstrating your care for all.
You have called us together:
send us out to work for your kingdom.
Lord, hear us,
graciously hear us.
Amen.

362

Father God,
forgive us,
for too often we say no to others
and no to you.
We see situations of need around us,
but we hold back,
whether through apathy, selfishness or fear of getting involved.
Remind us of what you endured,
what you sacrificed,
to transform our broken world,
and help us to give just a little of ourselves in turn.
Amen.

363

Give us, Lord, a vision not just of your kingdom in heaven,
but of your kingdom on earth,
a sense of what you want to do and are able to do,
here and now among us,
and may that inspire us each day to greater service
and more faithful discipleship.
Give us love for you and for others;
deeper faith in you
and in what you can achieve in the hearts and lives of all.
Send us out to live and work for you,
for your kingdom's sake.
Amen.

364

Gracious God,
give us genuine compassion for others:
not merely a passing concern,
an occasional nod in the direction of the needy,
but a real desire,
as best we can,
to make a difference.
Help us in our caring, helping, loving and giving
to put our faith into action,
expressing in some small way your love for all.
Inspire and enable us to minister in your name.
Amen.

365

Help us, Lord, not only to call for change,
but to work for it,
playing our part before we ask others to play theirs.
Amen.

366

Living God,
we can lose sight sometimes of the unsung work so many do behind the scenes,
of the invaluable contribution made to society by those in untrumpeted walks of life.
Too easily, we can overlook faithful service offered in our own fellowship,
what's out of sight also being out of mind.
Save us from ever assuming that a job is less necessary than others
simply because it fails to win plaudits or catch the eye.
Remind us that Jesus came to serve rather than be served,
and grant us similar humility to do the same.
Amen.

367

Lord Jesus Christ,
as you served,
so may we serve in turn;
as you loved,
so may we love in turn;
as you cared,
so may we care in turn;
as you lived,
so may we live in turn;
until that day when we are one with you and your people everywhere,
and you are all in all.
Amen.

368

Lord Jesus Christ,
thank you for not simply speaking of love but showing what it means;
for not merely talking of forgiveness but offering it freely.
Thank you that, in all things,
you practised what you preached,
your words and deeds being as one.
Help us to walk your way in turn,
to demonstrate our commitment to you by putting it into practice,
so that everything we say and do will likewise be consistent with the faith we profess.
We know that our words and deeds will never fully be one,
for we are weak, foolish and faithless,
but by your grace work within us
so that they may at least approximate more closely.
Grant that people may see in our lives a little less of us
and a little more of you.
Amen.

369

Lord Jesus Christ,
too easily we forget one of the truths at the heart of the gospel:
that you came to serve rather than be served.
Inadvertently, we turn faith into triumphalist dogma,
proclaiming you as the King of kings and Lord of lords
before whom all must bow the knee
yet overlooking the fact that, while you are indeed enthroned on high,
your glory was won through a cross and a crown of thorns,

through enduring suffering and humiliation,
and surrendering your life.
Remind us that you came not to lord it over us but to meet our needs,
not to claim your rights but to grant your blessing,
your way being one of gentleness,
love
and humility.
Help us to celebrate that awesome truth
and, in a world where the rich prosper and the poor are crushed,
where the strong thrive and the weak go to the wall,
teach us your way of putting the interests of others before our own.
Amen.

370

Lord Jesus Christ,
we are good at talking about service
but not very good at showing it.
We speak of your love for the helpless and hopeless,
but all too rarely translate concern into action.
Forgive us the way we have neglected opportunities to help others,
through deeds large or small.
Forgive the selfishness that has obscured love,
the greed that has denied compassion
and the laziness of body, mind and spirit that has so often prevented any meaningful response.
Show us where and how we can serve in your name,
and inspire us to reach out in love,
offering something of ourselves to others,
even as you offered your all for us.
By your grace we ask it.
Amen.

371

Lord Jesus Christ,
we claim to be your followers working for your kingdom,
yet all too often we are hesitant about getting involved in the needs of our world.
We talk of service but are reluctant to roll our sleeves up.
We speak of compassion but keep the needy at arm's length.
Teach us not merely to talk of faith or speak of love,
but to show it.
Amen.

372

Lord Jesus Christ,
we want to serve you,
and we like to believe we do,
but unwittingly we can turn even our faith into a way of serving ourselves.
We gain strength through fellowship and worship,
but neglect your call to mission.
We focus on our own concerns in prayer
and forget about the world beyond.
Even our deeds of kindness
can finally be more about our own sense of righteousness
than the needs of those we think we are serving.
Lord Jesus,
help us to overcome the stranglehold of self
and to understand that true discipleship brings its own reward,
for the more we give the more we shall receive.
In your mercy,
hear our prayer.
Amen.

373

Loving God,
instead of leaving it to you to carry other people's burdens,
help us to do whatever we can to share the load.
Amen.

374

Loving God,
thank you for the part so many play in our lives,
frequently passing unrecognised but integral to much that we take for granted.
Thank you for the teamwork that helps to put money in our pockets,
food on our tables,
products in shops and supermarkets,
crops in our fields,
energy in our homes,
treatment in our hospitals,
vehicles to drive and roads to drive them on –
all this and so much more.

Remind us that we need others just as they need us;
that life is not lived in a vacuum but in networks and relationships;
that we are all interconnected and interdependent.
Help us better to appreciate all that we owe to others,
and to play our part in contributing to their well-being in turn.
Amen.

375

As well as opening our mouths, Lord,
may we learn to open our hearts –
to you and to others.
Amen.

376

Loving Lord,
teach us to give generously,
to others and to you;
to use the resources you put our disposal in your service,
striving in some small way to build a better world,
bringing your kingdom closer here on earth.
Help us to love you more truly
and to show that love in both our worship and service,
reaching out where we can to those in need.
Through responding to them
may we respond also to you.
Amen.

377

Teach us, Lord, that though we can never lift every burden
we can help to carry a few.
Help us to do that,
lovingly and faithfully.
Amen.

378

Teach us, Lord, that when we turn our back on those in need,
we turn it on you,
and that when we respond to even the least of one of these
we are responding to you in turn.
Amen.

379

Teach us, Lord, to think not just of ourselves
but of others,
and to seek their welfare and happiness
as well as our own.
Amen.

Social justice

see also Themed prayers: Serving others

A fairer world

380

Almighty and all-powerful God,
we pray to you for the weak and powerless of the world,
those who yearn for change,
but who can find no opportunity to help themselves.
Lord of all,
reach out in love.

We pray for those in our own society –
the homeless and unemployed,
the disabled, sick and mentally ill,
those caught up in circumstances beyond their control
and who feel unable to cope with the problems of life.
Lord of all,
reach out in love.

We pray for those in other countries and continents –
the poor, under-privileged, hungry and dispossessed;
those who are persecuted for their beliefs
or who have been driven from their homelands as refugees;
those whose labour is exploited
or whose livelihoods have been destroyed by famine, disaster or war.
Lord of all,
reach out in love.

Almighty and all-powerful God,
give strength to everyone who is powerless –
strength to survive,
to hope,
and to work for a better future.
Give help to those who campaign for freedom,
for peace,
and for a more just world.

Grant that those who are strong may help those who are weak,
so that the voice of all may be heard,
and the rights of every individual be respected.
Lord of all,
reach out in love.
Amen.

381

Loving God,
we thank you for the many blessings that we have –
homes,
food,
clothing,
modern appliances,
public amenities,
opportunities for education,
access to healthcare,
and so much more.
Loving God,
hear our prayer for the 'have-nots' of this world.

We pray for those who have no homes,
living as refugees,
or living rough on our streets.
Loving God,
hear our prayer for the 'have-nots' of this world.

We pray for those who live in inadequate housing,
the shacks and huts of shanty towns,
or in bed-and-breakfast accommodation
because there is nowhere else for them to go.
Loving God,
hear our prayer for the 'have-nots' of this world.

We pray for those who have no food,
their crops having failed,
their economies burdened by debt,
or their labours not fairly rewarded.
Loving God,
hear our prayer for the 'have-nots' of this world.

We pray for those who have no fresh water,
daily facing the threat of disease and the nightmare of drought,
and for those who have no resources,
condemned to a life of poverty with no prospect of respite,
no opportunity to help themselves.
Loving God,
hear our prayer for the 'have-nots' of this world.

We pray for those who have no access to education,
to a health service or a welfare system;
no one to turn to for help or support.
Loving God,
hear our prayer for the 'have-nots' of this world.

Loving God,
in the context of this world of ours we are the 'haves',
those who have been fortunate,
who enjoy plenty.
Stir our hearts to respond to the 'have-nots'.
Help us to be ready to say no to ourselves
so that we may say yes to them;
to sacrifice a little so that they may receive much.
Loving God,
hear our prayer for the 'have-nots' of this world.
Amen.

382

Righteous God,
we pray for those who work to promote justice in our world –
those who campaign for fair trade
and an easing of international debts,
for a just sharing of the earth's resources,
for freedom of conscience and basic human rights,
for deliverance from dictatorship and the establishing of democracy.
Grant them encouragement and support in their struggle for change.
Lord of all,
hear our prayer.

We pray for those who work to promote justice in our country –
those who pass laws in our Parliament,
who administer them in our courts,
who deal with offenders in prisons,
remand centres

or the local community,
and who strive to uphold law and order in our society.
Grant them wisdom in all they do.
Lord of all,
hear our prayer.

We pray for those who work for justice in our society –
who petition for the poor and disadvantaged,
who fight abuse and exploitation in all its many forms,
who support the cause of the wronged and the falsely accused,
who stand up against crime and corruption.
Grant them courage and integrity.
Lord of all,
hear our prayer.

Righteous God,
we know that you want us to deal justly with one another,
to work for the good of all rather than a few,
and we thank you for those with sufficient passion to devote their lives to such ends.
Support them in all they do,
and inspire us to pursue the same goals in turn.
Lord of all,
hear our prayer.
Amen.

383

Living God,
we praise you for all that is good and precious in human life;
the value,
potential,
and uniqueness of every individual.
For our family of humankind,
hear our prayer.

We pray for all whose humanity is abused and exploited –
victims of violence, torture and rape,
children drawn into the world of prostitution,
people addicted to drugs,
those living under corrupt and oppressive regimes.
For our family of humankind,
hear our prayer.

We pray for those whose humanity is diminished by prejudice and discrimination,
subjected to insults, intimidation, hatred and suspicion,
day after day denied justice,
time and again deprived of the opportunity to prove themselves.
For our family of humankind,
hear our prayer.

We pray for those denied the chance to fulfil their potential,
whether through lack of education,
insufficient resources,
limited opportunities,
or a denial of their human rights.
For our family of humankind,
hear our prayer.

We pray for those whose lives are blighted by need,
burdened by debt or unemployment,
oppressed by poverty, hunger and homelessness,
crushed by natural catastrophe or personal disaster.
For our family of humankind,
hear our prayer.

We pray for those who have lost belief in their own worth,
overwhelmed by self-doubt,
beset by inner fears,
their confidence broken,
their faith in the future destroyed.
For our family of humankind,
hear our prayer.

We pray for those who mourn loved ones,
life suddenly seeming empty of meaning and stripped of joy,
and we pray for those who battle against sickness and disease,
unable to live life to the full,
and fearful as to what the future may hold.
For our family of humankind,
hear our prayer.

Living God,
grant that the day will come
when the worth of all will be recognised,
the rights of all respected,

the good of all pursued,
and harmony among all be enjoyed.
Reach out in love,
and show us how we can respond to the needs around us.
For our family of humankind,
hear our prayer.
Amen.

384

Loving God,
we pray for those who are denied access to what we take for granted –
food and clothing,
work,
a basic education,
proper housing,
mobility,
health,
companionship,
love,
human rights,
liberty,
freedom of speech,
justice,
peace.
Lord, in your mercy,
hear our prayer.

Prosper the efforts of all who fight for their rights,
all who labour to give them help and hope.
Lord, in your mercy,
hear our prayer.

We pray for those who feel themselves denied access to you,
separated by guilt,
doubts,
past mistakes,
or lack of faith.
Lord, in your mercy,
hear our prayer.

May all who seek your presence,
all who ask for your forgiveness,
and all who long for your love,
find in Jesus Christ the way, the truth and the life.
Lord, in your mercy,
hear our prayer.
Amen.

385

Loving God,
we bring to you our world of so much pain,
so much need and sorrow;
a world you care for so deeply that you willingly gave your all for it,
living and dying among us through your Son, Jesus Christ.
Reach out again in mercy,
and heal our wounds.

We bring to you the causes of so much suffering –
the sin of greed,
denying the many their share of this earth's riches
to the benefit of the few;
the sin of waste,
wantonly squandering the resources you have given
with no thought of future generations;
the sin of intolerance,
dividing families, communities and nations
through a refusal to engage in dialogue;
the sin of pride,
thinking too highly of ourselves and too poorly of others;
the sin of indifference,
caring too little about you,
too little about anything.
Reach out again in mercy,
and heal our wounds.

We pray for those who pay the price of human folly –
the poor and the hungry,
the homeless and dispossessed,
victims of war and violence, crime and cruelty;
the distressed, isolated, crushed and forgotten,
all who are deprived of love and denied hope.
Reach out again in mercy
and heal our wounds.

Loving God,
come again to our world
through your Son, our Saviour.
Mend our divisions,
forgive our folly,
and guide all our affairs.
Reach out again in mercy,
and heal our wounds.
Amen.

386

Almighty God,
too easily we blame you for the evils of this world,
shaking our fist at heaven and asking why you let them be.
Yet we know in our hearts that so many of the wrongs that have blighted history
and that continue to destroy lives today
are down to us rather than you;
to man's inhumanity to man:
to our greed,
pride,
envy,
prejudice
and intolerance.
Forgive, Lord,
and in your love bring new beginnings.

Forgive our share of responsibility:
our turning a blind eye to injustice,
our neglect of the need of others,
our failure to work for good.
Forgive, Lord,
and in your love bring new beginnings.

Forgive the selfishness that refuses to make sacrifices for the greater good.
Reach out into our broken world
and put an end to its madness,
so that whatever divides and destroys may be overcome.
Forgive, Lord,
and in your love bring new beginnings.

Give us, and all, not merely the vision of a better, fairer world,
but the resolve to work for it.
Amen.

387

Forgive us, Lord,
for we are part of an unjust and unequal world
in which *we* have plenty at the cost of others.
Your kingdom come,
on earth as it is in heaven.

Help us to do what we can to redress the balance,
not just through giving to charity and so forth,
but through truly working for change.
Your kingdom come,
on earth as it is in heaven.

Though economic issues are complex,
save us from hiding behind them,
exonerating ourselves from all responsibility.
Your kingdom come,
on earth as it is in heaven.

And save us also from serving self rather than you,
as though life to come can be separated from life now,
our relationship with you from our interaction with others.
Your kingdom come,
on earth as it is in heaven.

Give us a love of justice,
a hunger for a fairer world,
and help us in some way to bring them closer.
Your kingdom come,
on earth as it is in heaven.
Amen.

388

Gracious God,
we bring to you our broken world,
racked by injustice and exploitation,
suffering and sorrow,
hatred and division –
so few signs of hope in our world,
so much that invites despair.
Loving Lord,
bring hope and new beginnings.

We pray for those who work for change;
all who strive to bring help and healing,
hope and wholeness.
Loving Lord,
bring hope and new beginnings.

We pray for those who have stopped believing things can change:
all who have lost faith in themselves,
in others,
in life
or in you.
Loving Lord,
bring hope and new beginnings.

Gracious God,
bring healing and renewal;
finish your new creation among us.
May your will be done and your kingdom come,
through Jesus Christ our Lord.
Amen.

389

Living God,
thank you for the place we have in your heart;
for the way you value us as individuals,
each of us being precious in your sight.
Your kingdom come,
your will be done.

Thank you for the place we have in society:
the right to be ourselves,
respected for who we are,
each entitled to freedom of speech and opinion.
Your kingdom come,
your will be done.

Help us to recognise what all that means,
and to rejoice in it,
understanding what we owe to generations before us
who have secured a voice and rights that we too easily take for granted.
Your kingdom come,
your will be done.

Speak to us today through the example of those who have stood up for the voiceless,
and who have campaigned for the dignity and freedom of the oppressed.
Raise up more people like them to challenge the evils and injustices of today,
and give us the courage and vision we need to speak out as your people
and to offer support for their cause,
working as best we can for the dawn of your kingdom
on earth as it is in heaven.
Your kingdom come,
your will be done.
Amen.

390

Living God,
in a world of hunger and need,
give us hearts full of compassion.
Lord, hear us,
graciously hear us.

In a world of evil and injustice,
give us a determination to make a difference.
Lord, hear us,
graciously hear us.

In a world of greed and selfishness,
give us an open and generous spirit.
Lord, hear us,
graciously hear us.

In a world of putting self first,
give us a genuine concern for others.
Lord, hear us,
graciously hear us.

In a world of oppression and exploitation,
give us a yearning for justice.
Lord, hear us,
graciously hear us.

Send us out to live and work for you.
Amen.

391

Living God,
we have met you here –
help us to see you everywhere.
Lord,
hear us.

Where lives are broken,
truth is crushed
or justice is denied,
bring new beginnings.
Lord,
hear us.

Where hopes are thwarted,
faith is destroyed
or life is ended,
bring resurrection.
Lord,
hear us.

Where suffering scars,
sorrow weighs heavy
or hurts are hard to bear,
bring life in all its fullness.
Lord,
hear us.

Go with us now into our world of need,
and help us to walk there,
through your Spirit,
with the risen Christ.
Lord,
hear us.
Amen.

392

Living God,
thank you for those who have had the courage, across the years,
to stand up for their convictions,
even when doing so has proved costly.
Thank you for all who have stood up against evil, injustice and exploitation,
determined to help build a better world.
Help them, and us, to put you and others before ourselves,
and to do everything possible to conquer evil with good,
falsehood with truth
and hatred with love,
even when it proves costly to do so.
Amen.

393

Loving God,
you call us to seek justice,
not just for ourselves but for all.
Move in us,
work through us.

You urge us to be compassionate in our dealings with others,
to put their interests before our own,
to care for the poor, the weak and the needy,
and to do what we can in making this world a fairer place for all.
Move in us,
work through us.

Speak today through the example of those who have done just that,
and inspire us, in turn, to respond to you and to others more faithfully,
reaching out in the name of Christ, through word and deed,
to minister something of your love.
Move in us,
work through us.

Help us to build on what has been good in the history of your people,
and to move away from what has been bad,
so that we may contribute towards a more fitting and lasting legacy,
that truly redounds to your glory.
Move in us,
work through us.
Amen.

394

Loving God,
you came in Christ to proclaim good news to the poor
and hope to the oppressed,
and you call us in turn to show love and compassion to others,
in some small way continuing his ministry here on earth.
Open our hearts to you
and to all.

You came in Christ to confront injustice,
to challenge selfishness and complacency that turns its back on others,
and you call us in turn to confront self-interest and exploitation.
Open our hearts to you
and to all.

You came in Christ to change lives
and you call us in turn to change,
to look outwards rather than inwards,
to see beyond our own narrow concerns to the wider world.
Open our hearts to you
and to all.
Amen.

395

Lord Jesus Christ,
friend of the friendless,
hope of the hopeless
and joy of the joyless,
reach out into the hurt and pain of our world,
the injustice, hunger and hatred,
and may the seeds of your kingdom take root and grow.
In all this world's sorrow and suffering,
bring a harvest of justice and peace,
love and celebration,
for your name's sake.
Amen.

396

Help us, Lord, not simply to look forward to a day when justice is done,
when poverty is ended
and when none go needy,
but to attempt in whatever way we can to help bring that day closer.
Amen.

397

Father God,
so many people endure hardships we can scarcely imagine.
May that matter as much to us as it does to you.
Amen.

398

Father God,
speak through the example of those who,
though they barely have enough to survive,
somehow still get by.
Challenge us through their courage and resourcefulness,
and help us to live simply
so that they may simply live.
Amen.

399

Give us a faith, Lord,
that is as much about others
as it is about us.
Amen.

400

God of grace,
in the darkness of hatred, evil, sorrow and suffering
may your light shine,
this and every day.
Amen.

401

Lord Jesus,
build your kingdom here on earth.
Saviour Christ,
rescue your people.
Light of the world,
scatter our darkness.
Prince of peace,
heal our wounds.
Lamb of God,
have mercy upon us.
Word made flesh,
make us new.
Emmanuel,
God with us,
come and be with *all*.
Amen.

402

Lord of all,
it gets harder over the years to believe that this world can change for the better –
that love can overcome hate,
good conquer evil
and right triumph over wrong.
Hopes are raised for a time,
only to be dashed as new ills rear up to replace the old.
Help us, though, to remember everything that has been achieved in your name,
the lives that have been changed and situations transformed.
Break through the walls of disillusionment and despondency
and rekindle faith in all you are able to do.
Amen.

403

Lord of all,
should we ever fall victim to charity fatigue,
remind us of those who suffer from hunger and hardship,
and of how much more weary they must be of their circumstances,
and may that truth inspire us to give afresh,
however often we have given
or however futile it may seem.
Amen.

404

Lord of all,
there is so much evil in our world,
yet so much good;
so much ugliness,
yet so much beauty.
Nurture whatever enriches and builds up,
and overcome that which demeans and degrades.
Amen.

405

Work in the hearts of people everywhere, Lord,
to build a fairer and more caring society in which no one,
whatever their circumstances,
is left feeling they are an optional extra or a faceless statistic.
Bring closer a world that respects the value of all.
Amen.

406

Sovereign God,
strength of the weak,
hope of the despairing,
comfort of the sorrowful,
restorer of the broken,
send us out renewed by your grace
and help us to do all in our power
to bring your transforming touch to others,
through the healing power of Christ.
Amen.

407

Lord of the nations,
when we consider the scale of human need,
the enormous suffering, injustice and deprivation faced by so many,
we feel despondent,
overwhelmed,
for we seem powerless to change anything,
to do anything meaningful to help.

The world is so big,
and we are so small,
insignificant in terms of the forces that shape and control it.
Help us, nonetheless, in our living and loving,
our speaking and doing,
to work for change,
in partnership with you and others.
Remind us that what *we* can't do,
you can.
Amen.

408

Lord,
we look at the world sometimes,
and it seems desecrated beyond redemption,
stained by so much that destroys life and denies hope.
We see hatred,
violence,
injustice
and greed;
a world where good is crushed by evil,
where the innocent suffer
and people are divided by colour,
culture
and creed.
But we cannot judge,
still less condemn,
for much of what we see to be wrong in others
is wrong also in us.
Reach out to us in our need,
and bring the new beginnings you alone can give.
Cleanse our world of everything that demeans and diminishes,
and through your transforming touch make all things new.
Amen.

409

Loving God,
continue to work in the world,
giving strength to the weak,
hope to the oppressed,
joy to the sorrowful
and peace to the perplexed.

Reach out in your mercy,
conquering evil with good and hatred with love.
Despite everything that seems to deny your love and frustrate your purpose,
make known your renewing power and redeeming love,
and help bring your kingdom closer here on earth,
as it is in heaven.
Amen.

410

Loving God,
day after day pictures of hunger, squalor, violence and suffering
are beamed into our living rooms from across the world,
and our hearts go out to those enduring such misery.
But we are able to turn away,
dismissing such things from our minds.
Only there's no such option for them:
this is the daily reality of their lives.
Remind us that they are real people,
each one our neighbour,
and instead of pushing them aside,
as if they are part of another world,
teach us, whenever and wherever we can,
to respond in love.
Amen.

411

Loving God,
hear our prayers for all those who seek to further your will here on earth –
those who work for peace,
who campaign for justice,
who strive to relieve poverty,
who fight for the hungry –
all who struggle for the oppressed,
the exploited,
the under-privileged
and those denied their proper rights.
Prosper their efforts and grant them inspiration
so that they may challenge people everywhere to give of themselves in the service of others.
God of justice and mercy,
hear our prayer.
Amen.

412

Loving God,
save us from turning our back on issues of social justice
as though they are not our concern;
from adopting an attitude of 'never mind the rest so long as we're all right'.
Remind us that you came in Christ to bring good news to the poor
and hope to the oppressed;
that you care about people's welfare here and now
and expect us to do the same.
Teach us, then, to work in whatever ways we can towards a better and fairer world.
Amen.

413

Loving God,
we know that if evils are to be tackled
it needs the will of politicians, governments and leaders.
Help them, wisely and diligently, to do their bit.
We know it needs fairer trade and relief of debt
coupled with generous, genuine aid.
Grant that these may be achieved.
But save us from passing the buck,
as though the ills of this world are not also down to us.
As well as *calling* for change,
help us to change in turn,
ready to play our part before we ask others to play *theirs*.
Amen.

414

Loving God,
when it comes to loving and hating,
as with so much else,
we get things the wrong way round,
failing to hate what is evil as much as we should
and neglecting to love others,
let alone our enemies.
We may not *hate* anyone,
but we can dislike people more than we like to admit,
our attitude towards them being anything but loving.

Yet when it comes to the evils of this world,
the things that demean lives and debase society,
we can be strangely indifferent,
dismissing them as not our concern,
even colluding implicitly with them.
Teach us your way –
the way that overturns the values and expectations of this world.
Teach us truly to hate evil and love good,
and to live accordingly.
Amen.

415

Living God,
we don't think of ourselves as greedy,
not in the sense that people usually understand it.
Yet we are part, nonetheless, of a consumerist throwaway society,
of those who enjoy the lion's share of this world's resources
while so many suffer want.
Give us a greater passion for social and economic justice,
and help us to play our part in working towards it.
Stir the hearts of politicians, governments and world leaders everywhere
to right wrongs and seek the good of all;
to think of others as well as themselves
and of tomorrow as well as today.
Amen.

416

Holy God,
our world is stained by injustice,
intolerance,
fear
and hatred –
so much that desecrates and destroys countless lives –
and, for all our so-called advances,
we're no nearer to containing it than we've ever been.
Come to our aid,
and cleanse us of all that denies and divides –
that precludes joy and crushes hope.
Transform what we can never change ourselves,
and make all things new.
Amen.

417

Loving God,
you care for the broken-hearted,
the poor and weak,
the casualties of this world,
but we can't leave it all to you.
Remind us of our responsibilities
and help us to care too.
Amen.

418

Mighty God,
in a world where the powerful prosper
and the weak are exploited,
teach us to think generously,
deal gently
and love all.
Amen.

The homeless

see also Themed prayers: Society – Homeless shelters

419

Reach out, Lord, to those who walk the streets –
young people who've run away from home,
vagrants sleeping rough,
the destitute and dispossessed.
Grant help,
bring hope.

Remind them that though they may not have a roof over their head,
they have a place in your heart,
each of them being important to you.
Grant help,
bring hope.

Bless the work of churches, charities, hostels and agencies –
all who strive to provide food and shelter,
and who offer the prospect of new beginnings,
opportunities for the future.
Grant help,
bring hope.

Teach us where and how we can best respond to others,
and so also to you.
Amen.

420

Lord Jesus Christ,
you know what it is to have nowhere to lay your head.
Hear then our prayer for those who are homeless,
who live as refugees
or who are forced to live in makeshift and inadequate housing.
Support the work of all who campaign on their behalf
and challenge the consciences of those in authority
so that they may do all in their power
to provide somewhere for everyone to call their home.
Amen.

The poor and needy

421

Sovereign God,
we pray for the weak and vulnerable in our world –
those who feel powerless in the face of the problems that confront them.
Help of the helpless,
reach out to strengthen and support.

We pray for the poor,
the hungry,
the diseased,
the dying.
Help of the helpless,
reach out to strengthen and support.

We pray for the oppressed,
the exploited,
the abused,
the tortured.
Help of the helpless,
reach out to strengthen and support.

We pray for the frightened,
the lonely,
the hurt,
the depressed.
Help of the helpless,
reach out to strengthen and support.

We pray for those who live in lands racked by tension,
those who face famine and starvation,
those who are unemployed,
those who are homeless.
Help of the helpless,
reach out to strengthen and support.

Sovereign God,
you have expressed a special concern for the bruised,
the needy
and the weak of our world.
May that concern bring strength to all in such need,
and may it inspire people everywhere to work for a more just society,
standing up for the needy,
and working to bring an end to suffering, mourning and pain;
to establish that time when your kingdom will come
and your will be done.
Help of the helpless,
reach out to strengthen and support.
Amen.

422

Living God,
you came to our world through Christ
to help,
to heal,
and to save.
So now we pray for all those in any kind of need.
In your love,
reach out to them.

We pray for the sick and suffering,
the poor and hungry,
the oppressed and exploited,
the lonely and unloved,
the aged and infirm,
the frightened and anxious,
the sorrowful and the bereaved,
the helpless and the hopeless.
In your love,
reach out to them.

Living God,
there is so much need around us,
in our neighbourhood,
our town,
our country,
our world –
so many people crying out for help.
In your love,
reach out to them.

Show us where and how we can respond.
Give us the means, the will, the commitment and the love to reach out in the name of Christ,
offering something of ourselves to others,
even as he offered his all for us.
In your love,
reach out to them.
Amen.

423

Gracious God,
we long for the day when your world will be as you want it to be:
a world in which you will lift up the lowly
and fill the hungry with good things;
in which love and justice shall triumph,
evil be ended
and the meek inherit the earth.
Work in us, Lord.
Work through us.

Give us confidence that such a day will come,
and, more than that, give us the resolve to help make it happen.
Work in us, Lord.
Work through us.

Help us to respond as best we can
to the many millions who cry out for help,
and so to play our part in bringing the dawn of your kingdom closer
and turning vision into reality.
Work in us, Lord.
Work through us.
Amen.

424

Living God,
in terms of this world's resources,
we know that we're some of the lucky ones.
We may not be rich compared to many,
but in contrast to most we have enough and more than enough.
As we have received,
so may we give.

Whereas many barely survive,
we enjoy a standard of living they can only dream of.
Teach us to appreciate all we have
and to consider the needs of those who have so much less.
As we have received,
so may we give.

Instead of being snared by the tentacles of materialism –
of being so preoccupied with the desires of the body that we neglect the needs of the Spirit –
help us to remember that true fulfilment is a treasure to be received
rather than a commodity to be plucked off a shelf;
that we need to nourish the soul as well as the body if we are to be truly whole.
Open our hearts, then, to you and to others,
and deliver us from greed.
As we have received,
so may we give.
Amen.

425

God of all,
we're concerned about the poor,
or at least we say we are.
We watch news reports of famine, starvation and human need,
and we're truly moved,
keenly aware of how much we have to be thankful for
compared to the desperation of their plight.
Freely we have received;
freely may we give in turn.

Yet though we briefly respond,
too often we forget that their need continues;
that poverty and hunger are endemic to our world,
part of an order that we're complicit in maintaining.
Freely we have received;
freely may we give in turn.

Give us genuine compassion,
a real desire to make a difference,
and help us –
as part of our response –
to be willing to have less so that others might have more.
Freely we have received;
freely may we give in turn.
Amen.

426

Father God,
we cannot constantly carry the troubles of this world on our shoulders,
for they would overwhelm us.
We cannot respond to all those in need,
for our resources are limited
and deserving cases seemingly endless.
Yet save us from using that as an excuse to do nothing,
for allowing it to become a case of out of sight and out of mind.
Give us a truly caring heart and a compassionate spirit
so that we may be genuinely moved by the plight of others
and seek to do something about it.
As well as celebrating life ourselves,
may we help others to do the same.
Amen.

427

Forgive us, Lord,
for though we wring our hands at the suffering of the poor,
calling for justice and change,
too often we ignore their plight.
We speak of being generous
but display a meanness of spirit that denies your love.
For all our talk of love and compassion,
we're repeatedly more concerned with ourselves than others,
our fine words and good intentions being exposed as hollow.
Help us to give gladly and freely,
not waiting to be asked
but seeing the need and instinctively responding.
Amen.

428

Forgive us, Lord,
for in a world of need,
of hunger, injustice and oppression,
we turn our back on others,
concerned too often with our own welfare.
Remind us that in ignoring them,
we ignore you too.
Amen.

429

God of all,
we switch on the news or pick up a newspaper
and time after time we see pictures of appalling poverty –
scenes that bring tears to our eyes and a lump to our throat.
Yet too often we're no longer truly shocked,
for we've grown used to such images,
coming to assume that this is the way things are and have to be.
Forgive the injustices that continue to scar our world,
and give us a resolve to somehow make a difference
so that one day poverty may finally be ended,
and life be celebrated by all.
Amen.

430

God of all,
we wonder sometimes why you allow hardship to persist –
why you permit so many lives to be scarred by hunger,
disease,
poverty
and pain –
but though the question is real enough,
too often we forget that the answer lies in part with *us* –
so much misery being possible to avoid or relieve
if only we have sufficient will to work for change.
Teach us that you long to bring comfort, hope and justice to those who cry out in need,
and help us to play our part in that ministry,
refusing to leave to you what we are able to do ourselves.
Amen.

431

Gracious God,
we have enough and more than enough,
but we know there are many deprived of even the basic necessities of life:
who go hungry while we eat our fill;
who have nothing to drink or wear,
no place to call their home,
no access to medicine or hospital care
and no opportunity to improve their lot.
Teach us not only to pray for them
but to respond to their plight by giving generously from our plenty,
in Christ's name.
Amen.

432

Gracious God,
we read in Scripture of good news for the poor
and liberty for the oppressed,
yet sometimes the reality appears very different.
Day after day,
we hear stories of poverty, sickness, sorrow and suffering –
some from far afield,
some on our own doorstep.

All around us there seems to be so much injustice and oppression,
hatred and evil.
We try to trust in your purpose,
but the reality of this world seems to belie your will
and contradict the gospel.
Reach out, we pray, wherever there is need,
and grant that the light of your love may shine in our hearts
and in the hearts of all,
to the glory of your name.
Amen.

433

In a world of hunger, Lord,
teach us to appreciate our plenty
and to share it with those whose plate is empty.
Remind us of how lucky we are
and help us never to forget those less fortunate.
May our gratitude to you spill over in generosity towards all.
Amen.

434

In a world where so many go hungry, Lord,
teach us to deny ourselves:
to have a little less
so that those in need may have a little more.
Amen.

435

Living God,
respond to the cry of the poor
and the entreaties of the needy,
and grant that the time will come
when people everywhere receive a fair reward for their labours,
sufficient for all their needs;
a time when this world's resources will be distributed justly,
all having enough and none too much.
Amen.

436

Living Lord,
we don't think of ourselves as gluttonous,
but we're not far off that sometimes,
eating far more than we need while others go hungry.
Help us to recognise when enough is enough
and, instead of overfeeding ourselves,
to think of those not fed at all.
Amen.

437

Lord Jesus Christ,
you have promised that those who hunger and thirst after righteousness will be filled,
but we pray today for those who simply hunger for food
and thirst for water.
In our fractured world of rich and poor,
haves and have-nots,
create a yearning for change and a passion for justice,
and may that begin in us,
our willingness to share and identify with others marking us out as your people,
to the glory of your name.
Amen.

438

Lord of all,
hear the cry of the oppressed and exploited,
the hungry and homeless,
the sick and suffering,
and help us to hear it too
and to respond in your name.
Amen.

439

Lord of all,
we think of the millions in this world for whom water is a luxury.
We think of dehydrated children,
dying of thirst;

of communities whose supplies are polluted and diseased;
of lands parched,
pasture turned to dust.
And we're ashamed, for,
like so many,
we're swift to bemoan our lot
and slow to count our blessings.
Teach us to understand how lucky we are
and to think, for a change, of others instead of ourselves.
Amen.

440

Lord of all,
in a world where so many cannot fight their corner;
where the rich prosper and the poor are crushed,
the strong thrive and the weak go to the wall;
where naked self-interest leads to friendships being broken,
people estranged,
societies divided
and nations driven to conflict;
teach us your way of love and humility,
of putting the interests of others before our own.
If we would serve *you*,
teach us to serve *all*.
Amen.

441

When we're tempted to overindulge, Lord,
teach us to think of those who are unable to indulge themselves at all,
and help us, in some meaningful way, to respond.
Amen.

442

Lord of all,
help us to remember that so many in this world simply *survive*,
struggling each day to get by as best they can;
that far from enjoying the trappings of life we take for granted,
they are happy to find even the barest essentials,
let alone more.

Help us to remember how lucky we are,
how much we have to celebrate,
and teach us to respond,
generously and lovingly,
so that others may rejoice in turn.
Amen.

443

Lord of the nations,
we speak of making poverty history,
and we've done that,
but not in the way intended.
We've made it part of our world,
an accepted norm,
a fact of life . . .
and death . . .
for countless millions,
and though it's not all our doing,
much of it being down to forces beyond our control,
we're all still complicit in the crime,
none of us able to absolve ourselves fully of responsibility.
Forgive the evil of our world,
and our share within it,
and give us all a common resolve to tackle poverty
and *truly* consign it to history.
Amen.

444

Loving God,
we have so much to be grateful for,
a standard of living that many would understandably envy.
Help us to remember the poor and oppressed,
the hungry and homeless,
the millions across the planet who endure crushing poverty and need.
Teach us to appreciate the many blessings we have received,
and gratefully to respond to those with so much less.
Amen.

445

Loving God,
we don't consider ourselves to be mean,
hard-hearted or indifferent to the plight of the poor.
On the contrary,
we like to think that we're generous,
compassionate,
sympathetic towards others,
caring enough to offer help as best we can.
Yet in our hearts we know that's not as true as it should be;
that more often than we'd like to admit we turn our back on need,
reluctant to offer costly discipleship.
We tell ourselves that any money we give will make no difference;
that it will be wasted in administration or siphoned off by corrupt dictators;
and there's a grain of truth in such excuses.
But we know also that they are a way of washing our hands of responsibility
and avoiding doing anything meaningful.
Forgive us,
and give us genuine compassion for the poor.
Just as Jesus reached out to them in love,
help us to do the same,
offering a little more in the name of him who gave his all.
Amen.

446

Loving God,
we should pause each day to remember how lucky we are,
to give thanks for the material comforts we not only enjoy
but too often take for granted.
And we should pause also to remember those who are so much less
fortunate than us –
those who live in lands ravaged by drought, famine and war;
who have no roof over their heads,
no supply of fresh water,
no access to anything but the most basic medical care –
and our hearts should go out to them,
resolved to share something of our plenty to alleviate their suffering.
Forgive our subconscious attitude that says never mind the rest
so long as we and our loved ones are all right.
Teach us to respond to those in need,
gladly and generously.
Amen.

447

Loving God,
we're so fortunate,
for we have a roof over our head,
food in our stomach,
money in our pocket
and clothes on our back –
all this and so much more in a society that, though it is far from perfect,
seeks to ensure that none goes completely to the wall.
Yet we take all this for granted,
presuming it is ours by right
and feeling sorry for ourselves because we have less than the next person.
Teach us truly to appreciate everything we have
and to spare a thought for those who have so much less.
Grant us a generous, impulsive heart,
so that we may respond not grudgingly or counting the cost,
but gladly,
out of love for others
and for you.
Amen.

448

Loving God,
when we fill our trolley,
when we queue at the checkout,
when we unpack and restock our cupboards at home,
help us to remember those whose provisions for a day,
a week,
even a month,
would fit into one shopping bag several times over.
Remind us that what we see as a snack is a luxury for others,
that our meal for one could feed a family of many.
Help us not just to *remember* those with so much less,
but to share with them from our plenty.
Amen.

449

Merciful God,
forgive us,
for we have received so much yet give so little,
frittering away money on trivia and luxuries we do not need,
while a multitude suffer and die for want of a pittance.

Remind us of how fortunate we are
and of all we can do for others at such minimal cost,
and teach us to respond,
ready to give not just our small change,
but sacrificially,
just as you gave your all for us.
Amen.

450

Open our hearts, Lord, to our neighbours everywhere
and to our responsibilities towards them.
In the hunger of the poor,
the misery of the homeless,
and the plight of the refugee;
in the despair of the oppressed
and anger of the exploited;
in the victims of natural disaster,
terrorism,
violence
and war;
help us to recognise your call,
your need,
our summons to loving response.
Amen.

Self-denial

see also Christian Seasons: Lent

451

Loving Lord,
we mean to be generous,
but find it hard to let go;
we mean to respond to others,
but struggle to put *them* first
and *self* second.
As you have given,
so may we give too.

For all our talk of treasure in heaven
it's treasures on earth that consume us . . .
even as we consume them!
Work within us,
and overcome our greed.
As you have given,
so may we give too.

In a world where so many,
all too literally,
can barely keep body and soul together,
help us to open our hearts to you
and to all.
As you have given,
so may we give too.
Amen.

452

Have we done enough, Lord?
We've given, certainly,
but was our donation a meaningful gift or a token gesture,
a response from the heart or an attempt to salve our conscience?
We've offered a little but not much,
what we spare for others over a lifetime
barely being what we spend on ourselves in a few months.
Forgive us,
and teach us to deal generously,
as you have dealt generously with us.
Amen.

453

Inspire us, Lord, to give as generously to others as you have given to us;
to share from our plenty in the name of him who shared his all.
Amen.

454

Loving God,
forgive us,
for we spend more sometimes on one treat for ourselves
than on what we give to others combined.
We extol the virtue of a generous heart
yet display the meanest of spirits,
our talk of concern and compassion repeatedly being exposed as a sham.
Teach us, next time we're asked to give,
to respond gladly,
and to offer not the least we can get away with
but more than we can truly afford.
Amen.

Society

Firefighters

455

Sovereign God,
watch over firefighters everywhere
and help them in the difficult and often dangerous work they undertake.
Grant them skill in all they do,
courage when it means putting their safety at risk,
protection from accident and injury,
stamina in the harrowing and demanding situations they so often face.
Strengthen them in times of crisis,
guide them in moments of uncertainty,
and minister to them in experiences of trauma.
Equip them with the resources they need,
so that, confidently, safely and effectively,
they may continue the vital service they offer.
Amen.

Homeless shelters

see also Themed prayers: Social justice – The homeless

456

Lord Jesus Christ,
so often during your ministry you had nowhere to lay your head.
Reach out through the work of hostels for the homeless to all in a similar plight today –
youngsters who have run away from home,
victims of abuse,
those who abuse themselves,
the poor and destitute,
people of the street,
alcoholics and drug addicts,
those who have dropped out of society.
Lord, in your mercy,
hear our prayer.

May they find food and shelter,
warmth and compassion,
company and acceptance –
the knowledge that they are not completely on their own,
that someone, somewhere, cares.
Lord, in your mercy,
hear our prayer.

Guide,
protect
and enable all who serve in hostels,
and provide them with the resources they need to continue their work,
and bring hope to those whom society so easily forgets.
Lord, in your mercy,
hear our prayer.
Amen.

Justice and the judicial system

457

Loving God,
we pray for those who serve within the judicial system –
barristers, lawyers, judges,
magistrates, jurors and court officials –
all whose responsibility it is to see that justice is administered fairly,
and to all.
Give them wisdom, integrity, courage and dedication,
so that they may discharge their duties faithfully.
God of justice and mercy,
hear our prayer.

We pray for the police
and all those involved in the prevention or detection of crime,
and we pray too for those who work in our prisons,
whether as officers or governors.
Grant them your protection,
and help them in all they do to be firm but fair.
God of justice and mercy,
hear our prayer.

We pray for those who have strayed into a life of crime –
prisoners on remand,
those serving their sentences,
and those who have been released.
Lead them to true repentance
and give them the will and the opportunity to start afresh.
God of justice and mercy,
hear our prayer.

Finally we pray for those who have experienced a miscarriage of justice –
falsely accused,
wrongfully imprisoned,
unfairly punished.
Help them to come to terms with their experience,
and to receive proper recompense.
God of justice and mercy,
hear our prayer.
Amen.

458

Loving God,
reach out into this world of so much beauty yet so much ugliness.
Minister to those caught up in its dark side –
victims of injustice,
crime,
exploitation,
violence
and abuse –
and challenge the perpetrators of such evils,
all who knowingly and heartlessly add to the sum of human suffering.
Lord, in your mercy,
hear our prayer.

Support those who work in our police and security forces,
our prisons and legal system,
our caring professions and government,
our churches and social services –
all who play a part in seeking to build a safer and fairer society.
Lord, in your mercy,
hear our prayer.

Nurture whatever enriches and enhances life,
and help to get rid of everything that degrades,
demeans,
devalues
and destroys.
Lord, in your mercy,
hear our prayer.
Amen.

459

Loving God,
we pray for all those in our world who knowingly take the path of evil –
those who follow a life of crime,
those who cheat and deceive,
who exploit their fellow human beings,
who wound in body or mind,
who kill and destroy.
Open their eyes to the reality of your judgement,
their minds to the damage caused by their actions,
and their hearts to the transforming power of your grace.
Amen.

The police

460

Living God,
we bring to you those who serve in our police forces,
with all the demands and duties that involves.
Guide and prosper them in their work,
helping them to enforce justice
and to promote stability and security within the community they serve.
Protect them from danger,
provide them with courage,
imbue them with integrity
and endow them with strength,
so that they may discharge their responsibilities wisely and fairly,
honouring the trust shown in them,
to the good of all.
Amen.

Politicians, leaders and decision makers

461

Almighty God,
ruler of the ends of the earth,
we pray for those to whom you have entrusted power and responsibility.
We think first of our own country
and those elected to office as members of Parliament –
those who serve in government,
whether in cabinet office, junior posts or on backbench committees;
those in opposition,
with their mandate to challenge and debate government policies and decisions;
and especially we pray for our Prime Minister
and the leaders of all other parties.
Lord, in your mercy,
hear our prayer.

Grant them wisdom,
insight,
patience,
dedication,
integrity,
open-mindedness,
and humility,
that each may be equipped to honour the trust placed in them.
Lord, in your mercy,
hear our prayer.

We pray for those in local government,
entrusted with representing the interests of local people in their communities,
taking decisions that will directly influence their lives,
wrestling with limited resources and numerous demands.
Give them the qualities they need to serve faithfully,
staying true to their convictions
yet putting people before party.
Lord, in your mercy,
hear our prayer.

We pray for those in authority in other lands,
leaders of nations large and small,
super-powers and tiny states,
shaping the lives of millions or relatively few.
Grant them also the guidance and the gifts they need to govern wisely,
that they may work for the good of all their people,
and strive to promote justice,
freedom of speech and opportunity,
inner harmony and international peace.
Lord, in your mercy,
hear our prayer.

Finally we pray for those nations affected by an abuse of power,
divided by rival factions,
oppressed by military dictatorships,
exploited by corrupt regimes,
suppressed by totalitarian authorities.
Support those who suffer under such government,
and strengthen those who struggle to bring justice to those places,
so that the time may come when truth and justice prevail.
Lord, in your mercy,
hear our prayer.
Amen.

462

Living God,
you call us to pray for our leaders,
to remember those set over us,
so we pray now for all those in positions of authority.
We pray for those in our Parliament,
both government and opposition.
In all their decisions give them a proper sense
of the responsibility entrusted to them,
and grant that they may work not for themselves
but for the good of all.
Lord, in your mercy,
hear our prayer.

We pray for the Queen and the royal family.
Help them to cope with the constant glare of publicity and media interest,
and to use their position wisely,
offering inspiration and encouragement to the nation.
Lord, in your mercy,
hear our prayer.

We pray for those in the police force,
with all the dangers and difficulties their work involves.
Give them integrity, courage, patience and resolve,
and grant them your strength and protection.
Lord, in your mercy,
hear our prayer.

We pray for judges, barristers and jurors,
for magistrates and solicitors;
all those faced by complex moral and legal questions,
and having the power to irrevocably shape people's lives.
Grant them honesty and wisdom,
firmness yet sensitivity.
Lord, in your mercy,
hear our prayer.

We pray for head teachers,
lecturers
and all those involved in education,
entrusted with shaping the lives of young people.
Give them insight and understanding,
the ability to communicate their knowledge in a way that enthuses their students.
Lord, in your mercy,
hear our prayer.

We pray for managers and directors in industry and commerce –
those whose decisions will affect not just firms or businesses
but the lives of countless individuals, at home and overseas.
Give them the acumen they need to ensure financial success,
coupled with a genuine concern for the welfare of their employees
and of the wider community.
Lord, in your mercy,
hear our prayer.

We pray for leaders in the Church –
ministers, elders, bishops and deacons,
all those entrusted with positions of oversight,
and called to teach the faith through word and deed.
Grant them vision and discernment,
a living knowledge of your presence,
and a daily sense of your guidance.
Lord, in your mercy,
hear our prayer.

Living God,
we thank you for those who are willing to take on the burden of responsibility,
the onerous privilege of leadership.
Support them in their work,
and help them to fulfil their calling faithfully,
recognising that the day will come when they have to answer to a higher authority,
and when you will pronounce your verdict on all.
Lord, in your mercy,
hear our prayer.
Amen.

463

Living God,
we pray for all whose decisions influence the stability of this world:
for international leaders and rulers,
for politicians and diplomats,
for national governments and the United Nations Security Council –
those whose decisions and negotiations affect the lives of so many
and in whose hands peace ultimately lies.
Grant them wisdom in all they do,
courage to make tough decisions when necessary
but also a desire to work for justice and peace whenever possible.
Lord, hear us,
graciously hear us.

We pray for those in the armed forces,
charged with keeping the peace in countries across the world –
their work involving months away from family and friends
and often danger to themselves.
Grant them courage and sensitivity,
and protect them in all they do.
Lord, hear us,
graciously hear us.

We pray for security and intelligence services in this world of so much uncertainty –
those who work to forestall and prevent terrorism;
to track down those who aim to destroy human life randomly and indiscriminately;
to ensure the safety of all.
Grant them insight,
determination,
and skill.
Lord, hear us,
graciously hear us.

Sovereign God,
guide those entrusted with the future of this planet,
so that the causes of conflict may be overcome
and a more secure future ensured for all.
Lord, hear us,
graciously hear us.
Amen.

464

Lord of all,
too often we condemn politicians;
criticising,
castigating,
even ridiculing their efforts.
Grant them guidance, Lord,
and give them wisdom.

We find fault with their decisions and question their motives,
yet we know that their task is not only a thankless one
but almost impossible,
that they frequently have to choose the lesser of two evils,
making the best of a bad job,
or settling for the least damaging compromise.
Grant them guidance, Lord,
and give them wisdom.

Give us, then, a greater appreciation of everything they do;
and to leaders of all kinds –
locally, nationally and internationally –
give wisdom,
integrity,
courage,
strength of purpose,
compassion,
and, above all,
a determination truly to serve others for the greater good.
Grant them guidance, Lord,
and give them wisdom.
Amen.

465

Lord of all,
we pray for those whose responsibility it is to pass judgement and make decisions –
judges, magistrates and those called to jury service.
Give them guidance;
grant them wisdom.

We pray for those in the probation service
or other areas of social work.
Give them guidance;
grant them wisdom.

We pray for those interviewing candidates for jobs,
university places
or other opportunities.
Give them guidance;
grant them wisdom.

We pray for those serving on local councils
or in national and international government,
taking decisions that will affect local communities,
countries
and the world itself.
Give them guidance;
grant them wisdom.

We pray for schoolteachers and examiners assessing pupils' work,
their decisions potentially shaping the course of young lives.
Give them guidance;
grant them wisdom.

We pray for those involved in arbitration,
negotiation
or reconciliation,
seeking to bring people together
and to overcome division.
Give them guidance;
grant them wisdom.

Lord of all,
give to all entrusted with such positions an open mind,
the ability to make impartial and fair decisions,
insight to discern the right way forward,
and strength to bear their responsibility faithfully.
Give them guidance;
grant them wisdom.
Amen.

466

All-seeing God,
some say moral issues are simple,
the right course of action being written in tablets of stone,
but far from seeming black or white
they can appear to us as shades of grey,
what's right in one case appearing wrong in another.
Grant wisdom and guidance to all facing complex moral decisions,
and encircle in your everlasting arms those whose future depends upon them.
Amen.

467

Sovereign God,
hear our prayer for all entrusted with positions of leadership and responsibility.
Grant them wisdom in their decisions,
courage to hold fast to what is right,
integrity in their dealings
and a genuine commitment to the good of all those they serve.
Guide them to know and do your will,
for your kingdom's sake.
Amen.

A General Election

468

Sovereign God,
you have called us to pray for those set over us,
and to respect those in authority.
So now we think of the coming election
and of all those who will be standing in it.
Lord, in your mercy,
hear our prayer.

We pray for those standing as candidates –
may they seek the good of others
rather than be concerned with self-advancement;
for those who will cast their votes –
may they look beyond self-interest to the wider needs of our country as a whole;
for those who will be elected as MPs –
may they strive to represent all their constituency members,
irrespective of political affiliation.
Lord, in your mercy,
hear our prayer.

We pray for whichever party forms our new government –
may they see further than factional and even national interest
to the needs of the wider global community;
for those who will sit in opposition –
may they challenge complacency, injustice or abuse of power;

for those who will be appointed to the Cabinet
and other government positions –
may they honour the responsibility entrusted to them;
for the Prime Minister as *he/she* looks to lead this nation –
may *he/she* be equipped for the onerous responsibilities of office.
Lord, in your mercy,
hear our prayer.

Sovereign God,
grant to all called to serve in any position,
large or small,
the gifts they will need –
wisdom,
patience,
dedication,
integrity,
vision
and humility –
and help them to fulfil their calling faithfully,
mindful of all,
and mindful of you.
Lord, in your mercy,
hear our prayer.
Amen.

Prisons

469

Lord Jesus Christ,
hear our prayer for those in our prisons,
whether working or serving time there.
In your mercy,
hear our prayer.

Give wisdom to governors and staff –
the ability to be firm but fair,
strict but supportive,
hard when necessary but human where possible.
In your mercy,
hear our prayer.

And to the inmates give true remorse
and the desire to make amends –
a resolve to use their time there to move on from past mistakes
and begin again.
In your mercy,
hear our prayer.

In imprisonment, may those held there find true liberty,
the freedom that you alone can bring,
through your redeeming, renewing grace.
In your mercy,
hear our prayer.
Amen.

Supermarkets

470

God of all,
speak, we pray, through the bustle of supermarkets,
both of your love
but also of the needs and circumstances of others.
Lord hear us,
graciously hear us.

Through shelves piled high with food,
remind us of how fortunate we are,
how much we have to celebrate and thank you for.
Lord hear us,
graciously hear us.

Through the bewildering variety of produce,
daily replenished,
remind us of those, both near and far,
whose livelihoods are interwoven with what is sold there,
all too many being so much less fortunate than ourselves;
to them what we take for granted
seeming unimaginable luxury, an impossible dream.
Lord hear us,
graciously hear us.

Recognised or unrecognised,
speak to those who work and shop in our supermarkets of realities beyond themselves,
highlighting blessings,
quickening consciences
and inviting a response.
Lord hear us,
graciously hear us.
Amen.

Worth, of all

471

Creator God,
save us, as individuals or as a society,
from treating people as objects to be exploited,
statistics processed,
consumers targeted,
resources managed.
Remind us that in your eyes we are all unique and precious,
valued for who we are,
each seen not as an object but as a person.
Help us, then, in our dealings with others,
to see behind the labels
and to recognise the intrinsic worth of all.
Amen.

472

Father God,
in a world where so many feel left on the scrapheap,
discarded by society and of no use to anyone,
teach us to see the worth not just of objects but equally of people.
Open our eyes to look more deeply,
recognising the gifts, qualities and potential of those around us,
and, wherever we can, help us to nurture them,
so that they may bloom again.
Remind us that *you* value everyone,
and help us to do the same.
Amen.

473

God of grace,
forgive us, for we judge people by what we see,
too often failing to delve deeper,
and, in consequence, we miss hidden gems,
the pearl within the oyster.
Teach us never to dismiss anyone,
however ordinary they may seem.
Open our hearts instead to the value in all.
Amen.

474

Lord of all,
reach out to those behind the statistics:
the mother whose partner has walked out on her and the children,
the worker whose factory has closed down,
the trader whose business has folded,
the victim of the industrial accident,
the manager made redundant,
the casual labourer whose services are no longer required.
However hopeless they may feel,
however disheartened, disillusioned or despondent,
assure them of their worth as individuals,
and help us as a society to do the same.
Amen.

475

Creator God,
forgive us for overlooking the worth of others,
seeing them as part of a nameless crowd rather than as individuals,
as objects instead of people.
Forgive us for dismissing what we don't understand,
closing our eyes and ears to what is outside our experience
or challenges our preconceptions.
Open the hearts of people everywhere to the true value of all.
Amen.

Young people

476

Lord of all,
hear our prayer for the young people of our town,
our country
and our world;
young people with so much to offer,
so many gifts,
so many fresh ideas,
so much vigour and enthusiasm,
yet faced today as never before by all kinds of pressures, demands and temptations.
Lord in your mercy,
hear our prayer.

Hear our prayer for the young people of this church.
Help us to appreciate them,
to be open to their insights,
to use their gifts,
to nurture their faith,
and to care about their welfare.
Guide them in their work and studies,
protect them from all that may harm or lead them astray,
encourage them in all they are doing among us,
and show them your way for the future.
Lord in your mercy,
hear our prayer.

Hear our prayer for the young people of the wider world,
so often maligned on account of the few.
We pray for those in our schools and universities,
those from broken or needy homes,
those whose gifts lie wasted through unemployment,
those faced by the temptation of alcohol and drug abuse,
those burdened by the problem of debt,
those coming to terms with the complex world of human relationships,
those who are denied the resources they need to realise their full potential,
and those who, because of hunger and disease,
will almost certainly never reach adulthood.
Lord in your mercy,
hear our prayer.

Give guidance to all who work with young people –
those in our own church,
in youth organisations,
in schools and colleges,
in organisations dedicated to childcare.
Lord in your mercy,
hear our prayer.

Loving Lord,
we thank you for young people.
Through our giving to and receiving from them,
help us to make that gratitude real.
Lord in your mercy,
hear our prayer.
Amen.

Trouble, those facing

see also under Poetic prayers: For an awareness of God's presence where life is dark; For God's healing touch in times of trouble; *and under* Themed prayers: The anxious and fearful; The bruised and broken; Health

477

Living God,
we pray for all who feel they have lost control in their lives –
overwhelmed perhaps by tragedy,
or relationships having broken down;
battling against the rigours of old age,
or wrestling with terminal illness;
in pain of body,
or turmoil of mind.
Out of despair bring hope;
out of darkness, light.

We pray for the victims of other people's lack of control,
wounded in body or mind –
abused children,
battered wives,
broken homes,
victims of burglary, rape or assault.
Out of despair bring hope;
out of darkness, light.

We pray for those who struggle
to control aspects of their character –
lust,
temper,
greed,
impatience,
envy,
intolerance.
Out of despair bring hope;
out of darkness, light.

Living God,
give to all near the end of their tether
the assurance that you are with them;
to those who are hurt
the comfort of your healing love;
to those troubled in mind
the inner peace that you alone can give;
and to those dismayed by their repeated failings
the gift of self-control.
Out of despair bring hope;
out of darkness, light.
Amen.

478

Loving God,
there are times when we look at people's lives
and find it hard to believe things can ever change for the better.
We see them racked by illness,
weighed down by anxiety,
tormented by depression,
crippled by debt,
broken by alcohol,
destroyed by drugs,
scarred by bereavement,
shattered through unemployment,
and we wonder what their prospects really are,
what hope we can realistically offer them,
what help we can possibly give.
Transforming God,
may your light shine where there is darkness.

We pray for such people known to us now –
family,
friends,
members of our fellowship,
colleagues at work,
neighbours,
acquaintances;
as well as the countless people unknown to us,
each struggling under their own particular burdens.
Transforming God,
may your light shine where there is darkness.

We pray for our world –
for those many people who face suffering,
injustice,
hardship,
and death.
Transforming God,
may your light shine where there is darkness.

Reach out to all who are in despair,
all who long for change but see only hopelessness stretching before them.
Touch their lives,
and bring help, hope, healing and wholeness.
Transforming God,
may your light shine where there is darkness.

Reach out to countries broken by war
and to continents ravaged by famine –
to people living in fear of disease,
disaster
and death.
Transforming God,
may your light shine where there is darkness.

Help us to see beneath the surface,
recognising you are at work and that things can change.
Give to us,
and to all,
the assurance that there is no one,
and no situation,
unable to be transformed by your power.
Transforming God,
may your light shine where there is darkness.
Amen.

479

Loving God,
so often we act with little thought as to the repercussions of our words or deeds,
only to find later that decisions taken,
whether our own or others,
are hard to bear.

Hear now our prayer for all those suffering as a result of unforeseen consequences.
Take what is and has been,
and direct what shall be.

We pray for those who wish they could go back on their decisions –
those whose consciences are troubled,
who are burdened by thoughts of what might have been,
who wish they had taken another course,
or who simply find they have taken on more than they can cope with.
Take what is and has been,
and direct what shall be.

We pray for those who regret decisions they made or failed to make –
unhappy in their relationships,
their work,
their homes,
or in life itself.
Take what is and has been,
and direct what shall be.

We pray for those suffering the consequences of other people's decisions –
those whose marriages have been destroyed,
whose careers have been wrecked,
whose confidence has been undermined,
or whose feelings have been hurt.
Take what is and has been,
and direct what shall be.

We pray for those suffering the consequences of war –
their way of life overturned,
their livelihoods shattered,
their country destroyed,
their loved ones killed or injured,
Take what is and has been,
and direct what shall be.

We pray for the victims of economic systems and structures –
the poor,
the hungry,
the sick
and the exploited.
Take what is and has been,
and direct what shall be.

We pray for the casualties of thoughtless or careless actions –
victims of road or industrial accidents,
of misdiagnoses or inappropriate treatment,
of nuclear, biological and chemical testing,
of crime or miscarriages of justice.
Take what is and has been,
and direct what shall be.

Hear our prayer for all whose lives have been changed for ever
by the consequences of their own or other people's actions.
Give to each the ability to live with decisions that have been taken,
to reshape the results as best they are able,
to pick up the pieces of their lives and to begin again,
in the knowledge that you are able to make all things new.
Take what is and has been,
and direct what shall be.
Amen.

480

Hear, Lord, our prayers for those facing difficulty and trouble.

We think of those whose hopes have been dashed –
their plans laid to waste,
their dreams destroyed.
Rekindle their faith in the future.
Lord, in your mercy,
hear our prayer.

We pray for those who have been let down –
wounded by loved ones,
betrayed by those in whom they put their trust.
Save them from succumbing to bitterness or cynicism.
Lord, in your mercy,
hear our prayer.

We pray for those wrestling with depression –
those for whom life seems empty
and the future dark.
Show them a light at the end of the tunnel.
Lord, in your mercy,
hear our prayer.

We pray for those who are unwell –
afflicted by chronic disease,
suffering from terminal illness.
Support them through all that they face.
Lord, in your mercy,
hear our prayer.

Reach out to all for whom life is hard,
testing them to the limit,
and through your grace uphold them
and see them through.
Lord, in your mercy,
hear our prayer.
Amen.

481

Living God,
reach out to those overwhelmed by trials and testing:
those faced with the loss of a loved one,
the breakdown of a relationship,
financial troubles,
a threat to their job,
or the prospect of ill-health,
even death.
Reach out to hold,
reach out to help.

Give them the assurance that even there –
especially there –
you are with them,
reaching out to strengthen, support and sustain;
to hold them in your arms and set them on their feet once again.
Reach out to hold,
reach out to help.

Teach them that out of darkness you bring light;
out of tears, laughter;
out of despair, hope;
out of sorrow, joy;
and out of death, life –

that no matter what may bring us down,
you will always raise us up.
Reach out to hold,
reach out to help.
Amen.

482

Lord Jesus Christ,
still the storms in our lives –
of fear and anxiety,
of sudden crises,
of tragedy, trauma and trouble.
Lord hear us,
graciously hear us.

Still the storms in our world –
of injustice and intolerance,
of manmade and natural disaster,
or hatred, bloodshed and war.
Lord hear us,
graciously hear us.

Through your divine power,
reach out wherever life brings turmoil
and calm the waves,
bringing true and lasting peace,
rest for our souls.
Lord hear us,
graciously hear us.
Amen.

483

Loving God,
thank you for so often having been there when we've needed you most;
for the times you've picked us up when we've fallen,
tended our wounds when we've been hurting,
restored us when we've been broken.
Reach out now,
and enfold all in your love.

Thank you for the knowledge that in the darkest moments of life,
our pain is *your* pain and *our* sorrow *your* sorrow;
for the assurance that in moments of trouble
you will continue to be with us,
always looking to restore and renew.
Reach out now,
and enfold all in your love.

Minister to those for whom life is demanding,
for whom testing is hard to bear,
and grant the joy,
strength,
peace
and hope that you alone can bring,
through the healing touch of Christ.
Reach out now,
and enfold all in your love.
Amen.

484

God of all comfort,
we bring you this world of so much pain:
our own and that of those around us.
Reach out to hold.
Reach out to heal.

We bring you our hurts, troubles, anxieties and fears,
placing them into your hands,
and we pray for those countless others facing sorrow or suffering:
hopes dashed,
dreams broken,
let down by those they counted dear;
betrayed,
abused,
wrestling with depression or illness,
mourning loved ones.
Reach out to hold.
Reach out to heal.

Hold on to us and to all who walk through the valley of tears,
and grant the knowledge that you are with us, even there,
sharing our pain and moved by our sorrow.
Reach out to hold.
Reach out to heal.

Minister the consolation that you alone can offer,
and give the assurance that those who mourn will be comforted
and those who weep will laugh.
Reach out to hold.
Reach out to heal.
Amen.

485

Gracious God,
hear our prayer for those who are battered by the storms of life,
those who suddenly find themselves caught in a downpour of despair,
fear,
sorrow
or suffering.
May your grace bring hope;
your love bring help.

Reach out to all who are overwhelmed by trouble,
and assure them that, though the clouds hang heavy,
the world seems dark,
and the rain beats relentlessly upon them,
your light is still shining
and will eventually break through once more into their lives.
May your grace bring hope;
your love bring help.

In that promise may we likewise trust when,
as they surely will,
storms break also upon us.
May your grace bring hope;
your love bring help.

However distant you may sometimes seem,
however hopeless life may feel,
teach us and all to trust in you,
confident that the clouds will break
and the sun will shine once more.
May your grace bring hope;
your love bring help.
Amen.

486

Living God,
hear our prayer for those who are struggling to cope with bad news,
those who are frightened and helpless
or who have lost hope altogether.
Wherever there is sorrow,
grant your joy.

Hear our prayer for those who are troubled by the *prospect* of bad news
and fret anxiously about the future.
Wherever there is sorrow,
grant your joy.

Hear our prayer for all who have grown so accustomed to bad news
that they struggle to believe in the future,
their faith in life and in you having been shaken or broken altogether.
Wherever there is sorrow,
grant your joy.

Make known again the good news of your love in Christ,
and into our hurting world bring peace,
strength,
comfort,
delight
and trust –
glad tidings for all.
Wherever there is sorrow,
grant your joy.
Amen.

487

Lord Jesus Christ,
you spoke,
and you brought hope, comfort and renewal;
you touched,
and you brought love, peace, healing and wholeness.
Come now,
and speak again,
bringing your word of life to all who suffer or are hurting.
Shine now.
Shine always.

Reach out afresh,
bringing your touch of love to all whose hearts are aching
and who cry out for help.
Shine now.
Shine always.

Where there is despair and turmoil,
may your voice renew.
Where there is pain and sickness,
may your hand restore.
Shine now.
Shine always.

Lord Jesus Christ,
you came once,
you shall come again,
but we ask you,
come now,
and minister your grace afresh.
Shine now.
Shine always.
Amen.

488

Loving God,
we pray for those who specially need your guidance,
those facing problems unknown to us,
those for whom advancing years bring illness or infirmity,
those who have drifted away from us and from you,
those for whom life is dark and difficult.
May your grace bring hope;
your love bring healing.

May each in their different situations feel your presence,
and know your support,
May your grace bring hope;
your love bring healing.

May they know they are remembered and valued,
by us and by you,
and may that knowledge give them strength,
encouragement
and inspiration,
this and every day.
May your grace bring hope;
your love bring healing.
Amen.

489

Gracious God,
reach out to those for whom life is bleak,
and help them even in the darkest moments to glimpse a little of your light.
Though the night of sorrow, fear, pain or death closes in,
cold and forbidding,
may a glimmer of your love shine through –
a ray of sunshine sufficient to sustain faith,
nourish hope
and impart peace.
Amen.

490

In the trials and troubles of life, Lord,
minister your love.
In sorrow, bring comfort;
in sickness, bring healing;
in despair, bring hope;
in death, bring life.
Wherever lives are broken,
make them whole.
Amen.

491

Loving God,
reach out to all who feel overwhelmed by problems,
up to their necks in difficulties that threaten to sweep them away
and to which they see answer.
Teach them never to despair;
that, however daunting the obstacles,
your strength can make up for their weakness,
and your power see them through.
Amen.

492

Loving God,
to all facing the storms of life,
when the clouds hang heavy and the world seems dark,
give the assurance that your light continues to shine
though everything may seem in turmoil.
Teach them, however distant you may seem,
still to trust you,
confident that your love will break through
and its radiance enfold them once more.
Amen.

493

Loving God,
to all for whom life brings bad news,
disappointment,
trouble

or tragedy,
bring comfort,
strength,
hope
and healing –
faith that joy will come again.
Amen.

494

Loving God,
where hatred seems to have conquered love,
falsehood eclipsed truth,
darkness extinguished light,
and evil defeated good,
somehow turn the tables
and bring good out of evil,
joy out of sorrow,
life out of death.
To all wrestling with trouble and despair,
bring the knowledge that even in life's bleakest moments you are at work,
and that no situation is beyond the scope of your grace to transform.
Amen.

495

Loving Lord,
hear our prayer for those for whom life is hard at the moment.
In times of testing,
give strength.
In times of despair,
give hope.
In times of sorrow,
give comfort.
In times of hurt,
give healing.
Share their load
and help us to do the same
until such time that they feel ready to shoulder it themselves again
and step forward once more on their journey of life.
Amen.

496

Reach out, Lord, to those for whom life has got too much,
its demands and difficulties too hard to bear.
Remind them that you are there to share the load,
so that, instead of struggling on alone,
they may learn to place themselves and their problems in your hands,
assured that you are able to carry all.
Help them to focus not on their limited resources
but on your limitless power,
secure in the knowledge that you are able to offer support
as often as they need it
for as long as it takes.
Amen.

497

Reach out, Lord, to all who are troubled,
who crave peace yet cannot find it,
and answer their fears,
their hurts,
their emptiness.
Bring them true and lasting inner contentment
through the one who can meet our deepest needs,
Jesus Christ our Lord.
Amen.

The weary and disillusioned

498

Great and gracious God,
we pray for all those in life who carry heavy loads
and long for rest.
We pray for people weighed down by remorse,
carrying with them a burden of guilt –
those who have made mistakes,
who have said or done foolish things,
who have acted unthinkingly,
and who feel they can never find pardon.
Assure them of your constant forgiveness open to all.
Lord, in your mercy,
hear our prayer.

We pray for those weighed down by a sense that life has lost its meaning,
carrying with them a burden of despair –
those who drift aimlessly through each day,
who look to the future with a sense of weariness,
who feel trapped in a rut from which there is no escape.
Assure them that you have a purpose for all.
Lord, in your mercy,
hear our prayer.

We pray for those weighed down by injustice,
carrying with them a burden of helplessness –
the poor, sick and homeless,
the oppressed, persecuted and wrongfully imprisoned –
all who are deprived of their basic human rights
and who feel powerless to do anything about it.
Assure them that you are able to transform all things,
however hopeless they may seem.
Lord, in your mercy,
hear our prayer.

We pray for those weighed down by advancing years,
carrying with them the burden of age –
those who wrestle with declining health,
who are confused by the pace of change,
who feel lonely and unloved,
or who grieve for old friends who have passed away.

Assure them that your word and love endure for ever.
Lord, in your mercy,
hear our prayer.

We pray for those weighed down by the burden of doubt,
carrying with them a sense of shame at having lost their faith –
those who feel cut off from you,
troubled by all kinds of questions,
unable to believe as they once did,
alone in a cold and empty world.
Assure them of your involvement in every part of life,
even when they cannot understand it.
Lord, in your mercy,
hear our prayer.

Great and gracious God
bring hope,
bring joy,
bring peace,
bring trust –
bring renewal of life to all who struggle under heavy loads.
May they find in Christ the one whose yoke is easy
and whose burden is light,
and through him find rest for their souls.
Lord, in your mercy,
hear our prayer.
Amen.

499

Loving God,
we pray for those who are weary –
exhausted in body, mind and soul.
Lord of life,
renew their strength and refresh their spirits.

We think of those whose daily work hangs heavy upon them –
those in dull, soul-destroying employment,
in stressful and pressurised careers,
in labour that is heavy and physically exhausting,
or in jobs involving long and unsociable hours.
Lord of life,
renew their strength and refresh their spirits.

We think of those who have no job –
yearning for the opportunity to use their skills,
deprived of a sense of self-respect,
unable to provide for their loved ones as they would like to,
their life seeming empty and frustrating.
Lord of life,
renew their strength and refresh their spirits.

We think of those who are suffering –
battling against illness,
wrestling with infirmity,
crushed by physical disability,
or enduring long-term physical or emotional pain.
Lord of life,
renew their strength and refresh their spirits.

We pray for those who have lost their enthusiasm for life –
the depressed and downhearted,
the mentally disturbed,
the sad and disillusioned,
the frightened and anxious;
all those for whom just getting through another day has become an effort.
Lord of life,
renew their strength and refresh their spirits.

We think of those who have nothing to sustain their hope –
those whose dreams have been crushed by the harsh realities of life,
who struggle with doubt and uncertainty,
whose faith in you and the future has been battered beyond repair,
their ability to bounce back finally exhausted.
Lord of life,
renew their strength and refresh their spirits.

Loving God,
draw near to all through Christ.
Grant the peace of your presence,
the healing of your touch,
the blessing of your guidance,
and the assurance of your constant love,
so that all who are weary may walk in hope
and look forward in faith.
Lord of life,
renew their strength and refresh their spirits.
Amen.

The wider Church

The Bible

500

Loving God,
we thank you today for the Scriptures,
and the opportunity we have each day to read and study them for ourselves.
Hear now our prayer for all those denied that privilege.

We pray for those who have not heard the challenge of the Bible,
who do not possess a copy of it in their own language,
or who are denied the right to own a Bible or study it freely.
Lord, in your mercy,
hear our prayer.

We pray for those who have heard but closed their minds,
for those who read but do not understand,
and for those who have read the Bible so often that it fails to challenge as it used to.
Lord, in your mercy,
hear our prayer.

We pray for those who work to make the Scriptures known and available to all –
those who translate the Bible into modern language and other tongues,
who print and distribute it across the world,
who strive to open its message afresh to each and every generation;
and who preach from it, witnessing to Christ from its pages.
Lord, in your mercy,
hear our prayer.

Loving God,
may your word be made known
with clarity, wisdom, faithfulness and power,
so that many may hear its challenge
and respond in faith to your loving purpose.
Lord, in your mercy,
hear our prayer.
Amen.

Church halls and premises

501

Lord of life,
grant your blessing on church halls and other premises,
and everything they are used for.
May they be places of sharing and befriending,
of refreshment and relaxation,
and of service to others.
May they function not just as a resource for church members
but also for the wider community,
and may people meet you as much in events arranged and activities held there
as in any act of worship.
Amen.

502

Sovereign God,
we pray for the churches of our town,
our country
and our world.
Grant that they may be more than bricks and mortar,
fittings and furnishings,
offering, rather, a sacred space that speaks of you –
hallowed ground set aside for praise and worship,
preaching and teaching,
word and sacrament.
Above all, may they speak of what the Church is really all about:
those who life and ministry serves as a visible sign of your love,
an expression of your grace
and a symbol of service and witness offered in your name.
Amen.

Church workers behind the scenes

503

Loving God,
thank you for those who work behind the scenes in our churches,
quietly and faithfully contributing to the life of your people –
preparing refreshments after worship,
staging social events,

cooking meals,
washing up,
preparing flowers,
cleaning, dusting and polishing.
Bless their service –
all too often and easily overlooked,
yet so vital to countless fellowships –
that they in turn may be a blessing to others.
Amen.

Interfaith work

504

Holy God,
in a broken world,
torn by fear and hatred,
scarred by prejudice and intolerance,
grant your blessing on all instances of interfaith dialogue and working together.
Lord, hear us,
graciously hear us.

May they be a sign of hope,
a visible testimony to the healing power of your love.
Lord, hear us,
graciously hear us.

Despite differences in faith, creed and culture,
may people learn to focus on what unites rather than divides,
discovering that it is possible to stay true to one's traditions while being open to others,
to move beyond mere tolerance to respect,
beyond discord to dialogue,
beyond passive acceptance to an active working together,
building bridges within a fragmented society,
healing the wounds,
and working for the good of all.
Lord, hear us,
graciously hear us.
Amen.

Local Ecumenical Projects

505

Sovereign God,
grant your blessing on ecumenical projects and ventures.
May the vision that called them into being burn brightly in the years ahead,
whatever challenges may confront them.
Bind us together, Lord,
and make us one.

When the daily reality of living and working together throws up complications,
when unforeseen issues expose differences and disagreements,
may the knowledge of what unites –
the all-embracing love of Christ –
prove more compelling than what divides,
offering ways to resolve conflict
and to emerge the stronger.
Bind us together, Lord,
and make us one.

Shine through the life and work of ecumenical projects everywhere,
that they may be a living expression of your reconciling purpose
and the harmony that you desire among all.
Bind us together, Lord,
and make us one.
Amen.

Mission

506

Living God,
we pray for all those who witness for you,
all who preach and proclaim the message of Christ,
who challenge people with the message of the gospel.
Give them inspiration, courage and sincerity,
so that their witness may lead others to know Jesus for themselves.
Lord, in your mercy,
hear our prayer.

We pray for all those who hear,
all who in different ways are confronted with the challenge to respond to Christ.
May those who earnestly seek find faith,
those who are undecided be convinced,
those who glimpse a little see more clearly,
those whose faith is shallow be led to deeper understanding,
and those who refuse to listen be challenged to think again.
Lord, in your mercy,
hear our prayer.
Amen.

507

Loving God,
hear our prayer for your servants in every place.
Grant your blessing upon their life and witness,
and upon all you have called to service.
Build up your Church
and so bring closer your kingdom.

We pray for those involved in mission,
either at home or overseas –
evangelists,
preachers,
chaplains,
missionaries –
all those who seek to proclaim the gospel
and make known the love of Christ.
Build up your Church
and so bring closer your kingdom.

We pray for those who exercise roles of leadership,
whether it be over individual fellowships,
dioceses,
districts,
associations,
denominations,
or ecumenical groupings.
Build up your Church
and so bring closer your kingdom.

We pray for those who witness to you in their daily life and work,
expressing their faith in all kinds of occupations and vocations,
fleshing out the gospel,
putting it into practice,
exploring what it means in concrete and sometimes difficult situations.
Build up your Church
and so bring closer your kingdom.

We pray for those who work for Christian unity,
striving to draw your divided Church together,
breaking down barriers,
and building bridges of trust, respect and cooperation.
Build up your Church
and so bring closer your kingdom.

Loving God,
guide your people,
strengthen, equip and inspire each one for service,
and so may we, with them, joyfully serve you,
sensitively proclaim you,
and faithfully express your love for all.
Build up your Church
and so bring closer your kingdom.
Amen.

508

Lord Jesus Christ,
we pray once more for your Church
and for its ministry to the world.
May it be a source of love, hope and comfort,
compassion, challenge and inspiration.
Make known your love,
to us and to all.

May your followers in every place find the faith and courage,
vision and commitment,
to live as beatitude people,
poor and humble in spirit,
merciful in attitude,
pure in heart,
hungry for peace
and thirsty for righteousness,

and so, as individuals and together,
may your Church testify to your redeeming love and renewing power,
speaking through word and deed of your care for all,
your desire for justice,
and your willingness to show mercy.
Make known your love,
to us and to all.

Reach out through all whom you specially call to proclaim your name –
those gifted as evangelists,
those working abroad as missionaries
or here in our own country,
each seeking to share their faith
and to communicate your love.
Make known your love,
to us and to all.

But reach out also through everyday believers such as us,
ordinary Christians telling others about their experience of your goodness
and about the difference you have made to their lives.
Make known your love,
to us and to all.

Grant to all your people the inspiration of your Holy Spirit,
and the light of Christ in their hearts.
Help them to recognise the opportunities you provide,
to respond to your guidance
and so, faithfully, to proclaim the good news.
Make known your love,
to us and to all.
Amen.

509

Loving God,
guide those who in any way seek to speak of you:
preachers,
teachers,
evangelists,
Sunday school staff,
or ordinary individuals attempting to share their faith with others.
Make known your love, Lord,
to us and to all.

Help them, and us, to avoid,
as far as possible,
using religious jargon;
terms that we may understand ourselves
but that communicate little if anything to our hearers.
Make known your love, Lord,
to us and to all.

Teach us to avoid using clichés,
language that borders on the meaningless.
Make known your love, Lord,
to us and to all.

Prompt us to speak from the heart
rather than simply repeating the ideas of others;
to put across the message of the gospel,
but to do so in a way that people can relate to,
so that they, in turn, can make it their own.
Make known your love, Lord,
to us and to all.

Help us to witness sincerely and effectively to you,
through Jesus Christ our Lord.
Amen.

510

Loving God,
you call us all to the task of mission,
to make known the good news of Christ,
to proclaim the gospel to all we meet
through word and deed.
Teach us what that means,
and to be ready to fulfil that calling when the opportunity arises.
Speak your word,
to us and to all.

You call us all to be witnesses for Christ,
but there are some you set apart for a particular calling –
evangelists,
ministers,
preachers and teachers of your word,
each with a special responsibility to lead others to you.
Speak your word,
to us and to all.

You call others to more specialised ministries –
working in industry or shops, prisons or hospitals,
the armed forces, sport, youth work, charities,
or ecumenical projects.
Speak your word,
to us and to all.

You call others again to missionary service,
either at home or overseas,
to share the gospel through their preaching and teaching,
or through offering practical skills
as a testimony to the love and compassion of Christ.
Speak your word,
to us and to all.

Loving God,
we thank you for all who in different ways strive to fulfil the great commission,
taking the gospel to the ends of the earth.
Speak your word,
to us and to all.

Teach us to see their work as our work,
their needs as our needs,
their opportunities as our opportunities;
and so challenge us and your people everywhere to support them always,
through our prayers, our money and our love,
demonstrating our appreciation of their work
and our concern for your kingdom.
Speak your word,
to us and to all.

Grant your wisdom, guidance and inspiration,
so that many will hear and respond,
in the name of Christ.
Amen.

511

Lord Jesus Christ,
we thank you for those who have fulfilled your call to mission –
those who first made the gospel known to us,
those who proclaim it to others,
those who sow, nurture and bring to fruition the seeds of faith.

We pray for all you have specially gifted to proclaim the good news –
preachers and evangelists,
ministers and missionaries,
teachers and writers.
May many meet with you through their labours
and come to know you as their living Lord and Saviour.
Amen.

512

Loving God,
we ask for guidance in our witness –
help us to draw closer to the community around our building,
to serve wherever we see need,
and faithfully to proclaim the good news of Christ
whenever and wherever the opportunity arises.
Amen.

513

Loving God,
we prayer for all those you have called to the work of mission.
Help them both to give,
and receive;
to teach,
and learn;
to speak,
and listen;
to serve,
and be served.
Help them not simply to speak of Christ,
but to embody his presence
and to meet him in others,
sharing with him and them in a continuing journey of faith.
Amen.

514

Loving God,
we pray for those who are indifferent to you –
those who have not heard the challenge of the gospel,
or who have not considered the claims of Christ for themselves,
or who have a nominal faith but no real commitment.

Open their ears to the message of Christ,
their spirits to the reality of your presence,
and their lives to the joy of knowing you.
Amen.

Preachers and teachers

515

Sovereign God,
when it comes to knowing you,
to growing in faith,
we need help to get the picture,
for there are gaps in our knowledge,
details we find hard to grasp,
not least in the study of your word.
Teach us to appreciate those who offer guidance –
preachers, teachers, scholars, writers –
all whose insights lead to deeper perception
and a fuller experience of your love,
and, in humility, may we listen and learn.
Amen.

Sunday schools and youth work

516

Sovereign God,
hear our prayer for Sunday schools
and those in our churches who work among young people.
Speak through them of your love for all –
of your purpose,
your mercy,
your grace.
Equip those entrusted with communicating the gospel to young people.
Reach out through their words and deeds to nourish and nurture,
provide and prepare;
your joy and peace touching young lives and hearts,
through Jesus Christ our Lord.
Amen.

Those not able or unwilling to attend church

517

Loving God,
as we come together today we bring you our thanks –
for this place where, week by week,
we can come and share fellowship;
for this church, dedicated to worshipping you;
and for this time set aside from the daily tasks of life
so that we can offer you our praise,
reflect on your word
and seek your will.
We thank you for everything our coming here has meant
and continues to mean.
Lord of the Church,
unite us through the love of Christ.

But we pray now for those who, for a variety of reasons,
are unable to worship with us –
those confined to their homes,
those no longer fit enough to get out and about,
those in hospital,
those having to work on Sundays,
those looking after loved ones.
Lord of the Church,
unite us through the love of Christ.

We pray too for those who have drifted away from regular attendance –
those who have lost their faith,
or joined other churches,
or moved to a new area among new people.
Lord of the Church,
unite us through the love of Christ.

Loving God,
may each of these, our friends,
know that they are still much remembered,
much valued,
and much cared about.
May we find ways of expressing our concern,
showing our support,
and expressing our interest in their welfare.

And, whatever their situation,
may they know you close by their side,
joined with us and all your people in the fellowship that only Christ can bring.
Lord of the Church,
unite us through the love of Christ.
Amen.

518

Living God,
we do not think only of ourselves
but also of those not with us at this time –
those prevented from coming through ill-health,
age,
infirmity,
or other commitments;
those who have lost their faith
or their sense of belonging to this fellowship;
those still uncertain of their commitment;
those who have not yet reached the point of expressing their faith.
Teach us to respond sensitively to each one,
making real our love in Christ,
and showing a genuine concern for all.
Amen.

519

Loving God,
hear our prayer for those whose minds are closed to you,
unable or unwilling to recognise your love.
Speak your word to all who can or will not hear –
those who angrily reject you
or who simply dismiss you as irrelevant to their lives.
And speak also to us,
for though we may have responded to you in faith
we are still guilty at times of shutting you out,
selective in what we accept and what we prefer not to.
Break through the walls of hostility,
doubt,
arrogance
and apathy,
and reveal your grace and goodness in Christ.
Amen.

World peace and harmony

see also under The Church Year: Remembrance Day; One World Week; *also* Poetic prayers: For reconciliation in a divided world; Themed prayers: Social justice

520

Almighty God,
so many within our world seek to know and serve you better,
yet that very seeking and knowing seems often to divide and estrange
rather than draw people together,
alienating people from you
and from one another.
Come afresh to our world, Lord,
and heal our wounds.

Open the hearts of all to traditions other than their own,
and to everything that might be learnt from them.
Come afresh to our world, Lord,
and heal our wounds.

Open our minds to people who think differently from us,
and to insights that might share be shared.
Come afresh to our world, Lord,
and heal our wounds.

Save anyone from assuming they are right about everything –
that they have grasped the truth,
the whole truth
and nothing but the truth –
and from turning on those who disagree with them.
Come afresh to our world, Lord,
and heal our wounds.

Teach us to stay true to our convictions,
but to treat others also with respect,
always being open to you speaking in ways
and through people,
that we least expect.
Come afresh to our world, Lord,
and heal our wounds.
Amen.

521

Lord Jesus Christ,
you came as the Prince of Peace to bring healing to the nations –
to overcome hatred with love,
evil with good and darkness with light.
Prince of peace,
heal our wounds.

Teach us what that means in today's complex and troubled world,
where tension and unrest continue to dominate,
where violence and the threat of war are all too real,
and where mistrust, intolerance and prejudice still hold sway.
Prince of peace,
heal our wounds.

Grant wisdom to leaders of nations,
to all whose decisions will shape the future of this world
and, by your Spirit,
break down the barriers that divide us
and bring closer the day of your kingdom.
Prince of peace,
heal our wounds.
Amen.

522

Loving God,
reach out into this broken world,
and bring hope, help and healing.
Bind up our wounds,
and heal our divisions.

Come and mend the schisms that tear us apart,
the wounds inflicted by pride,
greed,
prejudice,
corruption,
hatred
and mistrust –
so much that separates person from person and nation from nation.
Bind up our wounds,
and heal our divisions.

In place of conflict foster cooperation;
in place of dogma promote dialogue.
Break down the barriers we erect against those who are different from us,
those whose views challenge our comfortable and complacent view of reality.
Bind up our wounds,
and heal our divisions.

Above all, save us from a narrow, intolerant faith
that proclaims harmony yet creates discord;
that extols love but harbours hate.
Bind up our wounds,
and heal our divisions.
Amen.

523

Creator God,
heal our broken world,
and put an end to its madness,
so that, whatever divides,
and whatever our colour, creed or culture,
we may see beyond cause or grievance
to the common humanity that unites us all.
Amen.

524

Eternal God,
overcome the barriers that estrange person from person
and nation from nation–
our selfishness,
greed,
prejudice
and intolerance;
so much that keeps us apart –
and establish an enduring bond between all that will never be broken.
Give us a love for you that is as real as yours is for us.
Amen.

525

Healing God,
bring closer the day when our divisions will be overcome,
our differences put aside,
and our fear and mistrust ended –
a time when we will live in peace together,
and you will be all in all.
Amen.

526

Lord Jesus Christ,
despised and rejected during your ministry,
reach out to the marginalised –
those pushed to the edge of society,
their identity denied,
rights ignored
and dignity destroyed.
Overcome the barriers of fear, suspicion and prejudice that divide us,
estranging person from person,
community from community,
and, whatever our differences,
help us to recognise the true worth of all –
to see beyond what keeps us apart
to the common humanity that binds us together.
Amen.

527

Lord Jesus Christ,
forgive us, for we can cause discord more easily than we imagine,
clashing with those around us
and even with you.
In all our relationships, help us to hit the right note;
to be in tune with you,
and, wherever possible, to live in harmony with others.
Amen.

528

Lord Jesus Christ,
forgive us,
for we're suspicious of differences,

interpreting them as threat instead of promise,
reason to fear rather than celebrate.
Overcome what divides person from person,
race from race
and faith from faith,
and make us one.
Amen.

529

Lord Jesus Christ,
in a world of conflict where so many are at loggerheads,
tussling for power and prestige,
bring an end to division.
Put an end to our posturing,
our endless conflict and confrontation,
and show us the way to peace.
Amen.

530

Lord Jesus Christ,
reach out to our broken world –
scarred by hatred,
fractured by division,
ravaged by war –
and, in your mercy, grant us peace.
Amen.

531

Lord Jesus Christ,
you broke down the barriers that separate us from God.
Forgive us that we are part of a world that busily creates all kinds of new barriers,
dividing person from person,
community from community
and country from country.
Draw us together,
and make us one.
Amen.

532

Lord of all,
grant not just peace but reconciliation in our world,
an end to all that divides and destroys,
so that those previously estranged may come together,
shoulder to shoulder,
heart to heart.
Amen.

533

Lord of all,
overcome the barriers that keep us apart,
dividing person from person and race from race –
East and West,
black and white,
male and female,
rich and poor.
Whatever our colour, culture or creed,
draw us together and heal our wounds –
so that we may live and work together as one people,
one world.
Amen.

534

Lord of all,
teach us, through the one made flesh –
the one who lived among us,
sharing our flesh and blood,
knowing our joys and sorrows,
experiencing our life and death –
to celebrate and honour our common humanity,
barriers broken and divisions overcome.
Amen.

535

Loving God,
our world lies broken,
fractured by prejudice,
splintered by hate,

scarred by fear,
and for all our efforts we cannot make it whole.
Pick up the pieces and bind them together,
bringing healing where there is hurt
and unity where there is division.
Hear our prayer
and meet us in our need.
Amen.

536

Loving God,
reach out to our broken world –
scarred by suspicion,
fractured by hatred,
ravaged by cruelty, violence and war –
and, in your mercy, heal our wounds,
overcome our divisions,
and grant us real and lasting peace.
Amen.

537

Overcome what keeps us apart, Lord.
Turn fear to trust,
hate to love
and war to peace.
Amen.

538

Renewing God,
grant not just superficial peace in our world,
but reconciliation,
an end to whatever divides and destroys –
all that fosters hatred, intolerance and injustice,
leading to misery for so many.
Break down religious, ethnic and social barriers,
so that those previously estranged may come together,
moving beyond their differences to a genuine meeting of minds,
and harmony among all.
Amen.

Peacemakers

539

Gracious God, in a divided world,
where chasms of fear, hatred, envy and injustice come between so many,
help us to build bridges –
to do what we can,
where we can,
to construct links,
create dialogue
and promote partnership,
bringing together those previously kept apart.
Where barriers estrange and rifts alienate,
help us to be peacemakers.
Amen.

540

Lord Jesus Christ,
help us to build bridges with others,
and help them to build bridges in turn,
so that, little by little,
we might help cross the chasms that still divide your world.
Amen.

541

Lord Jesus Christ,
though we're scared of what it might lead to,
afraid it may bounce back in our face,
help us to love our enemies
and to make the first move towards restoring peace.
Amen.

542

Lord Jesus Christ,
teach us, wherever and whenever we can,
to be peacemakers,
not poking our nose in where it's not wanted,
but ready, when we find ourselves caught in the middle of discord,
to serve as a go-between,
mediating your love.
Give us, then, sensitivity to calm the waters,
wisdom to break the deadlock
and love to heal the wounds.
Amen.

Poetic prayers

For an awareness of God's presence where life is dark

543

Where love is met with hatred,
and dreams have been snuffed out,
where days are full of suffering
and faith has turned to doubt,
where evil conquers goodness
and life is full of care,
grant through it all the knowledge
that you, O Lord, are there.

Where joy has turned to sorrow
and hope gives way to fear,
where peace is cruelly shattered
as sudden storms appear,
where life belies convictions
on which we once relied,
grant through it all the knowledge
you're always by our side.

Where darkness like a shadow
extinguishes the light,
where plans are brought to ruin
and nothing quite goes right,
where health begins to falter
and life begins to fade,
grant through it all the knowledge
we need not be afraid.

To those enduring trouble
with which they cannot cope,
to those for whom disaster
has put an end to hope,
to those who carry burdens
too difficult to bear,
grant through it all the knowledge
that you, O Lord, are there.

For the Church

544

You've called us as your Church, Lord,
your people here on earth,
a fellowship of equals
where all are given worth,
a family together,
distinguished by our care,
one faith, one hope, one gospel,
one vision that we share.

Yet we have been divided
by doctrine, dogma, creed,
estranged from one another –
we've left your wounds to bleed.
Too full of our convictions,
believing others wrong,
we've lost sight of the body
to which we all belong.

Our differences deny you,
betray the faith we claim;
instead of love uniting,
we squabble in your name.
Lord, heal the wounds that scar us –
suspicion, fear and pride;
reveal the good in others
that all our labels hide.

You've called us as your Church, Lord,
your people here on earth,
a fellowship of equals
where all are given worth.
May cords of love unite us,
too strong to be undone –
although we may be many,
equip us to be one.

For the elderly and infirm

545

Reach out to those who are ageing,
all for whom life is a strain,
those who are constantly waging
war against illness and pain.
Comfort the troubled and tearful,
give them your help to get by.
Strengthen those worried and fearful,
lovingly answer their cry.

Nurture the broken and ailing –
bodies grown weary and old,
faculties steadily failing –
scared what the future might hold.
Help those who, friendless and lonely,
wish that each day were their last,
those who find happiness only
when thinking of moments long past.

Lord, though the years lead to testing,
often too bitter to bear,
leaving some sadly protesting,
feeling you no longer care,
show that the future's not finished,
that your love still offers more,
carrying on undiminished,
holding the best things in store.

For God's healing touch in time of trouble

546

To all beset by fears,
by sickness, pain or tears,
reach out and make them whole,
in body and in soul.

To all who long for peace,
bid inner turmoil cease;
reach out and touch their life
and put an end to strife.

To all oppressed by care,
regrets, dismay, despair,
reach out and touch their mind;
help put the past behind.

To all who've gone astray,
give light to point the way;
reach out and touch their heart,
your love and life impart.

For healing, justice and peace in our world

547

Hear our prayer for others
in the trials they face –
fellow sisters, brothers:
grant to all your grace.
Heal the crushed and broken,
body, mind and soul –
let your word be spoken,
touch and make them whole.

Chide the rich and greedy,
strengthen the oppressed,
reach out to the needy,
comfort the distressed.
May the humble flourish
may the poor be fed,
in your mercy nourish
all who crave for bread.

Bring to every nation
harmony once more,
reconciliation,
peace instead of war.
Hear our intercession,
make our lives a prayer;
help us give expression
to your love and care.

For real and lasting change

548

An urgent voice is calling,
a voice from far away;
it's crying out for justice,
and yearning for that day
when no one need go hungry,
despair will be no more –
a day at last that heralds
a new start for the poor.

An urgent voice is calling,
a voice from somewhere near;
it's crying out with longing,
yet no one seems to hear;
despite long years of witness,
a multitude still search –
forgive us, Lord, and grant now
a new start for the Church.

An urgent voice is calling,
a voice from all around;
it's crying out in anguish,
the grim and tragic sound
of God's creation groaning,
stripped bare, denied her worth –
Lord, curb our greed, and bring now
a new start for the earth.

An urgent voice is calling,
a voice from close at hand;
it's crying out in anger,
campaigning for a land
where all will be respected,
and war will find no place –
a world of peace and friendship,
a new start for our race.

An urgent voice is calling,
the voice of God above;
it's crying out in sorrow,
and urging us to love,
for still a world lies bleeding,
the weak go to the wall –
Lord, help us build with others
a new start for us all.

For reconciliation in a divided world

549

Lord, to our world in its madness –
broken, bemused and concussed,
crushed by a burden of sadness,
ravaged by fear and mistrust –
grant your renewal and healing,
courage where hope seems in vain,
reach out to all who are reeling,
bring them relief from their pain;
break down the roots of division,
walls that destroy and estrange;
overcome hate and suspicion,
grant us the prospect of change.

For signs of God's kingdom here on earth

550

Grant, Lord, an end to our sorrow,
a halt at last to our pain,
the hope of a brighter tomorrow,
of sunshine, after the rain.
Assure us the day is dawning
when darkness will be no more,
no suffering, dying or mourning,
no violence, hatred or war –
a kingdom of joy unbounded,
of laughter, blessing and peace,
where evil will be confounded
and all divisions cease;

a time of celebration,
a place of rare delights –
Lord, finish your new creation
and set our world to rights.

For those struggling to come to terms with questions of faith

551

Lord, we see such goodness,
yet such evil too:
much that makes us question,
much that speaks of you.
All around are riddles
hard to understand –
help us find some answers,
help us see your hand.

Where there's pain and sorrow,
where your children bleed,
where there seems no future
for a world in need,
break into the darkness,
bring an end to night,
show that love continues,
shine again your light.

Where belief is shaken,
hope appearing vain,
where reserves are creaking,
sorely under strain,
grant the strength to trust you,
courage to hold out;
show us you are present;
speak, Lord, in our doubt.

For those under the shadow of death

552

Lord, we pray for those who weep,
mourning those they've loved and lost;
happiness that ran so deep
followed now by such a cost.

Each day brings now added pain,
memories of times they knew,
never to be shared again –
life a case of getting through.

When their hearts are fit to break –
hurt too bitter to express –
grant them solace, dull the ache,
comfort them in their distress.

In their anger, loss and shock,
help them find in you a friend;
in their turmoil be their rock,
one on whom they can depend.

Though they feel they cannot cope,
gracious God, reach out to save;
bring to each new life, new hope
in your love, beyond the grave.

For those who strive for social justice

553

For those who fight injustice
and make a stand for good,
who strive to give the poor a chance
to live life as they should,
for all who labour, heart and soul,
to make our world more fair,
we ask your courage, succour, strength –
Lord, answer, hear our prayer.

For those who show compassion,
who work to heal and mend,
who nurse the sick, support the weak,
encourage and befriend,
for all who reach out in your name
to offer love and care,
we ask your blessing, power, help –
Lord, answer, hear our prayer

For those who tackle conflict,
where wounds run red and raw,
who strive to conquer hatred
and put a stop to war,
who work to foster dialogue
despite the scars we bear,
we ask your guidance, vision, faith –
Lord, answer, hear our prayer.

For those who try to witness
to Christ through word and deed,
to show his love embraces
each colour, culture, creed,
who point to light and life and hope
in which the world can share,
we ask your wisdom, grace and truth –
Lord, answer, hear our prayer.

For ourselves, the Church and the world

554

Take this day, we ask you, Lord,
fashion all that it shall bring;
help us see your hand at work,
love transforming everything.

Take our lives, we ask you, Lord,
through your Spirit make us new;
help us now to do your will,
trusting you in all we do.

Take your Church, we ask you, Lord,
grant it strength to meet your call;
help it show through word and deed
something of your love for all.

Take our world, we ask you, Lord,
may its pain and sorrow cease;
help us heal each other's wounds,
show us how to live in peace.

For a world in need

555

In a world of hurt and fear,
teach us, Lord, that you are here.
Come and meet us in our pain;
show that faith is not in vain.
Touch the broken in their grief,
to the troubled bring relief;
grant to all who cannot cope
inner strength, rekindled hope.

In a world awash with need,
scarred by hatred, envy, greed,
come and show how much you care;
foster joy where there's despair.
Hear the pleading of the poor –
lives destroyed by debt and war.
Work to bring new hope to birth,
peace and justice on the earth.

In a world where faith has died,
yet where countless creeds divide,
come and put an end to strife,
all that scars or shatters life.
Heal, renew us, Lord, we pray,
show us where we've gone astray;
give us help to put things right,
turn our darkness into light.

For a world in which God seems absent

556

Where were you, Lord, when the planes struck
and the towers came crashing down?
What did you do to stop it?
Why were you out of town?
Where were you in the Balkans
when the streets ran red with blood?
And how about the shanty town
engulfed by streams of mud?
Why don't you end the famine?
Why don't you stop the war?
How can you let these happen?
What can it all be for?

Lord, is it wrong to ask you,
faithless to speak our mind?
Shouldn't we look for answers?
Don't you say 'seek and find'?
Yes, we know much is beyond us,
truth often hard to discern,
but we're ready and willing to listen,
eager and hungry to learn.
Don't think we're daring to judge you,
set ourselves up in your place –
some things, we know, must stay hidden,
at least till we meet face to face –
yet in a world where so many
feel faith and hope are in vain,
give us some sign, Lord, we beg you
to prove you are here in our pain.